For my wife, Dira

Contents

Preface

Whether the matter is about welfare or warfare, economic development or health, many public and nonprofit agencies continue to find ways of getting the job done. They take on new challenges helping their communities to move forward, and thereby make important, positive differences that affect the lives of their clients or citizens. Many fine examples of exemplary performance by public and nonprofit agencies exist that set standards for other agencies dealing with similar issues. The list of accomplishments by public and nonprofit organizations and their managers is a long and proud one, and every day new examples are added. Numerous awards programs such as Service to America Medals (2005) document and herald these accomplishments. Many agencies, even those that do not perform at high levels, aspire to improve themselves and increase their contribution in meaningful ways. There is good work to be done, and it is being done.

How do public and nonprofit organizations produce high performance results? What processes do they use? How can organizations improve themselves? This book examines the strategies and tactics used by senior, midlevel, and supervisory managers. These managers are key actors in the processes that their agencies use and the results that agencies produce. These managers bring mandates to life; they harness and transform the resources (economic, political, professional, etc.) of their agencies and communities into actual results. When public agencies win awards for best customer service or use information technology in innovative ways, one can be sure that their managers have played a key role. When the results are poor, managers have had their hands in that, too. Dreams are made real—or not. How well managers use the talents of their staff and other resources such as information technology, funding, and community goodwill all affect outcomes. It is not enough to merely proclaim by decree that this or that problem should be resolved; rather, the real work must be done. The actions by managers and employees of public and nonprofit organizations give form and shape to many of society's aspirations.

Of course, not all agencies and managers produce exemplary results; the evidence of mediocrity and failure are clearly around us, too. There are many challenges on the road to high performance, and there is a good deal to be learned from success, failure, and everything in between. If improvement is to be made, then we do well to understand challenges to high performance, and provide meaningful responses to them. This book examines these considerations. Indeed, one of the lessons of performance is that while not all barriers can be overcome, there is no situation that cannot be improved. The art is very much about taking stock of the situation and then leaving things better off. We need to make realistic assessments, and undertake strategies with a high chance of success. Readers will hopefully find this a useful guide, and also one that challenges them to consider some old things in a new light.

This book is a second, thoroughly revised edition. The previous edition was titled *Productivity in Public and Nonprofit Organizations: Strategies and Tactics* and was published in 1998. At that time, the implications of the then-new quality management strategies were becoming increasing clear and evident. Today, these strategies have become staples of modern management, and new strategies are now on the horizon. The time has come to update the first edition. There is progress. One change is reflected in the book title, which now includes the term "performance." In recent years, "performance" has become the preferred term that is now more in vogue. I agree with Holzer and Lee (2004) that the term productivity often is "simplified, misinterpreted and misapplied," sometimes synonymous with the limited meaning of ensuring efficiency or high production levels. These latter concepts are important but too limited to do justice to the nature of many public service goals. Performance, in the sense of achieving outcomes and being effective, is obviously central for public and nonprofit organizations.

Of course, many strengths of the previous edition remain in place. This book continues to emphasize the long and veritable tradition of management strategies for ensuring change and performance. Performance improvement is a slowly but surely developing body of knowledge and practice that is diffused throughout society. This book discusses new problems and strategies, as well as those that have endured and that give rise to a staple of "oldies, but goodies" management strategies. This edition also maintains a writing style that is accessible and which focuses on providing content that is useful. We also maintain a balanced presentation of practical strategies along with their underlying foundations and principles, as well as presentation of new empirical research about performance management efforts in public and nonprofit organizations. These are distinctive features of this book.

Some readers may ask whether a separate book on performance management in public and nonprofit organizations is really necessary, whereas others may ask whether combining public and nonprofit organizations in one book is not a bit much. As regarding the first question, public and nonprofit organizations have important missions, missions whose fulfillment matters, and justify a separate look at performance in these organizations. The strategies public and nonprofit organizations apply to their goals are also a bit unique. Consider that the average Space Shuttle mission costs about $2 billion and up, and involves numerous organizations working on research, construction, repair, training, and launch and flight control, for example. It also involves numerous stakeholders and, sometimes, political pressures. There is no off-the-shelf management approach for managing such a program; strategies must be adapted to their contexts. The need for careful consideration is also evident when adapting strategies originally developed for business purposes. For example, while inventory control may be a critical problem for Boeing, it is not so for most service agencies. Profitability is not a legitimate goal for most public and nonprofit organizations. The nature and context of public service goals and activities require a separate focus on performance and strategies for improving that performance.

The material here is relevant to many public administration and policy programs. Today's managers are expected to know and use strategic planning, empowerment, and process reengineering, for example. Analysts need to know about these things, too, as well as about partnerships, privatization, and other options for goal achievement. The accreditation standards of the National Association of Schools of Public Affairs and Administration (NASPAA) do not explicitly mention modern tools of management, but many faculty and departments recognize this need and wish to teach them. Clearly, graduates need to think critically as well as know the modern and customary tools of the trade.

Regarding the second question about combining both public and nonprofit organizations in a single study, we note that public service is increasingly less defined by whether one works in the public or private sector, and more by the task that one is doing—whether one is furthering public purposes. The public sector increasingly uses privatization and partnerships for achieving its objectives, and much of the actual work is now performed by the private sector. Many nonprofit organizations are uniquely focused to provide public service, and many businesses fulfill public service contracts, too. Some activities are also performed by government special districts—entities that are focused on a single purpose and designed to operate much like a business, such as some toll road and airport authorities. Many public service managers and students in Master of Public Administration (M.P.A.) programs increasingly pursue careers that take them to both the public and private sectors. Regardless of where public service is performed, managers need to be familiar with strategies and approaches to effectively manage public service programs. This book is for those whose aim is to provide effective public services through public or nonprofit organizations.

Finally, as in all endeavors, there are many people to thank. My professional frame of reference remains the American Society for Public Administration, through which I have met many wonderful colleagues and made so many friends. I especially thank my longtime friend and coauthor Jonathan West, as well as Marc Holzer, who asked me to serve as the managing editor of *Public Performance & Management Review.* This leading journal is devoted to advancing public performance through research and the dissemination of new ideas about performance. I thank my senior editor, Harry Briggs of M.E. Sharpe, for his support and suggestions as well as Elizabeth Granda and Amy Odum, who helped with the editing and manuscript preparation. I also acknowledge numerous colleagues who have supported me over the years, as well as clients who have given me opportunities to learn through their travails. I thank my students who provided feedback in my classes that covered this material. This book reflects all of their contributions.

Evan M. Berman

PERFORMANCE AND PRODUCTIVITY IN PUBLIC AND NONPROFIT ORGANIZATIONS

What Is Performance?
An Overview

Performance is about keeping public and nonprofit organizations up-to-date, vibrant, and relevant to society. It is about ensuring that agency programs and policies connect with the important challenges that people, communities, and the nation face. Schools need to teach children well, military procurement programs need to provide military personnel with the weapons and combat gear that they need, and environmental protection agencies should work to safeguard our natural heritage. Public and nonprofit organizations significantly affect, and have great potential to improve, the lives of citizens and communities in such areas as public safety, transportation, parks and recreation, economic development, education, housing, public health, environmental management, space exploration, social services, and more. In each of these areas there is interest, and sometimes very great interest, in ensuring that public and nonprofit organizations perform well and help society to move forward.

At heart, performance is about ensuring that organizations produce effective results, for example, that teen counseling services really do reduce suicide and pregnancy. But performance can also have additional dimensions. For example, there is also interest in ensuring that programs are equitably available to different population groups, and that programs are appropriately tailored to the needs of diverse groups. Today, program clients want choices, and to feel that they are attended to as human beings, not as numbers. The U.S. Internal Revenue Service has responded to this by providing counselors and flexible payment options to address the needs of millions of taxpayers. Another matter involves efficiency. It is important that programs use management methods that produce results at the lowest cost.

For example, modern information technology can increase efficiency by allowing employees to handle more transactions per hour. A dollar saved in one area is another dollar available to achieve other organizational goals.

Another dimension of performance is avoidance of waste and fraud. People want to know that monies are used wisely and that they serve legitimate purposes—rather than those of special interests, for example. People want public and nonprofit organizations to be effective and not wasteful. Focusing on performance draws attention toward the propriety of goals and means. Last but not least, many people also seek to participate in the process of deciding what gets done and how, and they want to feel that their voices have been heard. Public participation is an important part of performance improvement efforts, and can lead to many good ideas.

In short, performance matters in many different ways. By engaging in and ensuring performance, agencies and their managers contribute to the welfare of society, which, in turn, increases public trust in its public and nonprofit organizations. Performance helps connect organizations with the concerns of their stakeholders. Modern societies require effective public and nonprofit organizations, and those who contribute to performance also contribute to improving society. A vast literature provides numerous examples of performance in public and nonprofit organizations (e.g., Light 2002a; White and Newcomber 2005; Osborne and Plastrick 2000; Nanus 1999; Lemberg 2004; Ott 2000; Salamon 2003; Riggio, Orr, and Shakely, 2003).

For those working in public and nonprofit programs, the need to ensure performance can provide an important source of motivation and professional satisfaction. There are many reasons for emphasizing performance as part of the professional outlook of managers and their employees. For example, it is consistently supported by many professional associations, which state personal commitment to excellence as an expectation and even an ethical standard for their members. Performance can provide a sense of purpose and intrinsic satisfaction that is not contingent on external events. When new managers with a strong, personal commitment to performance join an agency, new performance efforts are often in the air. Not surprisingly, studies of high-performing agencies find that these organizations often adapt to change faster and better than others because of their internal processes and the commitment of their managers and employees. The personal motivation and commitment of managers matter (Light 2005).

For many managers, performance is not only about doing the right thing, it is also about doing the practical thing. For example, when programs are challenged by shifting funding priorities, performance management can help refocus priorities and assist programs to achieve their aims in more efficient ways. It can help track and understand customer satisfaction, and suggest

Table 1.1

Some Reasons for Performance Improvement

External relations
  • Increasing trust with external stakeholders
  • Getting organizations to be more responsive to clients
  • Improving communications with citizens and elected officials
  • Increasing the ability to effectively partner with other organizations
Management
  • Increasing effectiveness of services
  • Choosing better goals and targets
  • Reducing administrative overhead costs
  • Decreasing errors and mistakes
  • Improving accountability
  • Increasing efficiency or cost savings
  • Improving employee motivation and commitment
  • Increasing advantages from information technology
  • Getting employees to take responsibility for skill upgrading
  • Making work teams more productive
  • Improving the climate of trust in organizations
Marketing and fund-raising
  • Increasing yields from fund-raising efforts
  • Identifying new client groups for services
  • Improving the effectiveness of marketing efforts
  • Improving the yield from grant proposals
Volunteerism
  • Reducing turnover among volunteers
  • Identifying new groups of volunteers
  • Reducing complaints from supervisors and volunteers
  • Reducing training time for volunteers

ways to deal with client disapproval where that exists. Performance management also helps deal with unexpected changes in the program environment, such as unexpected spikes in client requests, drops in revenues, or natural or man-made disasters. In such cases, rethinking program objectives, response strategies, and performance is key. Performance management strategies help deal with many exigencies that organizations and their programs face. Table 1.1 shows additional reasons for performance.

Defining Performance

This book defines performance as *the effective and efficient use of resources to achieve results. Effectiveness* is defined as the level of results; for example, the number of arrests made by police officers, the number of welfare clients who find employment after being counseled by case workers, or the amount of money raised through fund-raisers. Such results are also referred to as accomplishments; the number of arrests by officers, for example, is appropriately referred to as a level of accomplishment. Many citizens and clients care greatly about public service effectiveness, and many public debates focus on it. They focus on both the level of results and, importantly, whether agencies are in fact pursuing the right accomplishments or targets. That is, that they are seeking to achieve the targets that matter most to them and their communities.

In recent years, increased attention to the measurement of results has given rise to a distinction between *outputs* and *outcomes* as measures of effectiveness: Outputs are defined as the *immediate results* of agency activities, and outcomes are measures of the extent that organizations attain their *goals* (or, ultimate purposes). By way of example, vocational training institutions provide education that helps students to acquire skills, pass tests, and graduate; these are immediate results of education and, hence, outputs. These outputs in turn help students get better jobs—an outcome. Similarly, police arrests (outputs) may result in reduced neighborhood crime (an outcome). Though outcomes are the ultimate purpose and raison d'etre of programs, outputs matter for two reasons. First, focusing on outputs provides faster feedback about accomplishment than focusing on eventual outcomes. Second, organizations often have more control over their outputs. Other circumstances also effect whether students get jobs and whether neighborhood crime is contained, for example.

Efficiency is defined as the *ratio of outcomes (and outputs) to inputs (O/I)*. It describes the cost per activity to achieve given outcomes; for example, the number of counseled clients per counselor who find employment or the number of graduating students per teacher. Efficiency is a ratio of the resources used (inputs) to achieve accomplishments (outcomes or outputs), or O/I. Efficiency is important because it helps budgets stretch further and thereby allows organizations to be more effective. For example, efficiency in fund-raising (e.g., dollars raised per staff member), police patrols (e.g., arrests or completed service calls per patrol member), or correctly handled service requests all help agencies do more. Efficiency has become very important in recent years as agencies struggle to meet rising demands. Efficiency is sometimes called productivity, and in this book we use these two terms as synonymous.[1]

It might be noted that the ratio "caseload per worker" is *not* an efficiency measure. Caseloads are not outputs or outcomes, but rather activities, which are also called *workloads*. The measure "caseload per worker" is therefore known as a *workload ratio*, or activity/input. The distinction between outcomes and workloads is important because, as many caseworkers know, high workload ratios are important only when outcomes or outputs are maintained. Merely seeing many or more clients does not ensure effectiveness in any way. Likewise, going on many patrols or for inspections should not be confused with making valid arrests or completing inspections in correct ways. Chapter 8 discusses in greater detail the measurement of performance.

Finally, the terms performance and performance improvement are not synonymous. The former is concerned with the level of effectiveness and efficiency, and the ways in which agencies achieve this. It may involve concern for equity and accountability as well. The latter is concerned with changing and improving these processes. *Performance improvement* involves diagnosis of performance problems, knowledge of alternative performance improvement strategies, analysis of the receptivity of organizations for performance efforts, implementation of skills and strategies, and assessment of outcomes. This book deals with both performance and performance improvement— managers want to know what to do, and how to make it a reality.

Performance in the Public and Private Sectors

The definition of performance suggests that managers should be concerned with *both* goal attainment (that is, effectiveness) and the efficiency of efforts. Public, nonprofit, and for-profit organizations vary in their relative emphasis on effectiveness and efficiency. Nonprofit and for-profit (business) organizations constitute the private sector, and although this book does not focus on for-profit organizations, these are discussed here for purposes of comparison. Effectiveness often is of paramount importance in the public sector: for example, the public (and, hence, elected officials) expect 911 emergency services to respond promptly, teachers to teach well, traffic to flow smoothly, museums to be open, space shuttles to fly, environmental toxins to be regulated, and defense systems to work. Although efficiency is important, it is often less important than effectiveness. Indeed, many citizens are more concerned with the effectiveness of 911 services (for example, that services arrive on time with effective personnel and equipment) than with the efficiency of 911 services (for example, the cost of a timely response). Getting on the scene quickly far outweighs any tax savings that causes delays or ineffective service. Likewise, the safety (effectiveness) of air travel or the educational attainment of students is of greater concern than the efficiency with which these goals are attained. Indeed, concerns about schools usually center on their effectiveness rather than on their efficiency; people wonder why they are paying so much for performance that so often is questioned.

Indeed, the lack of attention to effectiveness can bring severe repercussions to public organizations. Public organizations that are perceived as having low levels of effectiveness often encounter pressures to increase their workloads. In one such instance, a municipal unit of police detectives that had not communicated its effectiveness to the community faced significant pressures from elected officials to determine the "right" caseload for its detectives. Elected officials were also considering reallocating resources in favor of community-based policing efforts. The lack of sustained efforts to demonstrate and communicate its effectiveness—indeed, no such data had ever been gathered—contributed to the concern over caseloads which, in this case, was also seen as a prelude to downsizing. In short, public organizations need to make the case that they are effective, or else pay the price in diminished trust and support. This appears to be equally true for public schools, drug treatment programs, street cleaning—almost every public service.

This does not mean that efficiency is unimportant in public organizations. For example, the cost of environmental regulation, and its impact on business, is clearly an important concern. Efficient organizations stretch their resources further and thus are more effective. Efficient detectives solve more cases with the same resources. Efficient school systems will use teaching strategies that result in the highest learning accomplishment among their students per dollar spent. Exemplary public organizations will research such strategies know them, and implement them. In some situations, efficiency becomes a very important concern, such as when budget pressures are severe (for example, in some schools, jails, or health care organizations); when businesses compete for service delivery with public agencies (for example, emergency medical services or park maintenance); when regulatory burdens are thought to be too high (such as in drug regulation); when public embarrassments occur (e.g., cost overruns in major public projects such as airports or tunnels); and when overhead agencies pursue efficiency gains through procurement and contracting processes.

Consensus exists that efficiency is typically a *more important* goal in the for-profit (business) sector, where success tends to be more singularly defined as profit. Efficiency improvements are important because they result in cost savings that directly contribute to profitability, competitiveness, and corporate survival. Many productivity improvement efforts in for-profit organizations focus on applications that increase employee output, reduce inventories, speed up production, and reduce rework. All of these are designed to increase efficiency and serve business purposes. Some of these have been adapted by public and nonprofit organizations emphasizing efficiency, especially those that emphasize "quality" in relation to customer responsiveness and producing error-free services. In some cases, federal agencies have found new ways to improve efficiency and service delivery. Some agencies, such as the Social Security Administration, have even attained exemplary, award-winning levels of customer service.

Nonprofit organizations are often thought of as seeking effectiveness and efficiency in equal measure (e.g., Drucker 1990). Donors, public agencies funding nonprofit organizations, and employees and managers who work for these organizations often have high expectations about their ability to make an impact on the areas in which they are involved. The extent to which they provide services and affect important community issues is an important measure of the effectiveness of nonprofit organizations. Tax laws require that nonprofit organizations reinvest excess revenues, which furthers their commitment to effectiveness. However, efficiency is equally important. Resources are frequently scarce in nonprofit organizations, in part because their aims are huge (such as resolving homelessness), and partly because revenues streams are tight (for example, based on membership fees). Resource scarcity causes nonprofit organizations to seek out "free" resources such as volunteers and community donations. This can turn nonprofit organizations into highly efficient providers. Productivity efforts to better use volunteers and succeed at fundraising are especially important to these organizations, and are discussed elsewhere in this book.

Finally, organizations also differ to the extent that they value *equity* as an important goal. For-profit organizations usually have very little commitment to equity, other than avoiding discrimination lawsuits from their employees or clients. By contrast, public organizations often have great commitment to equity: they must provide services to all citizens, regardless of their ability to pay for such services. Public organizations must also ensure equal access to services, and they often provide help to disadvantaged populations to use their services. Nonprofit organizations also often serve disadvantaged populations, but they are seldom obligated to provide services to the entire population. Of course, both public and nonprofit organizations must avoid discrimination, as well.

In sum, performance is defined as the effective and efficient use of resources. Effectiveness is typically of greatest importance in the public sector, whereas nonprofit organizations often emphasize effectiveness and efficiency in equal measure. Public sector organizations also value providing services to all populations groups, that is, ensuring equity. The relative emphases of these values are shown in Figure 1.1.

Is Performance a Fad?

Performance improvement efforts sometime receive a bad rap. Employees are often concerned that managers are managing by the "fad of the month," thereby introducing and abandoning different performance efforts in rapid succession. Half-completed efforts often damage organizations by disrupting

Figure 1.1 **Productivity Values**

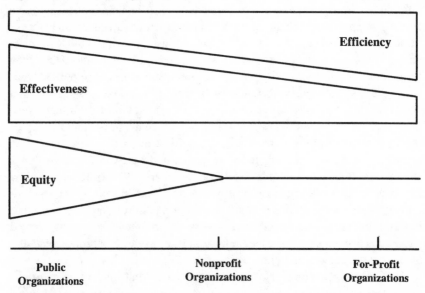

effective work activities and by reducing trust and confidence in management. The perception of performance as a fad is also reinforced by the media. Newspapers often report new tools that promise to solve important
problems. Success stories and "how-to" articles are quick to appear in professional trade journals, and sometimes in the popular press and even television. Organizations hire managers who are competent in implementing the
new strategies. Eventually, the number of articles about these efforts tapers
off as successful applications are no longer newsworthy. The rise and subsequent decrease in media coverage supports perceptions of performance improvement being a fad.

    In addition, success is often followed by the realization of challenges as
well. Not all organizations and managers experience total success. Subsequent reports reveal negative impacts of efforts and instances of outright
failure and rollback. Scholars contribute their views, too. When such critical
assessments occur, the judgment of the field changes from enthusiasm to
caution about these strategies. Media interest may briefly revive in response
to perceived failures and shortcomings. But, eventually, failure is also no longer
newsworthy, and the media then rushes on to report something else that is new.
The pattern repeats itself: the hot ticket of today is the dog of tomorrow. Does
all this mean that performance improvement is indeed a fad?

    A reassessment is in order. There is no question that organizations are
more customer-oriented today than in the past. They also make better use of

Figure 1.2 **Diffusion of Performance Strategies in Society**

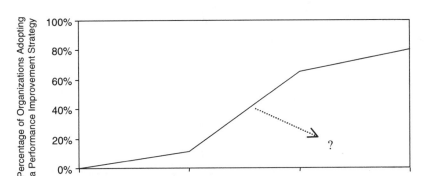

information technology and increasingly use performance measurement. There is progress for those who want to acknowledge it. We must better understand how organizations improve themselves through performance. What often occurs is that the initial, innovative, and pioneering efforts in some organizations are followed by similar efforts in many more organizations. The initial efforts may get the media attention, but in time, as more organizations acknowledge the importance of change objectives and the viability of response strategies, performance strategies find wider use, sometimes under a different name. Many people talk, but few act in the initial stages of new performance strategies. Rather, organizations learn in small steps, from trial-and-error, and from the replication of successful efforts elsewhere. The actual takeoff phase of diffusion in society often begins about three to five years after the initial introduction. The takeoff phase is built on proven applications, and often lasts another five to ten years, during which more and more organizations and managers adopt the new effort. This is shown in Figure 1.2.

It is not a given that an initial performance improvement strategy will be in fact widely used. Sometimes, good ideas and efforts turn to naught. The performance improvement strategy does not yield the effectiveness and efficiency that was hoped for. When performance improvement strategies falter, they may follow the broken arrow shown in Figure 1.2, only to be resurrected or reinvented some time later. An example is the effort to create "self-managed work teams in the late 1990s." This idea did not catch on widely, though it is now being revisited in some settings as the need persists for such teams. The term is no longer used, but the need for highly empowered and self-directed teams continues. Figure 1.2 also shows that usually not all organizations come to adopt improvement efforts. This may be because these organizations have no need for it, use alternative strategies, or are simply not prone to improving themselves; they remain stuck in the strategies of yester-year. This pattern of a characteristic S-shape diffusion curve is consistent with studies of innovation diffusion generally (e.g., Rogers 1995).

Total Quality Management (TQM) is an example of an at one time hot new performance improvement effort that was initially very well covered by the media. It first became popular in the federal government in the late 1980s, and among local governments in the early 1990s. It is associated with in-creased customer service and service quality, as discussed further in chapter 5. A few years after the initial efforts, the enthusiasm and hype seemed to wane; successes were no longer reported and there were articles that sounded caution, too. However, a more accurate reading was provided in an article entitled "Total Quality Management Is Dead" in the newspaper *USA Today* (October 17, 1995). This article noted that despite the alleged demise of TQM "some tenets of quality management are so ingrained that they aren't even recognized as such anymore." Though they no longer referred to TQM as such, government organizations were becoming increasingly customer-oriented and were beginning to use process reengineering and other TQM-based strategies. Today, customer service is much higher than it was a decade ago. In 1998, only one-third of U.S. counties with populations over 50,000 were using some level-of-performance measurement (a TQM-based strat-egy), and that of these, only 20 percent had made a serious investment (Berman and Wang 2000). But a more recent study found that performance measure-ment is now used by 47.8 percent of local governments in all departments, and another 20 percent in some departments (e.g., Melkers and Willoughby 2005). Such empirical studies confirm that performance improvement is not a fad, but a body of slowly diffusing knowledge and management practice.

Many older performance improvement strategies are now staples of man-agement. More than a decade ago, research found that financial forecasting was used by 76 percent of local governments, employee involvement efforts by 74 percent, and Management By Objectives (MBO) by 47 percent. Some efforts are organization-wide, whereas others are used only in some depart-ments (Poister and Streib 1994). Ninety-four percent of state budget offices use some form of performance analysis, and 66 percent use effectiveness analysis. For cities with populations over 50,000, 73.5 percent report having used strategic planning in at least one department during the past twelve months (Berman and West 1998). While there may be questions about the quality and effectiveness of some applications, performance improvement strategies clearly show increased use and diffusion over time.

The S-shape diffusion curve never fully reaches 100 percent. Poister and Streib (1994) note a ceiling effect at about the 75 percent adoption rate for

cities. In some cases usage rates are higher when strategies are widely required, such as certain audits or effectiveness analyses that may be required
by some state legislatures. This raises the question, if performance strategies
are so good, then why don't all organizations use all these strategies all the
time, regardless of whether or not they are required? Why is the eventual
diffusion rate not closer to 100 percent? Poister and Streib speculate that one
reason is because smaller organizations may lack resources for their use.
Some strategies require investment in training, personnel, and in some cases
information technology that is beyond their budget. But we suggest other
reasons, too. Some strategies can be used toward multiple purposes; there
may not be a need to use all strategies all the time in every organization.
There is also only so much that can be done at any point in time. Another
reason, elaborated upon in chapter 2, is that some organizations have a climate that resists change and improvement. Some organizations and managers just don't want to change. They might say that they want to change, but
their actions show complacency and resistance. They don't really want to
improve themselves. At best, change occurs at a very slow rate—much slower
than elsewhere in society. For all these reasons, the S-curve tapers off, and
some organizations and their communities are left behind.

Growing globalization means that performance strategies are increasingly
used by managers in other countries, too; diffusion is an international phenomenon. Efforts in TQM were quickly recognized by managers in other
countries—the Netherlands, Greece, Brazil, Trinidad and Tobago, Poland,
Lebanon, New Zeeland, Australia are just some examples of countries where
managers have quickly picked up modern strategies—some more than others, and some with more success than others. Agencies and managers in these
countries experience many of the same problems. Foreign managers adapt
these strategies to their unique circumstances, as do U.S. agencies when they
adapt these strategies to their problems and settings. Increased access to electronic journals and increased conference travel contributes to the rapid diffusion of knowledge and practice today. Based on publications in journals and
magazines, managers in other countries often pick up on new developments
reported in the United States within just a few years. Some, of course, may
be slower to adopt than others, giving rise to a likely S-curve in international
context as well.

One reason that performance improvement strategies are increasingly used
over time is because they are *useful*. In one survey, 48.6 percent of city managers agreed or strongly agreed with the statement that performance improvement strategies "are a useful vehicle of change" and an additional 41.7 percent
"somewhat agreed" with this statement; 90.3 percent agree or somewhat agree
that performance improvement strategies produce benefits that unfold over

time, and 44.7 percent of city managers agree that it produces large, immediate benefits to the organization. Likewise, 43.9 percent directors of large social service organizations agreed or strongly agreed, and an additional 37.8 percent "somewhat agreed" that performance improvement is a useful vehicle for change (Berman and West 1997, 1999). Many organizations and their managers see value in performance improvement strategies for helping the organization to move forward. Such support for performance improvement is clearly present in recent times.

The above has important implications for managers. First, at any point in time, there are many performance improvement strategies going on in society. The managers' job is to know what is going on elsewhere, so that they may be able to adapt a performance improvement strategy for their workplace. Managers need not reinvent the wheel, but they will need to be creative in adapting existing efforts to their organization. Second, notwithstanding the challenges of some organizations, most managers regard performance improvement as an opportunity for increased visibility and career advancement, as do their agencies. In one survey, 74.8 percent of senior local government managers agree or strongly agree that implementing new productivity improvement strategies makes them more attractive to other employers, and 68.4 percent agree or strongly agree that they have helped their careers (Berman and West 1999). Likewise, a review of managerial competencies by several national governments shows results orientation, leading people, communication skills, and problem solving as those most desired (Bhatta 2001). Familiarity with performance improvement strategies is also consistent with broader norms of both the American Society for Public Administration (ASPA) and the International City/County Managers Association (ICMA) that managers should strive for professional excellence. In short, being able to apply these strategies in productive ways that help communities and agencies move forward is a sought-after skill by agencies, one that helps managers distinguish themselves and build a positive reputation and career.

A Strategic Perspective

This book argues that a strategic perspective is needed. Managers must be clear about which goals they are pursing, the strategies for attaining these goals, and the conditions that may affect the implementation of strategies. The strategic perspective is threefold. The first step is identification of performance improvement problems and goals that are specific to the organization. There are numerous problems that may beset organizations. Some problems stem from inadequate alignment of actual organizational processes with the needs of stakeholders. Organizations often state that they are customer- or citizen-oriented, but how well do they measure up? How do customers or citizens assess the organization's responsiveness? Other problems involve misalignments between goals and the organizational structures and resources to achieve these goals. Delivery processes may be inefficient and not up to the task of meeting heightened expectations. Previous theories about impacts may have proven to be inaccurate or outdated, leading to calls for new efforts. Dysfunctional key actors are another source, such as those who ignore important problems and facts facing organizations. Chapter 2 provides an overview of many important performance problems.

Second, managers must choose from among different productivity improvement strategies to address the most important problems facing their organizations. This book discusses various strategies, such as quality management, strategic planning, partnering, organizational alignment, performance evaluation, use of information technology, and improving productivity through people. Each has its stated purposes, but can be used to address other concerns. For example, strategic planning is often issued to redirect agency objectives, as well as coordinate activities among different units. Some managers use strategic planning as a means to further the development of department capabilities. Performance improvement strategies often solve a variety of problems. Furthermore, productivity purposes that are not fully reached through one strategy are often reinforced using another. For example, the need for measurement is furthered by strategic planning, continuous improvement, program evaluation, and benchmarking.

Third, managers must address the manner in which they implement targeted improvements. Organizational realities and external constraints cannot be ignored. Neither can the strengths and weaknesses of managers who assist in implementing improvements, or in efforts needed to obtain the commitment and motivation of employees. Cynicism must be overcome and old and new foes must be reckoned with. There now exists a broad literature on implementing organizational change. Choosing a good implementation strategy is key to success, as important as the performance improvement strategy itself.

Another way of understanding the implementation challenge is that *performance improvement is an intervention in the existing state of the organization.* The magnitude of the required change effort not only depends on the nature of the performance improvement effort, but also on the present state of values, systems, tools, and behaviors. Organizations whose values are already consistent with various performance improvement strategies probably experience less resistance to using, say, benchmarking, than those that are committed to, for example, getting by with least effort. Depending on the organization, some changes will take multiple efforts over time. Discontinued efforts are not necessarily evidence of fads or failures but, like all efforts, must be evaluated in terms of their impact on existing cultures, practices, behaviors, and skills. This is the focus of chapter 3, which discusses strategies for successfully implementing performance and change.

In sum, the strategic perspective requires that managers (1) identify specific performance problems and goals, (2) identify a range of appropriate performance improvement strategies, and (3) develop an implementation strategy for successfully affecting change.

Performance Improvement in Historical Context

Performance improvement is a body of knowledge and management practice aimed at improving the effectiveness and efficiency of organizations. Performance strategies have been typically developed in response to past challenges or conditions. Thus, to understand the evolution of performance is in large measure to understand the challenges that organizations faced in historical context. Some of these challenges are still with us today; hence the use of these older strategies as well. Some strategies were altered to reflect changed conditions, but they can be traced to back to their origins (Bouckaert 1990; Schachter 2004; Spicer 2004; Washnis 1980).

1900 to 1939

The development of performance involves five periods. Many performance strategies date back to the first period between 1900 and 1939, which is called the *industrialization period* (see Table 1.2). During this period, the scale and scope of many organizations dramatically increased. In the for-profit sector, factories grew much larger, and companies became more complex as they added new divisions and departments (e.g., personnel). Increased size reflected both demand (many consumers wanted a Ford Model-T), as well as competitive advantages arising from economies of size and scope (e.g., integration with suppliers and distributors). The challenge of increased demand was revisited on federal agencies such as the Department of the Army, the Department of the Navy, and the Internal Revenue Service. The for-profit experience created many new performance strategies relating to the rationalization of work processes, supervisory management skills, the roles of executives, and principles of organization.

Performance strategies associated with the rationalization of work processes are often discussed in connection with Frederick Taylor's scientific management. The purpose of this approach, first described in 1911 (Taylor 1911), is to increase the efficiency and effectiveness of operations by identifying the best work practices, selecting employees to perform these practices,

Table 1.2

The Evolution of Productivity

Period	Problem	Selected strategies
1900–1939: "Industrialization"	Growth of organizations	(1) Hierarchical designs; (2) Rationalizing work process; (3) Supervising and motivating workers; (4) Functions of executives: PODSCORB
1939–1945: "World War II"	Quality war products	Quality production and control
1945–1965: "Postwar growth"	Controlling growth	Program and performance budgets
	Human motivation	Research: Theory X vs. Theory Y
1965–1980: "Program analysis"	Increasing program efficiency and effectiveness	Operations research, cost-benefit analysis, PPBS/ZBB, strategic planning
	Human motivation	Organizational development
1980–present: "Quality paradigm"	Increasing effectiveness and efficiency through organization	Outsourcing, partnering, flattening organizations, use of information technology
	Stakeholder trust	Broad-based strategic planning; Total Quality Management and related strategies

and ensuring implementation. Taylor also discussed economies that resulted from working in teams. An important challenge was the impact of new work processes on supervisory management, which was required to deal with more employees in a more impersonal manner than under previous craftsman-apprentice systems. In 1926 Mary Parker Follett described how supervisors can best get employees to follow instructions without creating resistance: Requests should be depersonalized, and bad work habits such as slothfulness or failure to follow procedures should be examined for their consequences (Shafritz and Hyde 1992). This is congruent with Dale Carnegie's work on making friends and influencing people by creating areas of agreement, cooperation, and conforming desires. According to Follett, psychology is an important part of scientific management, and managers require training and testing in both.

Another problem of the time was defining the functions of executives and departments. For example, the role of personnel departments (now renamed human resources departments) was defined as managing the flow and effectiveness of employees through such activities as designing job descriptions, recruitment, selection, hiring, training, appraisal, support, and exit. Effective and efficient strategies were developed in each of these areas. The job of the executive was described by Gullick (Gullick and Urwick 1937), based on the work of Henry Fayol, as POSDCORB, or: planning, organizing, staffing, directing, coordinating, reporting, and budgeting. Organization of the new bureaucracies was a critical concern. The "correct" design of organizations was advocated for based on the need for specialization (hence, different departments for personnel, marketing, etc.), the need for authority to coordinate different departments, and limits on the number of employees or departments that one person could effectively oversee. Although these principles helped, they were later challenged as somewhat vague and sometimes inconsistent. For example, the principle of clear and undistorted communication suggests that supervisors should deal directly with many subordinates, but the principle of limited span of control suggests that managers must limit the number of subordinates that they directly oversee.

These principles of scientific management and organizational design were used in public agencies as well as nonprofit organizations. Hospital administrators used the new techniques to distinguish themselves from doctors, even though most hospitals continued to be run by doctors. Bouckaert (1990) and others describe these strategies as the basis for reform movements to create a government less influenced by politics and corruption and more by professional, efficient management. During this period, schools of public administration were created to train public managers in these new techniques (e.g., Maxwell School of Citizenship at Syracuse, New York), and various commissions were created to further the use of business techniques in government at all levels.

1939 to 1945

The principles of organization and scientific management were widely applied during World War II (1939–1945), especially by the federal government. This is the second period of performance improvement. The war effort also created a need for increased performance and reliability in manufacturing. Consumer products sometimes malfunctioned, but higher standards were required on the battlefield for tanks, planes, and communications. Domestic manufacturers who converted to wartime production developed new techniques of quality control in mass production. This quality-based, industrial capacity of the United States is credited with being one of several factors that lead to the eventual success of the Allies. However, these high-quality manufacturing strategies were largely discontinued in the United States after the war because many companies considered them too costly and unnecessary for consumer goods. Some U.S. wartime production strategies were absorbed by Japanese companies in their rebuilding efforts, which improved and refined them, sometimes aided by U.S. engineers in the postwar period as part of the postwar reconstruction effort. Japanese companies were quite successful at doing so, and many of these strategies were later reintroduced in the United States in the late 1970s as TQM, to be discussed further below.

1945 to 1965

The third period is called "postwar growth" and occurred between 1945 and 1965. An important concern at the time was the sharp rise in government spending, and new budget strategies were introduced to control costs. Specifically, traditional line item budgets (used primarily for accountability in spending) were complemented by functional and performance budgets. Functional (or activity) budgets link resources to activity levels (e.g., expenditures related to street maintenance). Performance budgets relate resources to outcomes (for example, cost per street mile cleaned). They are efficiency budgets. Although these techniques had only limited impact at the time, the development of these budgets and measures has increased over time.

During this period, researchers undertook significant efforts to increase their understanding of human motivation as related to performance. Maslow conceived a hierarchy of needs (1954), suggesting that whereas some people only work to satisfy their physiological and safety needs (e.g., for food and shelter), others require social acceptance, recognition, and self-actualization. According to this model, workers could not be adequately motivated without meeting their particular needs. They might comply with management, but lack commitment. This causes performance to slump. McGregor (1960) described people as Theory X versus Theory Y types, whereby the former have a dislike for work ("lazy workers") and the latter view work as natural as play ("motivated workers"). These theories would become the foundation of later experimentation during the 1970s.

1965 to 1980

The fourth period, between 1965 and 1980, focused on program improvement. It had five developments. The first one is the development of operations research. These analytical techniques, invented during World War II, were greatly advanced by developments in computers, mathematics, and statistics. They include simulation and queuing modeling, linear programming, and decision-analysis, as well as advanced tools of project management. Operations research techniques are often used for logistical problems, such as those found in defense and transportation. These techniques optimize resources and outcomes, such as by identifying the optimum number of buses serving multiple routes, which minimizes waiting and transfer periods and limits expenditures. A second development was the use of economic techniques, specifically, cost-benefit/effectiveness analysis and risk assessment, which are often used in environmental management and infrastructure investment decisions. In addition, program evaluation was developed and refined to assess program outcomes, identify community needs, and evaluate service efficiency (Newland 1972). These became relevant to nonprofit organizations in their work under federal grants. A third development was the introduction of elaborate budget processes, such as Planning-Programming Budgeting and Zero-Based Budgeting, to better control costs and "force" discussion about the effectiveness of programs. These budgeting processes related program expenditures to other broader goals, other programs, and alternative spending amounts. But they failed to take hold. They were too encompassing and cumbersome, and often failed to take into account the incremental and political nature of programs. With few exceptions, these budget approaches are not much used today, but vestiges still shape some decisions in agencies.

A fourth development concerned the link between organization and strategy. Many companies diversified and became multinational. The disparate mix of services and products created a need for the strategic management of highly diversified portfolios and decision-making processes for making strategic decisions. From this challenge developed strategic planning. This was later adapted by the public sector as a broad-based, consensus-building strategy among public and private organizations (chapter 5). Finally, during this period research ideas about human motivation were put into practice through organizational development (OD). Early OD applications emphasized increased human expression, open communication, and team building (e.g., T-groups). Because these practices were not perceived as directly contributing to performance, many were discontinued in the mid-1970s. However, later applications pioneered concepts of planned organizational change for diffusing new processes throughout entire organizations. These are currently central to performance improvement strategies.

1980 to the Present

The period from 1980 to the present is the called the "Quality Paradigm" and focuses on broader and decidedly strategic concerns. Concern with client relations and the quality of services caused many organizations to consider TQM. First adopted by large U.S. multinational firms largely in response to competition from Japan, this practice rapidly spread through other sectors of the U.S. economy. By the mid-1990s, many governments had a first brush with TQM, and many nonprofit organizations were experimenting with it. Interest in improving quality also coincided with emerging public concerns in the 1970s about trust in public and private organizations; many of these concerns continue today. TQM helps organizations to address trust issues in the areas of customer service, service delivery, and accountability (Berman 2003). Today, TQM is a comprehensive management paradigm that emphasizes customer orientation, empowerment, objective data in decision making (including performance measurement), and a holistic view of delivery and production processes. Many applications of TQM begin with emphasizing and meeting customer expectations, and many organizations have greatly improved their customer service. However, many organizations find TQM involves too much change initially. Instead, they adopt different aspects of TQM over time: customer orientation, benchmarking, reengineering, and empowerment.

The present period also involves new uses of information technology and rethinking of organizational designs. Increased use of information technology has eliminated the need for middle managers who deal primarily with data or information processing. This enables flatter organizations with less overhead costs. Continued budget pressures also foster increased use of partnering and networking strategies; many organizations shed functions to other organizations with whom they contract or partner. This allows them to specialize and develop economies of scale, thus providing superior and more cost-effective services. Although partnering has been long used by nonprofit organizations, many of these organizations are finding new opportunities with government and business. As a result of budget pressures and information technologies, the closed model of organizations is being replaced with a fluid, flatter, and networked model of organizations. By comparison with earlier approaches to performance improvement, the present efforts are decidedly more strategic in nature.

In Conclusion

Public and nonprofit organizations significantly affect and improve the lives of their communities and clients. Performance is defined as the effectiveness and efficient use of resources to achieve results. Public and nonprofit organizations vary in their emphasis on effectiveness and efficiency. Performance improvement is viewed as a slowly diffusing body of strategies used by managers and their organizations, organizations vary in their use of strategies. A threefold strategic perspective is suggested for performance improvement, which addresses the importance of assessing goals, identifying performance

challenges and appropriate performance improvement strategies, and designing efficacious implementation efforts. There are many fine examples of high
performance in public and nonprofit organizations, and all organizations can
do better, and many try to. The strategies discussed in this book are designed
to help managers improve the performance of their organizations.

Application Exercises

1. Identify some performance improvement strategies that have found
   increased use in your agency. What is your agency doing better today than in the past? Is there improvement over time?
2. Make a list of current performance issues in your program or agency.
   Specifically, identify those relating to effectiveness and goal attainment, efficiency in operations, equity in services, and accountability. Consider how your list or priorities might change when viewing
   them from the perspective of program clients or citizens.
3. Can you imagine how your program would be different if it were
   undertaken in a public, nonprofit or a for-profit organization? What
   positive/negative consequences might that have?
4. "Managers need not reinvent the wheel, but need to be creative in
   adapting existing efforts to their organization." Explain.
5. Apply the strategic perspective described in the text to a specific
   problem in your organization.
6. Identify five performance improvement strategies in your workplace,
   and identify the historical period with which they are associated. Be
   sure to include some from previous eras in addition to the present
   era. How well are these strategies working in your workplace? By
   what measure(s) do you conclude this?

Note

1. In the first edition, productivity was defined as including both efficiency and
effectiveness, but in recent years the narrower definition has become commonplace.
Sometimes managers refer to activities, outputs, or outcomes as "productivity." For
example, in some educational institutions, the number of students taught is referred to
as a unit's "productivity." This may be activity, but it is not a measure of productivity
defined as efficiency.

Major Performance Challenges

There are many opportunities for improvement. This chapter looks at some areas in which improvement has often been recognized and sought in recent years. Taken together, these efforts provide an overview of commonly pursued performance goals. Specifically, improvement opportunities are discussed in the following four areas: (1) better serving external stakeholders' needs, (2) improving organizational effectiveness and using resources efficiently, (3) improving project management, and (4) increasing productivity through people. Modern performance improvements efforts often raise the bar in these areas, and managers are increasingly expected to be familiar with the strategies and standards that they involve. These areas offer important opportunities for increasing performance and productivity (White and Newcomber 2005; Ammons 2004; Covey 1992; Herman 2004).

Performance improvement often begins with a diagnosis of things that the organization is not achieving, and which managers and others think it should. This is consistent with the strategic perspective of performance improvement discussed in the preceding chapter. A gap is experienced between expectations and reality—the promise or hope of what an organization can do is not being met. Manifestations such as inefficient or shoddy service, cost overruns, low client satisfaction, failure to make key decisions—all indicate things are out of kilter, either a little or a lot. A disquiet or dissatisfaction exists about the status quo—something is not good enough. From this awareness of things not quite measuring up (something is seen as "way too much" or "much too little") begins the search for underlying problems, which eventually leads to the adoption of new goals, and the development of processes to help the organization move toward a more desirable state (Bardach 2000). Performance goals express the gap between what organizations experience, often undesired, and what they think they would like to experience.

It is clear that goals imply, implicitly or explicitly, a standard or vision of how things could be. Client complaints are a problem only in the presence of a standard or alternate future in which fewer clients complain; otherwise, they are just a statement of fact that people are complaining. Where there is no standard, there is no discussion about success or improvement. However, performance goals should not only reflect what can or should be improved, but also a realistic assessment about what can be changed. This chapter focuses on the former, whereas chapter 3 considers the reality of change in organizations that impose preferences or constraints that managers must consider. This chapter sketches the lay of the land, whereas the next chapter examines strategies for making change happen successfully.

The overview of possible performance improvement opportunities provided in this chapter can also be viewed as a list of problems of modern organizations. Where there exists an improvement opportunity, there also exists a problem. The tables in this chapter are designed as a checklist for possible performance problems. While there are many possible problems that organizations could address, most are able to work on only one or two major problems at a time. It takes time and dedication to make changes well and ensure that they are enduring. Thus, managers will want to select among those problems that appear most urgent for them.

Managers know well that performance problems are not always readily seen. What shows up as a low client satisfaction often is but a symptom of something else, such as a lack of information technology, uncaring employees, or an outdated and deficient delivery process. Symptoms of problems are also sometimes covered up—managers seldom want others to know that their unit experiences cost overruns or complaining clients. Reasons are given why problems or symptoms do not exist as such, but rather as "understandable phenomena" in the light of circumstances. All organizations experience the challenge of openness versus obfuscation to a greater or lesser extent. If we are to make improvements, then we need to look beyond the stories and excuses to the facts as they exist. We need to be willing to look deeply and honestly into how things are functioning. Is the lack of employee motivation a manifestation of something deeper, such as too much red tape? This chapter is more than an inventory of modern performance challenges; it is also an invitation to think more deeply about what is really going on inside your organization. It is an opportunity to get to the fundamental root causes of your organization's functioning. To that end, it also identifies symptoms that may point toward performance problems, and it concludes with thoughts on the process of problem diagnosis in performance improvement.

Stakeholders

In recent years, organizations are increasingly viewed as "open systems" that thrive through exchanges with their environment: organizations must satisfy the needs of their stakeholders: clients, citizens, elected officials, and community leaders. When the needs of these stakeholders are met, organizations benefit from increased support for their missions. However, when their stakeholders' needs are unmet, organizations suffer the consequences through democratic processes and the loss of clientele. Revenues and appropriations decline. Table 2.1 shows a range of major stakeholder problems, and variations that may occur. Each of these implies improvement opportunity.

Attention to customer and stakeholder needs is a key legacy of the efforts to embrace Total Quality Management (TQM) and other customer-oriented strategies that have been emphasized in the public and nonprofit sectors since the early 1990s (Boyne 2002). Communities expect programs to be tailored to their needs. The standard is now increasingly that organizations identify their target groups or constituencies, and then develop programs to meet their needs (Problem 1). For example, parks departments must tailor their services to teenagers, single mothers, and retirees—they must know what each group's needs are. These managers might be surprised that many retirees are as interested today in yoga and business development as they are in socializing and playing cards. Public safety departments must correctly assess the different needs and priorities of low-income populations and affluent neighborhoods if they are to serve these populations well. Different neighborhoods do have different problems. Tax collectors' offices must also serve people who are blind and those who do not speak English. Although public agencies typically cannot pick and choose their markets—they are chartered to serve the entire population—they need to correctly identify the needs of different groups. The challenge and opportunity is for managers to find new needs that they can meet.

This approach stands in sharp contrast with the one-size-fits-all mentalities of the past, whereby services are narrowly designed around their stated missions, irrespective of the needs of different groups and the impact of these services on community outcomes. For example, park departments would provide facilities with little consideration for serving the needs of different age groups. They developed community resources that were to be used by those who wanted to. Police departments would provide an equal number of patrols to different neighborhoods, regardless of whether this served the needs of different neighborhoods. Today, such approaches are considered ineffective, outdated, and unacceptable. The bar has been raised. Agencies are assessed by the results they produce for their different

Table 2.1

Major Performance Problems, Part 1

Major stakeholder problems

Typical symptoms of major stakeholder problems: stakeholder complaints, stakeholder apathy, low levels of stakeholder satisfaction, stakeholders or community leaders ganging up on the organization.

Problem 1:   Needs of target groups are not sufficiently met.

Variations: Programs are absent or too small to meet target group needs, programs or policies perform poorly, client groups feel disenfranchised or excluded from decision-making processes, target groups have unrealistic expectations.

Problem 2:   Individuals who interact with the agency are dissatisfied.

Variations: Unresponsiveness by agency staff, poor mix of interaction mechanisms, inadequate frontline service.

Problem 3:   Citizens, clients, or community leaders are apathetic about the program.

Variations: Inadequate enthusiasm for new programs, inadequate support of agency goals and staff.

Problem 4:   Individuals or groups are making politics at the expense of the organization.

Major organizational problems

Typical symptoms of major organizational problems: infighting in units, turf battles across units, efforts that consistently sound right but fail to produce results, perceptions of having too many meetings and not doing enough work, spending too much time managing coordination across units, generating plans that gather dust, excessve budget requests, and demotivated employees.

Problem 5:   The mission of the organization (or program) does not serve important society needs.

Variations: The mission(s) has become outdated, failure to obtain new authority and mandates.

Problem 6:   Missions are not being pursued.

Variations: Lack of focus, inadequate program development, the organization as a rudderless ship, poor or inadequate resources (financial, technology/skills, people).

Problem 7:   The organization or delivery technology is inefficient.

Variations: Organization does not take advantage of economies of scale, delivery process has too many people or units involved, doing it all in-house, inefficient or ineffective use of information technology, delivery process is not informed by state of art practice, red tape.

Problem 8:   Inadequate coordination.

Variations: Coordination omits organizations or departments, coordination is shoddy or incomplete, coordination exists, but the outcome does not serve mission or stakeholder needs.

Problem 9: Communication is unclear, contradictory, or ignored.
Variations: A lack of unitary command, contradictory demands, cultural and interpersonal differences cloud communication, communication is misinterpreted by the command structure.

Problem 10: Rewards do not support mission.
Variations: Rewards or acknowledgement are absent or support other priorities, rewards or consequences encourage perverse behavior.

client groups and communities. Nonprofit agencies have long been accustomed to the need for tailoring, but some do it much better than others, and grant-making agencies are increasingly raising the bar on accountability in this area, as well.

A challenge is to know which expectations communities and clients hold. Communities seldom speak with a single or even a clear voice, and they and their leaders also may make unrealistic and contradictory demands. Some residents measure performance by whether or not traffic jams disappear and if social services for infant children are provided for free—these are unrealistic, fantastic expectations. Drivers like to drive their cars at speeds they think are safe, but as residents they prefer that all drivers adhere to far lower speed limits—these are contradictory expectations. Another challenge for leaders is to articulate a vision for the stakeholders and explain how their services fit within that vision. Organizations need to provide the right services that help their communities and clients move forward. Residents and community leaders may not realize the possibilities of the agency, but the agency would be remiss not to develop programs and policies that help them move forward. This conundrum of conflicting, interdependent, and underdeveloped interests requires open communication (King and Zanetti 2005). Managers need to identify and assess community needs by talking with community leaders, and also by conducting focus groups, citizen surveys, and holding public hearings. Doing so helps to process and evaluate citizen expectations, avoid citizens' groups feeling disenfranchised, and helps raise and test new ideas. Through this dialogue, organizations are able to explain their policies as mindful of different interests and consistent with the broader interests of the community. Failure to gain workable community acceptance through these processes causes the credibility of organizations to suffer and complicates the job of the agency of meeting stakeholder needs. The improvement opportunity is to find new, effective ways of involving community leaders and citizens.

Many agencies have significantly improved their customer service and responsiveness in recent years. This, too, is a legacy of TQM. No longer is frontline service in public and nonprofit organizations often synonymous with long lines and uncaring employees (Problem 2). Expectations and performance have risen. High performing organizations set high standards for customer service and seek proactive ways to ensure high satisfaction, making even slight deviations a matter of internal import. They provide customers with a broad range of convenient and technology-based ways to interact with them; they make their services customer-friendly and develop them with the customers' needs in mind. Interactions with public and nonprofit organizations need not be an annoying and aggravating event—but in some organizations they still are. Phone calls are not returned, clients are given the runaround, environments are dirty and run down, employees are uncaring, and they offer clients fewer choices for interacting with them. In many organizations, there is still ample room for improvement.

Providing customer service in the public sector has its unique issues, some of which are "red herrings." Some public officials believe that customer service is more difficult in the public sector because some services are involuntary—such as getting a speeding ticket or being audited by the IRS. But saying "no" to customers is not unique to the public sector—private businesses do it every day. Experience shows that tax inspectors and police officers can get high marks for their courtesy and respect, even while explaining infractions and penalty options. Inspectors can be friendly and helpful, or not. Employees do not have to be rude or uncaring; more can be done than merely citing this or that rule or policy. In short, customer service standards can be set for all interactions. Of course, many public service interactions do not involve the above scenarios, but rather straightforward information and service requests, such as asking information about one's Social Security benefits.

Another problem is a lack of support by leadership networks and public apathy (Problem 3). Managing programs well does not automatically guarantee a cadre of committed supporters, which are necessary to help see public organizations and their programs through inevitable periods of controversy, and nonprofit organizations through inevitable times of resource scarcity and the need for lobbying. Leadership and public support are invaluable assets that help programs grow and contribute to their communities; the improvement opportunity is to cultivate and maintain leadership support. Such support can also deal with another problem, that of individuals or groups making politics at the expense of the agency (Problem 4). It is not uncommon for political candidates or political rivals to take shots at an agency, for example. When this occurs, managers must stand their ground, defending the achievements and integrity of the organization. They must communicate the pride of the organization and it's mission. Agencies and programs that fail to cultivate stakeholder support experience a lack of community and political support when it is needed. Table 2.1 shows typical symptoms that may indicate a need for improvement in dealing with stakeholders and addressing their needs: stakeholder complaints, apathy, dissatisfaction, and lack of stakeholder support for organizational objectives. Each of these attest to something "not quite right," suggesting a gap between actual and desired performance in one or more of the above areas.

Organization

Many performance problems are caused by failure to adhere to basic principles of organizational design. This can produce symptoms such as infighting, lack of direction, micromanagement, spending too much time on coordination, plans that gather dust, and the inefficient use of or acquisition of resources. Employee demotivation may occur as a secondary result. These problems affect programs as well as agencies as a whole. What are these basic principles that give rise to so many symptoms? Though authors define these differently, at heart, organizational design is about (1) deciding what the purpose of the organization is, and then (2) allocating responsibility, along with (3) resources, to getting the job done. Within this seemingly simple notion of focusing on the "what and how" lie a host of challenges and pitfalls.

One problem is that agency missions and program goals fail to serve important needs in society (Problem 5). For many years the Federal Bureau of Investigation (FBI) was slow to adapt to the growing need for counterterrorism intelligence. Even following the September 11, 2001, terrorist attacks against the New York World Trade Center and elsewhere, it was reluctant to expand its mission in this area. Instead, it remained rooted in its post–World War II missions, which included counterespionage of Communist activities in the United States, even though this mission had diminished significance and had become outdated. This also happened at NASA, the space agency that had come into existence in the late 1950s after the U.S.S.R. (Russia) launched the world's first satellite. Concerned about being dominated by the U.S.S.R. in space, President John F. Kennedy challenged the fledging U.S. space industry to land a man on the moon and safely return him by the end of the 1960s. Since that historic accomplishment in 1969, NASA has struggled to find an equally compelling mission. It redefined its mission around a mix of unmanned space exploration, manned space flight, and advanced aeronautics, but none has captured the public's imagination as the early Apollo missions did. Agency missions and programs need to be periodically updated and aligned with important societal needs, or they become outdated. Performance improvement can begin by asking what missions are being pursued, and how relevant these missions are.

Sometimes agencies fail to acquire new mandates or authority in a timely fashion. Many contemporary local problems have a regional or intergovern-mental focus, such as environmental protection, transportation, education, and public safety. In each of these areas, new goals and objectives often exceed mandates of existing jurisdictions. For example, transportation solutions re-quire regional approaches to managing growth that often require new policy mandates for local jurisdictions. Sometimes, the authority that is sought is less encompassing, such as the ability to access information in another agency's database. When agencies cannot acquire new mandates, progress becomes sty-mied, limited, and eventually unsatisfactory (Behn 1995).

Another problem occurs when well-aligned missions and necessary man-dates are inadequately pursued (Problem 6). A common occurrence is the ad-dition of new missions over time, sometimes reflecting stakeholder pressures. For example, many schools provide an ever-expanding range of nonacademic services to students, including after-school programs, teen counseling, sports activities, and so on. Diversification may dilute the main objective of learn-ing, and cause intra-organizational rivalry over resources and priorities. Non-profit organizations also sometimes overextend their resources in an effort to serve broad populations, thereby failing to serve client groups well. Not only does overreaching dilute grant writing and fundraising efforts, grant writing that is not closely linked to furthering core missions may take nonprofit or-ganizations into areas for which they are poorly equipped—the tail is wag-ging the dog. The lack of a clear mission-driven focus can cause missions to be inadequately pursued.

The improvement opportunity is for agencies to know what they are about, and what their priorities are (Bryson 2004). Problems arise when leaders fail to be clear about these points. Then, for example, the wrong people are as-signed to key positions. New ideas about how to pursue the mission are not solicited or followed up. Too little pressure is put on lower managers for performance. Work upon work is piled on. Leaders are overwhelmed, ill pre-pared, sidetracked, or excessively involved in operational program manage-ment. These problems can be exacerbated by leadership turnover, for example, causing too-frequent shifts in priorities; successive leaders set them, but they are not pursued long enough to create a focus for the agency. New programs are met with a sense of déjà vu. The agency, department, or program is seen as a rudderless ship (Caiden 1991).

Another consequence of leadership failure is that resources are not sought and acquired. In recent years, many organizations have hired grant writers to assist them in obtaining resources from federal and state agencies and pri-vate foundations. Those that have not may find themselves lacking resources to fully implement necessary programs. Leadership is needed to ensure that agencies have the direction and resources to carry out their missions.

After responsibilities have been determined and assigned, people, resources, and technology are brought together—an organization is created. There are many different ways of organizing, and many take advantage of economies of scale (that is, size), economies of scope (that is, diversification), and cost-effective delivery methods, while being mindful of modern standards, the need for continuity, and the ability to adapt to changing circumstances. These are some common standards for evaluating the effectiveness of organization. Problems occur when the organization or delivery technology is inefficient (Problem 7).

Obviously, there is no one best way of organizing; what works well for one organization may not work well for another. For example, medical imaging technology often has economies of scale that require minimum utilization rates. Hospitals can organize this technology by purchasing it as equipment for individual service departments, by establishing new units that are viewed as cost or profit centers, by purchasing imaging services from third-party providers, by forming partnerships with other hospitals (thereby minimizing utilization uncertainty and avoiding third-party profits). What is best depends on specific factors; form must follow purpose. But when conditions or missions change, it is necessary to consider the organizational form. Does the specific form still make sense given changes in the mission or operating conditions? Is there a better, more cost-effective way to address the need?

Increasingly, organizations are evaluating their use of departments as basic units of organization. Departments are justifiably used when there are well-defined areas of responsibility that have continuity of purpose, and when there are minimum economies of scale, scope, or a critical mass that must be met. Departments also shield organizations from resource uncertainty, for example, by ensuring a pool of qualified personnel. But concerns about the rigidity of departments and sometimes high cost structures cause top managers to consider partnerships, alliances, and outsourcing as alternative ways for obtaining capacity. The latter may provide a more flexible and cost-effective approach to mission accomplishment, especially in areas in which developing expertise or economies of scale are not the agency's main focus. For example, agencies increasingly contract out for their routine administrative and maintenance functions.

Modern thinking about delivery processes and the use of information technology has also changed organization forms. Internet and intranet pages now allow offsite access to electronic databases and help organizations deal efficiently with many routine client inquiries. Delivery approaches emphasize streamlining, fewer steps, and greater responsibility for outcomes. These often involve process reengineering and approaches to employee empowerment discussed in later chapters. When too many people or units become involved, errors and delays occur. The ability to utilize new forms of organization to increase responsiveness and achieve lower costs is a hallmark of modern organizations. When organizations fail to take advantage of these new forms, they often experience employee and stakeholder complaints about the inability to provide requested services.

The corollary of organization is coordination (Problem 8). Many managers spend much time coordinating the efforts of departments and people. There is truth in the expression that management is the art of getting work done through others. Organizations are increasingly networked, which means that they depend on cooperation and collaboration (Goldsmith and Eggers 2004). Reflecting this, the federal emergency response plan is now retitled as the National Response Plan, highlighting coordination with numerous local and state agencies. When people fail to cooperate and collaborate, programs become ineffective. This may be caused by lack of understanding of the mission, improper assignment of responsibility, failure to collaborate, political rivalry, or other reasons. Whatever the cause, lack of coordination reduces program effectiveness.

Coordination requires effective communication. Unclear or contradictory communication is an obvious area for improvement (Problem 9). Communication is seldom a matter of people not hearing each other well; it is more commonly a problem of not having a clear understanding of responsibilities, of what is expected from them in terms of both results and communication, and how their authority relates to that of others. Problems arise when people are confused about their roles and how they relate to others. People make assumptions, some of which cause conflict. A lack of unified command sends conflicting signals, cultural biases interpret messages in ways that add to confusion; major technology failures can sometimes be traced to command structures failing to heed warnings or giving unclear instructions (Garrett 2004).

People vary in how they interpret what is said between the lines. Complex rules breed uncertainty and confusion. A general guideline is to keep understandings, expectations, and relations as simple as possible. Ironically, policy manuals seldom dispel this confusion, either because they are quite complex or because they fail to communicate what is needed to get the job done. People forget their rules, or are confused about how they apply in a variety of different situations.

Finally, problems occur when rewards do not support the mission (Problem 10). Every formal structure depends on informal relations and goodwill to produce quality results. Individuals must be willing to go above and beyond that which is expected of them in order to deal with unforeseen situations. Feedback is the mechanism through which the effectiveness of past actions is assessed; rewards, incentives, and norms are means to encourage future productive behavior. People and organizations need to know through material recognition and other forms of acknowledgment that they are doing well; they also need to know when improvements are needed. When rewards are perceived as small and insignificant, managers lose an important tool of motivation, and morale and productivity may suffer. When positive feedback (praise, etc.) is withheld, employees receive the message that the impact was not noteworthy. Indeed, a frequent workplace complaint is that employees and managers are not given sufficient positive and consistent feedback or recognition for their work. Employees may also receive contradictory signals, which undermine the mission—encouraging risk while punishing failure encourages risk-avoidance and make-believe risk-taking.

Projects

Whereas the above focuses on organizations and programs, the following focuses on projects and work activities. When projects are managed poorly, they fall behind schedule, lack relevance, exceed costs, and fail to meet standards, yielding stakeholder dissatisfaction or apathy. They fail to contribute to the agency's mission. Project management is about avoiding these outcomes. The hallmark of properly managed programs is that they achieve their objectives (1) on time, (2) within budget, and (3) at or above quality and performance specifications.

Planning is more than developing to-do lists, though it involves these, too. Planning involves the assessment of goals, identifying resources and strategies, assessing the quality of resources, combining resources and strategies into a timetable, and anticipating challenges to performance and developing contingency plans. An important expression is: "people don't plan to fail, they fail to plan" (Problem 11, Table 2.2). Improvement begins by asking how well planning occurs.

Legislators and top leaders frequently formulate lofty goals that are broad, appealing, and . . . infeasible. During the 1960s and 1970s, neither the War on Poverty nor the War on Cancer could eliminate poverty or cancer; both persist. Of course, progress and very worthwhile achievements were made. When "stretch" goals are set that challenge current abilities, realistic targets should be set for evaluating progress toward final ends. Before the Apollo 11 mission could land a man on the moon, the Apollo 9 mission circled the moon and operated the lunar landing craft just to develop those capabilities. They were significant stretch objectives that allowed for subsequent missions. Progress is made in challenging but realistic steps; projects

Table 2.2

Major Performance Problems, Part 2

Major Project Problems
   Typical symptoms of project problems: insufficient relevance, falling behind schedule, not achieving results, going way over budget, and having upset or apathetic clients and other stakeholders.

Problem 11:   Inadequate planning.
   Variations: Unrealistic goals, misalignment between ends and strategies, resources are poor or inadequate, lack of a contingency strategy.

Problem 12:   Inadequate control of execution.
   Variations: Not sufficiently knowing the status of projects or events that affect projects, allowing partners and people to get sidetracked.

Problem 13:   Lack of satisfaction among clients or stakeholders.
   Variations: Clients insufficiently involved, clients' needs wrongly assumed (see Problem 1).

Major People Problems
   Typical symptoms of people problems: people shunning their work, manager, or coworkers, staff demotivation, formal or informal complaints against a person, projects falling behind, lack of new programs, successful programs, or program leadership.
   Note: These symptoms are not always caused by people problems. People may show these symptoms when caused by other problems such as poor coordination or red tape.

Problem 14:   Values are insufficiently professional.
   Variations: Unethical or a-ethical behavior, disinterest in skill development.

Problem 15:   Technical skills are lacking.
   Variations: Inability to acquire modern skills, avoiding activities that require technical skills, denial that skills are lacking, mediocrity, micromanagement.

Problem 16:   Poor social skills.
   Variations: Being too confrontational or too accommodating, being impulsive, being closed to constructive criticism or opportunities for growth.

fail when goals are too far beyond current abilities. The art is to get the learning steps just right.

After the goal has been determined, managers must ensure that they have sufficient resources and the right strategies to get the job done. If personnel or resources are lacking, or inefficiently deployed, then accomplishments (objectives) or timetables will suffer. A timetable is not a wish list; it reflects the fit among the goals, strategy, and resources. If the strategy is inefficient, it will take longer to accomplish the goal. If the strategy is ineffective, the goal may never be reached. If mediocre talent is assigned to projects that require expertise and judgment, the results will often be lesser results.

Another purpose of planning is to develop contingency plans by anticipating unexpected events. A lack of planning and foresight gives room for catastrophic events to occur which, according to Murphy's Law ("what can go wrong will go wrong") they have a tendency to do. The more managers know about a project and its conditions for success, the more managers will want to plan. Inadequate concern for possible failure is a red flag; it may be a sign of naiveté, wishful thinking, mediocrity, inadequate commitment to success, or unimaginative foresight about what can go wrong. The improvement opportunity is to take planning seriously, to acquire the right resources, have plans for contingencies, and be certain of the standards and timetables that are to be met.

Another project problem is inadequate control of execution (Problem 12). Delays have myriad causes and not everything can be foreseen. Contingency strategies can help provide a quick response when something goes wrong, but even the best-laid plans cannot predict every way in which something can go awry. What is certain is that something unforeseen will occur. Project execution is very much about knowing what is occurring, so that the right responses are made. When managers fail to follow what is happening, they get blindsided by major errors and problems. Staff gets tasked with competing projects, or partners squabble over an unforeseen obstacle. Some problems, such as shoddy work, become evident only by hands-on involvement and inspection. The point about execution is to get to the finish line and do that well. When managers fail to measure progress against milestones and target dates, slippage often occurs.

Problems of stakeholder dissatisfaction, discussed earlier in this chapter, are sometimes revisited in project management (Problem 13). When clients are inadequately involved in project decision making and fail, for whatever reason, to articulate their needs they may become dissatisfied later. For example, a parks and recreation department provides card games for seniors, who prefer aerobic exercise or even computer training. Or a public works department breaks open a road for repairs, assuming that residents won't mind the inconvenience for a month or two. When a budget office acquires a new software program for tracking expenditures and accomplishments without adequate input prior to purchase from users as internal clients, then these departments are apt to be dissatisfied and the program ill-suited to their needs. Failure to correctly know and manage client priorities increases the likelihood of their dissatisfaction and hence project failure, regardless of any technical mastery and execution.

People

It is obvious that people are key to making organizations work. When they fail, so too do many organizations and their programs. People are a critical resource. Typical symptoms of people problems are people shunning their work, their manager or their coworkers, staff demotivation, formal or informal complaints against a person, projects falling behind, and lack of new programs, successful programs, or program leadership.

Some people problems reflect having inadequate professional norms and standards (Problem 14). Professionalism is more than a set of skills or achievements: it involves personally held beliefs which, today, often emphasize orientation toward stakeholders, accountability, openness, integrity, and professional standards. These convictions are surely not omnipresent, and when managers fail to articulate or prioritize these norms, unethical and unprofessional behavior by some employees will likely result. Problems range from lack of courtesy and respect, to inadequate awareness and commitment to norms and high standards of professionalism, to lack of attention to blatant violations of agency rules and laws. This, then, gives rise to the symptoms of people problems in the above paragraph.

Organizations are increasingly requiring ethics workshops and short courses in order to reduce blatant disregard of important norms, and some are making ethics a criterion in hiring and promotion. Beyond these problems, the lack of commitment to professional standards may lower performance in ways that are only barely acceptable, as well as other problems discussed below (Bowman et al. 2004; Cooper 1998). The improvement opportunity is to set clear and consistent standards for professionalism, and to intervene at the earliest opportunity when standards are not sufficiently met.

Performance problems occur when people lack up-to-date technical skills for the work they are expected to do (Problem 15). For employees, these skills concern technical aspects related to work areas, including information technology applications, as well as basic aspects of project management. For managers, these skills include many of the organizational improvement strategies and techniques as well. When technical skills are deficient, work is performed at sub-standard levels or inefficiently. For example, a land surveyor who does not use the latest methods will take longer and be less accurate. Mental health workers who are unfamiliar with the latest therapies will be less effective. At worse, the lack of technical skills causes employees and managers to avoid activities that require these skills. Managers who lack quantitative skills may fail to undertake what-if analyses to maximize performance, for example. Such managers may also fail to appreciate the needs of subordinates who do have these skills, and to adequately plan the development of these skills in their units. When managers lack technical skills, they miss out on opportunities to improve their unit's performance.

However, technical skills alone do not ensure productivity by people. Social skills grease the wheels of human interaction (Problem 16). Different perspectives exist regarding critically needed social skills. Covey (1992) discusses the importance of refraining from saying unkind or negative things; the importance of exercising patience with others; keeping promises made to others; assuming the best in others; seeking to understand before reacting; giving an understanding response (rather than evaluative); admitting mistakes, apologizing and asking for forgiveness; allowing yourself to be influenced; and distinguishing between the person and the problem. According to Goleman (1995), the fundamentals of emotional intelligence (EQ) are: self-awareness (about one's feelings), impulse control, optimism in face of setbacks, the ability to identify and respond to the unspoken feelings of others, handling emotional reactions in others, interacting smoothly, and managing relations effectively. This is a broader perspective.

It is obvious that deficits in people skills, however defined, lead to problems in productivity. However, addressing social skill deficits can be challenging. Many workplaces lack patterns of communication in which social interactions and skills are discussed, and in which people receive feedback and support for improvement. In some environments, open communication is intentionally avoided (de Vries and Miller 1984). Unaware of such deficits, poor social skills go unchecked, and people falsely assume that others are aware of their own poor social skills. To help address this problem, chapter 7 discusses successful new ways of opening up the dialog. People may learn to adjust their responses through feedback and coaching.

Sometimes the social skill deficit problem runs deep and in ways that pose ongoing performance challenges for managers. Poor interactions may reflect severe problems that employees are unwilling or unable to change. People with significant depression or anxiety may not to be able to address deficits such as controlling one's impulses or identifying and being empathetic about the feelings of others. It may be difficult for obsessive-compulsive persons to refrain from saying unkind things, and codependency and addiction may cause people to be too accommodating, showing a lack of leadership. Rubbing people the wrong way may stem from deep personal insecurities and uncontrolled envy aimed at coworkers or colleagues who perform highly. Of course, not everyone with "people problems" has these underlying problems, or even to a strong extent. But for those who do become performance challenges for managers; the adage that 80 percent of the problems are caused by 20 percent of the people certainly applies. It is obvious that social skills continue to be an area of significant managerial concern.

Problem Definition as Activity

There are many possible performance problems, but for managers who are well familiar with their units, improvement opportunities in the above areas often are all too obvious. They know their unit's challenges well—too well, perhaps. Implicitly or explicitly, they have articulated standards, or others have told them what standards are to be met. They have prioritized their problems; they know what they need to work on first. The squeaky wheel is identified and needs to be addressed. But sometimes the underling problem may not always be so obvious, to them or to others. Supervisors of managers are apt to want to ascertain managers' diagnosis or statement of the problem; top leaders may want to engage in their own fact-finding. They will study the unit a bit, get some data and facts, and perhaps interview some employees or clients. This is also the case for new managers, consultants, and employees who are new to the organization. Things may not be fully as they appear. Sometimes problem definition is obvious, and sometimes it needs a bit of work. When problem definition is its own distinct activity, it is generally an iterative process that involves the following: (1) obtaining information about manifested symptoms, as well as associated circumstances and underlying causes; (2) assessing information about symptoms and causes against standards or a vision of the future, and developing a statement of the problem that expresses the gap between what is, and what should or could be; and (3) identifying strategies that help realize the future in ways that both address the manifest symptoms and their causes, and which move the organization forward in ways that are consistent with its broader priorities (Harrison 2004; Swanson 1996). These activities and their relationships are shown in Figure 2.1. This often is an iterative process that is not very linear. Information dribbles in, a bit from here and there, and managers assess initial conclusions until they are crystallized in a coherent and consistent way. Of course, at times the problem is straightforward—clients are not being attended to and the employees that should be doing so are all out for lunch. But sometimes the problem, standard, or intervention is not well defined, and managers must then develop their own understanding of these matters. Sometimes stakeholders have very strong opinions that are a given for managers, but even then managers will want to formulate their own understanding and determine what other problems might be resolved as well.

A core challenge to accurate problem definition often is that organizations present symptoms that do not fully reflect the range of problems that should be considered. For example, consider an organization in which manifest symptoms are infighting between units and low employee morale. But there may be more than meets the eye—there may be other relevant facts to

Figure 2.1 **Processes of Problem Definition**

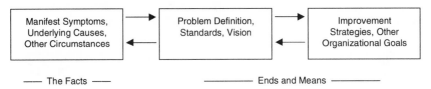

consider as part of problem diagnosis. For example, what if both infighting and low morale are caused by managers failing to identify priorities for the organization? Lack of leadership can readily give rise to these symptoms; units bicker to make their programs more important, and employees get caught up in this; for many, a loss of pride occurs. Yet, the lack of leadership may not be manifest, especially if it is covered up. If leadership is a problem and prioritization is not addressed, then the above problems are likely to persist or resurface at some point. Hasty diagnosis is the result of not digging deep enough, and thus making wrong conclusions. We need to ask why the manifest symptoms are occurring, before assuming that they constitute the entire problem. The following symptoms are red flags for the very likely possibility of deeper underlying problems: client complaints, infighting and prolonged turf battles, plans that gather dust, frequent lawsuits, excessive time in coordination and troubleshooting activities, employee demotivation, projects falling behind schedule or going over budget, and lack of new program development. Digging just a little deeper in any of these areas typically reveals a range of problems, many of which have been described in this chapter. Even experienced managers make the mistake of incorrectly identifying their unit's problems; they, too, need to dig deeply.

As an aside, some analogies exist between organizational performance and medical diagnosis. In both, symptoms can have different underlying causes; stomachaches could indicate indigestion or something far worse; low client satisfaction could be caused by many different things. We can't infer the problem from the symptom and vice versa; we need to establish the chain of causality. Analysis implies evaluating symptoms against contexts of what is normal and what is not. Poor doctors treat symptoms and fail to recognize underlying causes. Likewise, when defining performance problems we need know what normal organizational functioning is, the symptoms of malfunctioning, and processes (problems) that give rise to these symptoms. Finally, when considering possible problems, it makes sense to first consider commonly occurring problems, rather than those that are interesting and exotic but that rarely occur. This chapter's problems are certainly among those that frequently occur.

It is also well worth noting that the problem definition does not define the solution. The lack of leadership does not mean that the solution is more leadership. It may be to abolish the unit whose leadership has been lacking. Problem definition and problem solution are separate matters. Too many cost overruns in a program or activity does not mean doing less of the program or activity in order to reduce costs—it may be to do the program or activity in a more efficient way. There are options; there is more than one road that leads to Rome. However, the initial symptoms remain at the heart of the improvement effort, as it continues to define what needs to be improved.

A good problem definition is one that incorporates the manifest symptoms and includes a set of viable strategies for leading the organization forward. When managers want to be able to consider a broad range of possible strategies, it is helpful to formulate problems as community outcomes or social behaviors. For example, if there is too much disease (a community outcome), then possible strategies include improving communications, increasing access to medical services, providing consequences for certain behaviors, and so on. However, if only a smaller set is to be considered, then problems might be defined as shortcomings of agency processes and procedures. If the disease problem is defined as inadequate outreach by the agency, then solutions are more restrictedly focused toward that, and value-based preferences, such as for partnerships or limited government, can be used to further narrow the range of acceptable strategies. Problem definition does not determine the solution strategy, but it does help shape it.

In sum, the process of problem definition usually starts with taking inventory of manifest symptoms, and then searching for associated facts and underlying causes. Consider the following example. Clients complain about shoddy and untimely service, and we find this to be a fact. We then identify possible causes based on the service delivery process and consider factors suggested by the inventory of problems later in this chapter. We use our imagination about what that could be. Then, through analysis and dialog with clients and employees, through which additional facts are raised, a conclusion is reached about one or more factors constituting the problem that, if resolved, would address the symptoms and other issues that may have surfaced. Sometimes, a standard or vision for future performance needs to be separately generated, if it did not surface through this process. Talking with clients can bring up new standards, and elected officials often have their own ideas, too. Professional managers have their own training from which standards follow, and may know standards of best practices used elsewhere. Some are implied in this chapter. Sometimes, the standard is simply doing what the organization has already committed itself to, such as serving a broad range of populations, or completing service requests in a timely manner.

An important, final step in problem definition is to marshal evidence about the extent of the problem. Quantification of problems is not always possible, but whatever evidence is available should be brought to bear, including anecdotal evidence. One client complaint does not prove much, but twenty might. It matters whether 4 percent or 40 percent of road repairs exceed their estimated repair time or cost. To quantify the problem is to help evaluate the extent of it, but how much is too much or how little is too little? Rarely are published standards available; managers will need to set their own standards based on past performance and future expectations. Then, is there a big or little gap between reality and expectation? Quantification also suggests possible targets for improvement, of course, and it is a segue into further analysis about ends and means. What is the cost of reducing the road delays to from 40 percent to, say, 20 percent, 10 percent, or 5 percent? Maybe a new process can be introduced that is used elsewhere as a best practice. What is the cost of implementing the new process now and over the lifetime of the next twenty projects, compared to the cost of continuing with business as it is done now? Such analyses often help to sharpen the problem definition.

In Conclusion

There are many performance problems in organizations. Problem definition is about defining the gap between what is, and what should be—too much this, or too little that? This chapter identifies major problems in the areas of dealing with stakeholders, organization, project management, and working with people. It shows myriad variations of these problems. It is obvious that the job of managers is to become aware of the problems in their organizations, and then to successfully address them. This typically involves a little digging beyond the surface of manifest symptoms. Hasty diagnosis is the result of not digging deep enough, which may cause managers to address symptoms rather than their underlying causes.

At any point in time, managers will face numerous challenges—more than can be worked on at any time. Chapter 3 helps managers choose those that they will likely want to work on, and which doing so will increase the likelihood of implementation success. Subsequent chapters describe different performance improvement strategies. Problems of goal setting, stakeholder orientation, and customer-focus are often addressed by strategic planning (chapter 4) and quality management (chapter 5). Problems of delivery processes and customer satisfaction can sometimes involve information technology (chapter 6). Problems of standards, accountability, and feedback can sometimes be addressed through performance measurement (chapter 8). Strategies for dealing with problems of collaboration with external partners are discussed in chapter 9. Problems of individual motivation and behavior, communication, and the productivity of teams are discussed in chapter 7. A collection of classic tools discussed in chapter 10 discusses problems of project management, cost control, and raising revenues.

Application Exercises

1. Make a list of some manifest symptoms that are problematic in your organization. Then, for each, decide whether it is a performance problem as mentioned in this chapter, or whether there is some underlying process or cause that should be more appropriately targeted as the performance problem. Note any symptoms that often are used as red flags for indicating underlying problems. Some examples of manifest symptoms may include staff turnover or demotivation, client complaints, rework, or cost-overruns.

2. Identify one or more organizational problems in your organization, as shown in Table 2.1. Use this table as a checklist. Prioritize these problems, and then identify the most important one. What symptoms does the problem give rise to? What is the magnitude of this problem? How would you measure it, and progress toward resolving it?

3. Identify some problems of stakeholders as affecting your program or agency. How might these be addressed?

4. Research the literature for examples of best practices and standards in the areas that you identified as problems. How might these best practices be adopted in your organization?

5. Identify some opportunities for personal growth as identified in the section on people problems. Which skill(s) do you want to work on? How does the deficiency affect you? How can you make progress toward improving it?

6. "Problem definition does not define the solution." Explain, and give some examples.

3

Achieving Success

Performance improvement is an intervention, a change in existing roles, relationships, or expectations. Managers should not be surprised to find that while some people and organizations welcome the possibility of improvement, others are reluctant to embrace change. Grand schemes come to naught in the face of stakeholder indifference or resistance; even ardent supporters are likely to raise challenging concerns. Therefore, managers need a strategy for bringing organizations and their people along, to ensure that change is instilled and enduring. Strategies must deal with the realities of organizational behavior. This chapter first looks at the conditions for success, and then at specific implementation strategies for change in small and large settings. This chapter focuses on change within organizations; the following chapter discusses a strategy for creating change in communities.

Conditions for Success

Whereas some agencies and jurisdictions are repeatedly lauded for their high performance, others are not. Phoenix, Arizona, is repeatedly ranked among the very best, as is Fairfax County, Virginia, and the U.S. Social Security Agency, among others. Within agencies, some departments are viewed as progressive and are places where many managers and employees would like to work. But not all organizations and departments perform well or are seen as desirable places to work. Some are viewed as having mediocre or poor performance. Some places are to be avoided. Organizations are not all alike, and the differences tend to persist over some time. By analogy, some football teams repeatedly end up among the top ten or so in the country; others rank repeatedly in the middle or at the bottom. Why is this so?

A plausible answer is that leading organizations have more favorable starting conditions. For sports teams, the playing field is not level at the beginning of the season. Top football teams often have some players who are slightly or even markedly better than average, as well as coaches who produce schemes that take better advantage of their team's strengths, while concealing their weaknesses. They also have better strategies for ensuring that players stay out of trouble off the field. Of course, even top teams suffer their embarrassments and setbacks, but over the length of an entire season, the little advantages here and there make the difference.

Similarly, different starting conditions can make it easier for some public and nonprofit organizations to succeed more frequently than others at introducing new change and improvement strategies. When managers know these conditions, they can make markedly wiser decisions. Astute managers first survey the landscape; they lay the groundwork for further activity in years to come (Caravalho 2004). For example, managers may choose to postpone making changes and instead improve starting conditions, thereby implementing change later with a greater chance of success. Why fight an uphill or even losing battle? The purpose of managing is to make a difference, not to engage in valiant efforts that produce mediocre results.

Here are five conditions for successful change:

1. Support by top or senior management.
2. A real, urgent need (or crisis) for change.
3. Support by a critical mass of people.
4. Some early and easy successes, when appropriate.
5. Sufficient trust among people involved in the change.

That these conditions are imperative for success is clear. Assume that a manager wishes to a make a significant, but still modest change that improves client satisfaction, such as an expanded Internet customer service or an upgrade of the reception area. Imagine the chances of accomplishing any of these changes when they are not supported by senior managers whose support is needed, when the changes are not a response to any urgent need or crisis, when almost no one else is committed to the project, when employees do not trust the manager leading the project, and when the Internet effort is perceived as having a high risk of initial failure. A rational person quickly evaluates that the chance of success under these conditions as very, very low.

Next, imagine that top management supports these changes, that people perceive the changes as appropriate responses to some urgent need or crisis, that there is a critical mass of people who support these efforts, that it is quite likely that the manager will have some easy, early successes to be celebrated, and that people support and trust each other in working toward this expanded service. Managers may still experience some bumps in the road and bad luck—remember Murphy's Law, that what can go wrong will go wrong—but the chances of eventually succeeding are very good and certainly much better than in the previous example. They might even be aided by *Berman's Law,* which is hereby stated as, "no one can be unlucky all of the time."

The above conditions are a checklist for managers aspiring to make change. This is not to say that all of these conditions must be present, but the absence of even one or two of these items is clearly a handicap. For example, some savvy managers may be able to get around the lack of top management support, but it sure helps to have that and all of the other conditions in place, too. The following discusses how managers can assess their organization for these conditions, and what they can do to help ensure them. Throughout, a new management philosophy is introduced, called "the path of least resistance" or "easy is better." This is somewhat contrary to the commonly held opinion that when people know how to solve really difficult problems, then they can solve easy problems, too. Hence, people are told to practice on difficult problems. But in the business of change and improvement, this chapter suggests that managers go with the path of least resistance. The following discussion clarifies why this is so.

1. Top or Senior Management Support

The phrase "top or senior" manager is used as simply referring to the person above the manager making the change. Top or senior management support for change matters, not only because top managers provide legitimacy and needed resources, but also because they can prevent end-runs around the manager by those who oppose the change. The latter is a significant threat to change. The role of senior managers in change management in providing legitimacy, resources, and support greatly furthers change effort.

Top managers can be asked for their support, and typically are. If support is given, then agreements about timetables and resources need to be locked in, as well as understandings about how the risk of adversity will be dealt with. No one likes surprises, and being backed by superiors in the face of adversity is a true measure of support. More than one senior manager has been tentative about coming through when needed. Sometimes this is indicated by a waffling initial response.

Another approach to obtaining top management support is from time to time inquiring about top managers' agendas or ideas for change. Top managers may or may not have specific ideas, and the manager might offer his own ideas. Whatever improvement opportunity is then selected has top management support. Any source for improvement will do if it leads to managers being able to make improvement, even if it is not the manager's own idea.

Table 3.1

Performance Improvement Proposal (outline)

Title of performance improvement
1. Background: Current activities
    • Discussion of key activity or work processes.
        Add diagram or flowchart that clarifies.
    • Identification of improvement needs or opportunities.

2. Performance improvement effort
    • Definition of the performance improvement effort, and relationship to improve-
      ment opportunities or needs mentioned under 1.
    • Discussion of how the performance improvement effort (1) increases effective-
      ness, (2) increases efficiency, and (3) pays for itself (or, is otherwise imperative
      to undertake).
    • Discussion of any standards that the improvement effort seeks to attain, and
      comparison with existing performance.

3. Measurement matrix
    • Key performance measures of the program, performance improvement
      objectives, and efficiency savings.
    • Examples of measures (with past trend data, to the extent available).
    • Discussion of data collection strategies.

4. Implementation strategy
    • Summary of the purpose of the implementation effort, and discussion of the
      steps of the overall implementation strategy.
    • Discussion of the feasibility of the implementation plan 1: Manager identifies
      obstacles that can be overcome and discusses how this is accomplished.
    • Discussion of the feasibility of the implementation plan 2: Manager identifies
      constraints that are fixed and that cannot be overcome, and shows that the plan
      stays within these constraints.
    • Approximate milestones and timeframes for implementation.

5. Summary
    • Recap of the purpose of the intervention, the need for the intervention, expected
      outcomes and benefits of this effort for the organization.

Getting support requires a persuasive argument in favor of the proposed change. Though other factors also affect support, such as the presence of urgent needs (below) and funding availability, a persuasive argument needs to be made for whatever proposal is eventually accepted. Managers show leadership by formulating arguments for why something needs to be done, how it can be done, and how challenges can be met (Behn 2004). Table 3.1 shows an outline for a performance improvement proposal that addresses many issues that managers will want to consider. Although performance improvement proposals that emphasize effectiveness gains are important, those that also would achieve efficiency gains and have a low chance of failure are even better. Thus, managers will also need to identify specific cost savings and gains in efficiency. Beyond this, the performance improvement proposal calls attention to measuring success, strategies for implementing change, and resources, among other things. Though performance proposals are not always very thorough, they provide a disciplined way to think the issues through.

A problem that is sometimes mentioned in the public sector is the difficulty of obtaining support for change from elected officials. Performance improvement is not always a priority on the agenda of elected officials, and access to them by managers may be severely curtailed, especially in federal and state governments. While this is sometimes a problem, many performance improvements in fact do not require approval by elected officials or even changes in laws. Many improvement opportunities exist within present authority, policy, and guidelines. Federal and state agency managers continue to find many opportunities for improving performance in their programs; the art of management is to do what is possible, not to lament the impossible. It may be that, in the aggregate, dealing with many stakeholders slows improvement; however, many managers make improvements without the support of elected officials, but only with that of their superior managers.

2. A Real, Urgent Need (or Crisis) for Change

There's nothing like an urgent need or crisis to provide great impetus for action. Perhaps decisions ought to be made rationally and with foresight rather than as a response to crisis or an urgent need, but in the real world of overloaded and time-stressed executives, what gets done often is what must get done now. Hence, improvement suggestions that respond to an urgent crisis are more likely to find support from top managers and others than those that are worthy, but do not respond to a crisis. What is a crisis or urgent need? It is that which is the number one or two priority of the manager, both today and tomorrow.

Managers are typically not in control over which crisis or urgent need occurs. However, in the affairs of humans and their organizations, there is typically always some crisis or urgent need occurring. If it is not a really important one, a minor one will do—the local evening news always finds one to talk about, as do many members about their organizations. Some authors lament that some public organizations are shielded from major crises and thus are slow to change (Nutt 2004; Rainey and Fernandez 2004), but the experience of many managers is that there is usually something significant going on. Given the routine occurrence of crises and urgent needs, perceived or real, one rational approach is to have various improvements in store, just waiting for a crisis to occur for which one of them is the right response. This approach embodies well the Chinese expression that "luck is chance meeting preparation." When no improvement suggestion is handy and ready to adapt, managers will obviously do some quick thinking in the face of the urgent need or crisis.

In the absence of a crisis or urgent need, managers may try to argue why their proposal is needed anyway. They may be able to argue that something about their organization is "too much" or "too little," and that their proposal is the right thing to do. Or, that if the proposed change is not undertaken, surely worse things will or could happen; the sky will fall. Quantitative and other evidence sharpens the proposal (chapter 2). Alternatively, managers may be able to articulate some "lost opportunity" as something that would be a setback and embarrassment. The receptivity of the audience will likely vary, and when support for the proposal is not forthcoming, managers may have to wait until the problem grows and gains wider attention. Some folks just have to see to believe. Comparing these strategies it becomes clear that the first approach is clearly the path of least resistance—building on an already existing crisis or urgent need in order to further support for the change or improvement effort.

3. A Critical Mass of People Support the Change

Managers get work done through others; they need others to embrace their proposed change and improvement efforts. Often, change and improvement is done in small steps; managers need a few people to lead off and try to make the improvement work, usually through trial-and-error. The 25–50–25 rule states that when a new idea is suggested, about 25 percent of the manager's audience with embrace it (with varying degrees of enthusiasm), 50 percent will be indifferent, and 25 percent of the manager's audience will reject it (with varying degrees of enthusiasm); they may come to support it in time, if and when it works out and becomes a fait accompli. They are "fence sitters." The 25–50–25 rule has not been rigorously validated by scientific research, but many managers feel that it more or less accurately represents their experience when they propose any new idea.

Inexperienced managers often try to persuade everyone, or almost everyone, to embrace their idea. The theory is that this increases support and reduces resistance. Though this makes sense as an idea, the 25–50–25 rule states that some people will be against the change no matter what. They will find reasons to be against the change; maybe a past experience was unpleasant, maybe the manager gave them a hard time last month, or maybe they just like to be negative, hostile, and cynical. There will always be naysayers among us. This is the reality of organizations. The key element is that it is futile to try to get everyone or almost everyone behind an idea. Managers must accept the permanent reality of always having some resistance.

This reality is dealt with by developing effective strategies for each of the different groups. First, managers need to identify and work with those who support the change. A positive and supportive environment needs to be created for their endeavors (Kanter 1985; Abramson and Lawrence 2001). Second, managers need to provide fence sitters, over time, with evidence of successes that will encourage them to embrace the new effort. Eventually, managers will need them to support their efforts (Gilliland 2004; Shapiro 2003). People have a right to be initially skeptical and concerned, and they may be enthusiastic supporters in other areas. Also, although fence sitters might not volunteer for change, they might go along with it after it has been tried out, even if not enthusiastically. Third, managers need to manage the naysayers by shielding those who do support the proposal from their negative influence. Perhaps they can be excluded from early efforts, and some might become fence sitters over time as the results become positive or the change appears inevitable. In time, then, the strategy of increasing successes will cause some fence sitters to become enthusiastic supporters, and some naysayers who are not blinded by their negativity to become fence sitters. So, the initial 25–50–25 distribution may become more like 60–30–10 over time. Strategies for dealing with ardent naysayers are discussed later in this chapter.

The strategy of identifying and working with those who like our ideas is the strategy of least resistance. It assumes that managers are able to correctly classify people in these three groups. One approach is to simply ask people how they feel about the proposed change. Managers will soon know, from both verbal replies and body language. They might also look at the support and effectiveness surrounding other, similar efforts.

4. Some Early and Easy Successes

There is nothing like a success to inspire others to join in, and to quell the skeptical voice of critics. It is hard to argue with success. By contrast, failure, in any major or minor way, gives fuel to opponents. The purpose of the path of least resistance is to ensure that new change and improvement efforts are successful. A "ripe apple" is an application that is sure to be successful. It is among the easiest of possible targets. It is typically not very difficult to identify easy targets, and sometimes they are labeled as pilot projects (initial projects undertaken on a small scale to encourage learning and skill-building).

This approach is very different from the teaching strategy of trying oneself on the most challenging efforts first, in order to quickly go down the learning curve. The problem with this strategy is that it increases the chance of early failures, thus diminishing support and increasing the likelihood of early termination of the effort. It gives fuel to naysayers, and takes the wind out of the sails of those who are positive. Also, with little experience, managers may lack information to know which problems are insolvable, rather than just very difficult. Starting with very difficult problems robs managers of the chance to gain experience by starting with the easiest problems first. So, there are some good reasons to start off with easy targets and work toward progressively more difficult ones. Again, managers need to choose the path of least resistance.

5. Sufficient Trust Among People Involved in the Change

This is the most abstract of the conditions, but arguably the one of greatest importance. Sufficient trust must exist in order that people give up known ways and relationships and accept new, uncertain roles and relationships. Performance improvement requires a degree of trust; that is, the expectation that managers and coworkers will not take advantage of employees, and that managers will be honest with them about what is occurring (Barber 1983; Jennings 2002). Following someone else's lead on a new venture can be a scary business, especially when deviating from ways in which things have long been done (Rainey 1999). When people trust their leaders, speed bumps and setbacks are taken in stride. When people distrust their leaders, foot dragging, finger pointing, and dodging commitment and responsibility are common (Beccerra and Gupta 1999; McLain and Hackman 1999).

Trust is an emotion, resulting from our interactions with others. We tend to develop trust for people who (1) are supportive of our needs and desires, (2) are effective in what they do, and (3) allow their decisions to be shaped by our input and contributions. Trust develops when people are almost flawlessly consistent in these three aspects; one bad word can do away with the benefit of ten good words, and require ten more just to repair the damage done to trust. The path of least resistance in change and improvement is the path that is built on trust. To establish trust, managers must do those things that are likely to inspire trust in others. Managers need to give people a reason to trust them, notably by ensuring that their actions are mindful of others and efficacious. It is uncommon to experience feelings of trust for people who use their power to control and dominate. While managers may never get the trust of all, acts that consistently meet the above criteria will inspire some degree of trust among those that are positively predisposed to support the effort.

The above discusses the five conditions for successful change. It should be clear why the success of any effort is furthered by the presence of these conditions. Though not all five conditions are always necessarily present in successful change efforts, they are important conditions that make the task easier and less prone to failure when they are present. Imagine a manager not having trust, an urgent need, and leadership support—how likely will success be then? Add to that the lack of a critical mass of employees supporting the effort and an early flop, too. Even the absence of any one these conditions can complicate the manager's efforts. Clearly, not all playing fields are equal.

Managers do well to first assess the presence of these conditions; the above is a useful, short checklist. If some condition is lacking, managers will want to consider the implications, possible coping strategies, and whether or not they want to first ensure the condition before moving forward. Managers should create the most advantageous situation for success, and ensuring a condition is a worthy six-month objective. The above has important implications for new managers, too. The job of the manager assigned to a new department is to use the first six months to get to know the lay of the land, to assess and ensure the presence of these five conditions for success. If new managers act too soon, they may not know what they are getting themselves into. They will invite resistance. If they act soon, they have a high chance of being caught off-guard by something or somebody. New managers are often perceived as doing nothing for the first six months, when they in fact they are quietly creating the conditions for their future success.

Some people also identify planning as an important condition of success. Of course, the question is, planning for what? —which ripe apples to select, how to get top management support, and so on. Planning may also involve other issues, such as ensuring that resources are available, or that the right people are selected. (Some of these are discussed later in this chapter as implementation issues.) So planning is rather a general activity, and managers need to think about what they need to plan for, and what conditions they need to be successful. As the saying goes, "people don't plan to fail, they fail to plan." To which might be added: "fail to plan adequately," such as with regard to the considerations in this module.

Change in Small Units

The five conditions mentioned above set the stage for describing specific improvement strategies. Here, we look at change in a small unit of ten or fifteen employees, whose supervisor wants to make some change in how his or her unit conducts its business. Perhaps the change involves the use of some new technology, a revised process for handling service requests, increased use of teamwork, or something else. These are the steps for making change in a small unit:

1. Get a mandate to start the project.
2. Ensure that the change process has a clear reason (and, if appropriate, rewards).
3. Select a team, if appropriate.
4. Show confidence that the goals and target dates can be achieved, give some examples of how.
5. Undertake some initial first steps.
6. Empower people to operationalize the plan.
7. Monitor implementation, and keep the project on track. Intervene to keep the change moving forward. Be available for crisis intervention. Involve others in the change effort, if appropriate.

Though many of these steps are straightforward, the following discussion ties them to the five conditions discussed earlier and provides some additional helpful suggestions.

The first step clearly tests the first condition for change, getting top or senior management support. Obtaining such support—the mandate—provides legitimacy for any subordinate who might ask; it forecloses end-runs that naysayers might want to try. Managers might want to think about locking in any promises by senior managers about resources and other matters, such as through a confirmatory e-mail after the meeting in which promises and commitments have been made. In addition, managers might want to think of how employees will be rewarded for success later, and ensure that any resources or commitments that are needed (for example, recognition) are locked in as well.

The second step, ensuring a clear purpose, relates to the second condition for change, having an urgent need or crisis for change. People will want know why the change and improvement effort is needed; a reason must be given. The reason will be challenged. Some typical expressions of resistance are (Fournies 1999; Behn 2004):

- We don't need this
- We didn't do this before
- What's in it for us?
- Who is out to skin us?
- You don't understand the process
- We are understaffed
- There is not enough time or money

- It has been tried elsewhere and it didn't work
- It's too complicated
- Other things are more important
- We don't have the skills
- It will never work

Managers need to think how they will address these concerns. Openness and discussion are useful to bring these concerns out into the open. However, as Argyris has long argued, some issues in organizations are undiscussable, and their undiscussabilty is undiscussable as well (1990). The above may be symptoms of underlying resentment for past actions, fear of losing something in the process (power, job, authority, etc.), or feeling that they cannot do what is asked of them, and yet being unable or uncomfortable of raising these points. In short, resistance for whatever reason is likely to be present, and even openly and fully addressing stated issues is unlikely to completely eliminate it. As previously noted, resistance is a fact of organizations and their members.

Sometimes, project teams are given or develop a mandate or charter. This is somewhat formal, and perhaps more common when project teams operate outside a single line of control, such as a when the effort spans multiple departments or jurisdictions. A charter or mandate may lay out (1) the rationale for the project, (2) what it is expected to accomplish, (3) limitations as to what it is not expected to do, (4) a general statement about the nature of the change or improvement method, (5) resources and staffing issues, and (6) completion dates. Such a mandate justifies the team's existence and may help to keep the team focused later. However, it often is unnecessary to be so formal, especially when working within a small department. A verbal statement of these matters probably suffices just as well. The project rationale is also the basis for later evaluating whether the project has been successful. Managers will want to develop measures for monitoring progress and thereby determining success—closing the gap between what is, and what the future should be. Measuring and communicating progress toward goals establishes a clear sense of success, and thereby broadens buy-in and addresses concerns of critics.

The third step is team selection. Sometimes the improvement effort can be implemented on a small scale at first, among only a few employees. Small-scale trial-and-error promotes learning and helps work out the bugs. For example, a new Internet service or paper processing approach might be able to be implemented on a pilot scale, without involving the entire work group. When a team is put together, the following criteria can be used for selecting team members:

- Having enthusiasm about the proposed effort
- Having needed skills and knowledge
- Having prior experience concerning the type of improvement effort
- Being essential to initial or later implementation
- Being well-liked by others
- Able to look at the project from different angles, and not afraid to speak up

It is quite unlikely that each of these characteristics can be found in every member; employees will vary in their characteristics. Of course, when the change and improvement effort involves the entire unit, then managers cannot choose their members and they will have naysayers, too. Such people should be put in the role of followers, and their assignments, if any, should not be critical to the project's success.

The fourth step involves communicating goals, objectives, and specific target dates to employees. This is important, because it implicitly communicates to others confidence of the leader in the effort, and it sets standards for keeping the project team on track ("we need to get this done by next week!"). Questions will arise about how goals will be met, and leaders should have some specific examples of how the unit is going to move forward. Leaders must appear competent and in control.

It also is quite likely that at this point the leader will have to deal with the matter of rewards and incentives. Some employees will want to know what is in it for them. Although such questions may reflect a calculating self-interest to maximize returns for the lowest possible investment of effort, these questions may also reflect legitimate interest in the availability of rewards and recognition, as is appropriate for doing the right thing by helping the organization and its clients. There may also be concerns about possible downsides; what happens to employees or the department if the project fails?

A fundamental maxim is that managers cannot fall in the trap of thinking that they have to pay people extra for doing the right thing. As discussed in chapter 7, such a strategy is unsustainable for any organization—people get used to pay raises and then want more. Rather, organizations have to move forward and change with the times. They have to find ways of doing better. It is expected that employees and managers adjust to higher standards. Minor rewards, incentives, and acknowledgments may be available for a brief time among those who bite the bullet first, such as additional training or travel, and they may figure prominently for a year or so as criteria in awards and recognitions. But eventually the new practice must become the standard expectation. Though such a message will be unpopular with some people, there is not much that managers can do about it. Some people may resist or ignore the change, but they will be left behind, and possibly suffer career consequences for their decisions. This is clearly an area where managers set the norm, the expectations.

The fifth step is about undertaking the initial actions. Here, managers need to lead by example, showing commitment, and thereby making it easier for employees to see what is expected of them and how to get the job done. If there is trial-and-error, then the boss is going through that, too, while showing how to stay focused on the goal and improving the effort. By the end of the fifth step, there should be some successful applications (yes, ripe apples) that are examples for all. Various studies suggest that perceptions of success are pivotal to keeping the momentum; the experience of success must be shared by others (e.g., Walston and Chadwick 2003). Keep in mind *the rule of seven*: people become masters of new skills only after they have applied it seven times. While some say that seven times is a bit exaggerated, managers should expect some initial errors, and managers need to encourage people to keep trying to get things working, and acknowledge their effort.

This step is also an opportunity for the manager to once again signal commitment to the change and improvement effort. *Berman's rule of three* states that people only hear things that have been said three times. The reason is that so much that gets said in organizations is not followed up on, that it is rational to take what is said the first time with a little grain of salt. If it is important, the speaker will surely follow up on it. If it is not, why get worked up over it now? By the end of step five the manager will have stated at least three times, if not more, why the changes and improvements are important, what the goals are, how it will be done, what the manager has committed, and targets dates for implementation.

At about this stage, or perhaps the next, nonverbal forms of resistance may become evident, such as foot dragging, promising that something will be done only to explain later why it was not, feigning or exaggerating challenges to performance, performing in barely acceptable ways, and creating reasons for rework and unending delays. More aggressive forms of resistance include organized group resistance, playing managers off against each other, being sick or otherwise not available for the work to get done, filing or threatening to file complaints and grievances, and spreading rumors of problems. Managers as resisters have even more tools than employees, such as underspending the budget and assigning inept staff to work on the proposed change. Managers obviously have to guard against these tactics and be watchful for them.

The sixth step is to get employees to make change and improvement happen without managerial leadership; they are tasked with making the change and improvement effort happen in their area of operation. They are now accountable for producing the result, not merely the effort. The rule of seven suggests that managers should expect initial shortcomings, and thus work with individual employees to sort out what went wrong, or how improvements can be made for the next time. Manager, be patient! The goal of this step is to have employees now autonomously applying the new change and improvement strategy. This is the beginning of the change taking hold in the unit.

The last step then allows the manager to move on to other endeavors, while keeping a watchful eye on the change and improvement effort. Of course, something unexpected is fully expected to happen, and so managers find themselves troubleshooting, running interference, and putting out fires as needed. Managers should play the role of friendly supporters, there to aid employees when needed. Also, managers will now carefully monitor their timetable for accomplishment and ensure that things stay on track. They will share their performance measures with both employees and higher managers as evidence of the budding success. Whatever rewards and acknowledgments have been promised are now being rolled out.

Finally, if a team has been used that is a subunit of the unit, now is the time to get other members involved. Along the way, fence sitters have seen the change effort being executed and the results that it is producing. It is now time for them to engage in the change. Perhaps those employees who participated in the effort so far can help colleagues to quickly master the new technique. The manager will work with them, as was done with other employees, to offer support and advice for the inevitable errors that will occur. In this way, the initial 25–50–25 will shortly become 60–30–10 for the manager. The new way has thus become the expected way and, quite soon, the normal way in which the department does its business.

Large-Scale Change

The preceding section discussed change in a small unit. This section assesses how managers can change a state agency of perhaps 1,200 people or more. The model of small unit change does not discuss how managers can ensure change in possibly thirty different departments. It would surely be a Herculean task for top management to undertake the previously described effort in so many different settings. Most top managers simply do not have enough time for that. A modified model is needed.

In the late 1970s, theories of planned (organizational) change were first developed, which have since been tested and progressively refined and improved over time (e.g., Osland, Kolb, and Rubin 2000; Mento, Jones, and Dirndorfer 2002; Golembiewski 1997; Brescia 2004). The following strategy appears to be increasingly common and widely used; though data about this is nearly absent, it is supported by many anecdotal accounts. Planned organizational change strategies use project teams previously described, but the project team model is supplemented in the following ways to ensure learning and diffusion to other departments without ongoing top management involvement. The purpose is to create somewhat of a self-learning agency.

A site is chosen for an initial pilot effort. The site and effort will comply with the five conditions for success. Top leadership supports the effort and provides oversight for the initial effort. Supportive managers and employees are found, and a ripe apple application is identified. Top leaders articulate why the change is necessary and in the strategic, long-term interest of the agency, and provide a mandate for its execution. Typically, the pilot effort is rolled out with a minimum of fanfare, as the purpose is to learn and get it right for later. Many in the agency may even be unaware of the effort. An example of such a pilot effort is new procurement processes in public agencies that provide greater flexibility to vendors, hence leading to more innovation (Abramson and Lawrence 2001). These efforts are often tried out in few settings first.

The initial pilot effort is undertaken in a similar way as described in the small team approach. However, the initial change and improvement effort is supplemented by a few employees from other departments. These employees observe and learn from the efforts of the project team, and are part of future change and improvement teams in their own departments. These other employees or observers are selected by the supervisors in other departments as next in line for using the change and improvement effort. The manner in which these other employees participate is typically by attending a weekly discussion of the project, and other meetings as necessary. Importantly, by attending the meetings and discussing these efforts, these employees are able to make a few friends among the current change and improvement team who then can act as resources in the other departments' later change and improvement effort.

In addition to the above additional employees, a team of middle managers is formed from different departments (the management team). The purpose of the management team is to provide other middle managers an opportunity to learn from the department that is currently doing the change and improvement effort. In biweekly or monthly meetings, presentations are made describing where the change and improvement stands. It is expected that upon completion of the initial effort, these other departments will be tasked with implementing the effort in their departments, using the "other" employees discussed under point one, above. Thus, many of these additional middle managers will be from the same departments as the above additional other employees.

Because of the involvement of other departments and the need to ensure that the pilot effort is successful in the initial pilot phase, a top or very senior manager ensures that other employees and managers in fact attend to change and improvement efforts in their departments. This person is the de facto top management champion of the change and improvement effort in the organization, and one who urged the effort from the beginning. Top-down commitment is imperative, and it is typically a senior or top manager who has responsibility for a major program, who has interest in matters of administration. The paradoxical role of top leadership is captured well by the expression "top-down direction for bottom-up implementation" (Long and Franklin 2004).

It is easy to see how the initial management team and initial change and improvement team can lead to similar efforts in, for instance, half a dozen or more departments. This is the cascading process. When these second phase efforts are also undertaken with observing managers and employees from other departments that have yet to implement the change and improvement effort, then each second phase team can give rise to half a dozen or more third phase efforts. And so on. It is easy to calculate that this snowball or cascading strategy then results in a fourth phase effort that involves as many as 216 units (1 * 6 * 6 * 6) in this example. This, in turn, might involve about 2,500 employees (assuming about 12 employees per unit). Hence, three or four cascading efforts are sufficient to instill organizational change in the entire agency.

The formalization of the change and improvement through a statement of policy or similar instrument is typically made toward the end of the third or fourth phase of cascading efforts. This stands in marked contrast with traditional management strategies, in which top management issues order and edicts. While top management orders are seldom ignored, a serious problem is that the lack of ongoing interest by top management allows lower managers to backslide and eventually revert back to customary patterns: "this too shall pass" is not an uncommon thought among lower managers and employees. Although data are lacking, there is a widespread perception that top management edicts have little enduring effect, apart from perhaps in military-style, top-down organizations that are accustomed to following top commands. In more decentralized settings such edicts would have close to zero effect. The purpose of formalization is to codify agency-wide expectations, including perhaps rewards or appraisal standards. The strength of the cascading model is that it results in departments learning to do things better, not merely complying with rules and edicts. In the above model, there is no need to issue an agencywide edict to formalize what is already widespread practice.

Another interesting feature of the cascading model is that while it often takes a few years for an entire agency to go through three or four iterations of the effort, the model does not require a mastermind of sorts to be in place to oversee the effort through the entire period. People move around; what matters is that people step into the necessary roles. As long as there is sustained top-management interest to ensure that "management teams" are formed and are held accountable for subsequent implementation, the process will move forward. There is no need for a single coordinator. Also, from a career development perspective, managers need only show that they were responsible for some successful aspect of the overall effort. That is sufficient evidence to demonstrate their ability. They need only take responsibility for some part of the problem.

A second interesting consequence of the cascading process taking "a few years or more" comes from the fact that many people stay only five or so years with an employer, although some do stay ten years or more. Estimates are that agency turnover varies from about 6 percent to 10 percent annually. Hence, a process that takes, say, three or four years, will have seen about 20 to 40 percent turnover in the agency. For these people, the new way is in fact the only way they know. Hence, it is the "normal" way of doing business for them, and they will be a significant force toward ensuring that the new way takes hold. Turnover at lower levels of the organization can be an ally of the change effort.

Finally, many employees and managers have experience with change through this cascading model of change. But change efforts are not always successful in practice, where all kinds of problems may occur. Managers may be inept leaders, choose the wrong project team members, or attempt to tackle problems that are not ripe apples. They may have failed to provide adequate resources. Frequent turnover may have caused the organization to become something of a rudderless ship. Such occurrences do not invalidate the model, but point to implementation issues. Table 3.2 is a checklist for feasibility assessment that addresses many concerns that were raised earlier.

Dealing with Resistance

Managers must plan for dealing with employees who resist change. This includes employees who do not wish to adopt modern values but instead use tactics of self-aggrandizement, intimidation, backstabbing, and other means to reach their goals. The first response to such resisters consists of a rational process of identifying and addressing underlying reasons for resistance. The goal is to reach an accommodation with the employee about these concerns. For example, an employee might resist change because it would require him or her to periodically work during the weekends. An arrangement could be made whereby the employee is promised to work no more than one weekend

Table 3.2

Feasibility Assessment

People
- Are the people who will implement the change effective change agents?
- Do employees have adequate skills for the intervention? If not, how will required skills be obtained? Is training required? When will staff get it? How successful is training likely to be?
- Which incentives and rewards are required? Are they adequate? Are there promotion and compensation opportunities?
- Who will likely resist, and how will resisters be dealt with?
- Can proponents be shielded from possible retaliation?
- Who will monitor the change effort? Do change agents know what is expected from them? Who will evaluate the change agents?
- How will staff be evaluated?
- How will the change be explained to others in the organization? About how many interactions will this take? Over what period? What arguments explain the reason for change? What counterarguments might be raised? How will these be dealt with?
- Is there sufficient support outside the organization for the proposed change?
- How does the change affect the current expectations, roles, and responsibilities? Are there role models within the organization that can be assigned leadership responsibilities for implementing change?

Other
- What changes of policy does the intervention require, if any?
- Are the resources sufficient for the intervention (staff, technology, etc.)?
- Are adequate resources available to sustain the intervention?
- Are existing information, delivery, feedback, and other systems adequate to support the intervention? If not, what changes are needed?
- Are any physical plant changes needed that prevent the intervention?
- How will change affect decision-making structures within the organization? Can change be used to improve decision making?
- How does the intervention affect relations among units? Are new liaison functions needed?
- How does the intervention affect basic missions, goals, and objectives of units?
- How and when will we measure the success of the intervention?
- Is there a plan for the intervention? A timeline for accomplishment?

every other month. Strategies for reaching accommodations can follow processes of making the psychological contracts (discussed in a later chapter), as well as the specific suggestions for managing conflict-ridden negotiations in Fisher and Ury's (1981) well-known work, *Getting to Yes*: (1) separate the people from the problem; (2) focus on interests, not positions, (3) invent options for mutual gain; (4) insist on objective criteria. However, what can managers do when employees make unreasonable demands, resist for the sake of resisting or to settle old scores, or have a need to act out their malice and domination?

Indeed, the above approaches suggest a certain reasonableness and rationality among resisters. What if employees insist on being unreasonable? This does happen. The second response is to (1) separate the individual from the change process and (2) deal with the individual separately. Resisters and others who are obstacles to change should be identified early in the change effort. As noted above, change processes begin by identifying those who are enthusiastic about change, not those who resist. Change is created by involving more and more employees in the changes over time. Resisters are usually not involved until the very last. By then, a majority of employees should be supporting the change effort, and hopefully many resisters will now have become isolated. Resisters may yet fall into place when they lose their audience. However, when this does not occur, managers must consider other alternatives.

One alternative is doing nothing. Managers might ask whether they really need to have all employees on board for change and improvement. Do these employees really do more harm than good? The first priority of change and improvement is to isolate such employees from influencing the success of efforts. If this can be accomplished, then it may be worthwhile to tolerate the imperfection of some persistent naysayers. Doing nothing is often attractive in view of other alternatives, which involve personnel action. A second alternative is trying to transfer resisters whose services are no longer needed. Employees who resist are often poor performers and they may welcome a change of unit or supervisor. Their talents might be better suited in another position. Personnel managers often assist in finding alternative positions for such employees. But what is the manager to do when employees resist being transferred and no other manager wants them?

A third alternative is to seek dismissal of resisters. However, the complications of firing are well-documented in the public sector, and firing is no sinecure in the private sector either because of the prospect of expensive lawsuits later. The road to dismissal typically begins with progressive discipline and the documentation of poor performance (e.g., Teratanavat and Kleiner 2005). Legally, managers must create a paper trail documenting unacceptable behavior or performance. Employees must be given an opportunity to improve and provided with feedback about these efforts. However, management signals must be consistent. For example, dismissals are easily challenged when employees are also given satisfactory performance evaluations or managers fail to inform employees of poor behavior as soon as it occurs. When repeated written notices fail to produce desired results, managers provide notice of discipline. Most public agencies have arbitration processes, but a common complaint is that these processes include numerous appeals that are very time-consuming. However, some organizations now have expedited processes that provide a final ruling in about two months. In some cases, downsizing is used as an alternative to dismissal by eliminating employees with poor performance records.

Managers need to focus on their objective of improving performance and ensuring change. From this perspective, the best strategy is often to initially ignore resisters and isolate them over time. Strategies of transferring and dismissing resisters usually come into play at the end of implementation efforts after significant gains have already been achieved through employees who are committed to change.

In Conclusion

There is more to making change than meets the eye. Some organizations do well at implementing change, whereas others appear to lag and struggle. This chapter identified five conditions that increase successful change: top management support, an urgent need or crisis, a critical mass of support, some early and easy successes, and trust between the manager and those involved in the change. This chapter also identified strategies for implementing change in large and small units. These strategies emphasize the importance of learning and engaging those who participate in initial efforts in positive ways. Change efforts that are undertaken in settings that meet the five conditions for change and which follow the strategies discussed are said to have a much higher chance of success than those that do not.

Application Exercises

1. Think of a dozen problems in your workplace that would be significant improvements if addressed. Which, if any, of these problems are part of urgent crises facing your unit?
2. Consider a possible change and improvement effort in your workplace. Among people in your office, how would you classify each according to the 25–50–25 rule? That is, who is a likely supporter, resister, or fence sitter. How do you think your manager classifies you? Why? What would you have to do to change his or classification of you?
3. Identify two or three ripe apples that are designed to be successful and inspire confidence in the efficacy of a change and improvement effort.
4. Identify ten actions that would inspire trust in you among people in your environment.

5. Apply the seven-step process described in this chapter toward a possible change and improvement effort for your workplace.
6. Consider a past change and improvement effort in which you were associated. What was its result; did it work or did it fail? Analyze to what extent the results occurred due to the presence or absence of the previously mentioned five conditions, and the use or absence of the above steps.
7. Many managers operate by axioms, adages, or expressions that help them get through difficult situations. One such example is, "if you push people hard enough, they will sooner or later get it right." Identify a few axioms, adages, or expressions that you might have used in dealing with people. Consider what worked, and what didn't.
8. How have you dealt with resisters in the past? What worked? What didn't work? How might you handle resisters better in the future?

Strategic Planning: What's the Mission?

If you don't know where you are going, any road will take you there.
—Chinese proverb

New developments and changing environments often prompt organizations and communities to assess their priorities and missions. Adjustments are needed to better serve clients, citizens, and other stakeholders, and to better position themselves for the future. Strategic planning is a process that helps organizations and communities to align their priorities with changing conditions and opportunities. Through strategic planning, organizations develop new goals and strategies, update their missions, and create shared commitment among leaders, employees, and others regarding present and future endeavors. Strategic planning is often used in organizations that find themselves in fast- and ever-changing environments, and those that use it do so frequently (Alison and Kaye 2005; Bryson 2004; Bryson and Farnum 2004; Wheeland 2003).

Strategic planning does not assume that future events can be perfectly predicted. Rather, strategic planning asks such questions as: Which roles and missions should organizations seek to fulfill? Is the mission, and its rationale, widely shared by client groups and others inside and outside the organization? What are the unique competencies of the organization that make it qualified to fulfill this role? How do these competencies compare with the expertise and capacity of other organizations? How much external and internal commitment exists for goals that are pursued? How might future challenges affect the ability of the organization to fulfill its goals? Is collaboration with other organizations possible and desirable? Which objectives and strategies are being pursued in order to realize the above vision? Are these objectives specific, feasible, and credible? What resources are available to assist organizations in their efforts, and are these resources adequate? By which target date will strategies be implemented and completed? How will success be measured?

This is a handful of questions, for sure. A key purpose of strategic planning is to ensure that the mission of the organization better serves society's needs. This is noted as Problem 5 in chapter 2. Many leaders like strategic planning because, first, it helps establish new priorities and allows them to refer to these for some time. Second, the strategic planning process aims at getting stakeholder buy-in to change; it puts their contributions, and commitments in evidence. Third, leaders like strategic planning as a first step toward dealing with other issues of the organization such as inadequate mission pursuit (Problem 6), insufficiently meeting the needs of target groups (Problem 1) and those who interact with the organization (Problem 2), inadequate technology (Problem 7) or coordination (Problem 8), and many other problems noted in chapter 2, including problems of rewards (Problem 10) and professionalism (Problem 14). These problems often can be linked to realizing the goals and objectives that are adopted through strategic planning.

The flexible uses of strategic planning have undoubtedly contributed to its popularity among top managers. The use of strategic planning has become markedly widespread and is now increasingly used by managers at lower levels, too. Poister and Streib (2005) find that 44 percent of cities with populations over 25,000 had initiated citywide strategic planning over the past five years; ten years earlier, these authors found that 38 percent had done so (Poister and Streib 1994). Likewise, a survey of cities with populations over 50,000 shows that 41.7 percent prepare a citywide strategic plan at least once every two years and, among these, 83.1 percent agree or strongly that such planning results in establishing clear priorities for the organizations (Korosec and Berman 2005). In about half of the jurisdictions, 53.7 percent, departments are required to prepare a departmental strategic plan, and in 1997, 73.5 percent of cities reported having used strategic planning in at least one department during the past year (Berman and West 1998). That the usage rate for citywide planning is not higher probably reflects some cities solely relying on political processes for their strategic priorities; departments use it more often. Many state and federal agencies also prepare strategic plans, helping them to establish or integrate strategic priorities and develop strategies for realizing their goals. In some instances, strategic planning is required. Many nonprofit organizations also use strategic planning to similarly help establish priorities and opportunities for growth; in 1997, 89.9 percent of large social services organizations and 79.0 percent of large museums reported using strategic planning in at least one department in the past twelve months. Strategic planning is not the only vehicle for making strategic change, and some other approaches are mentioned at the end of this chapter (Berman and West 1998; Herman and Renz 1998; Stauber 2001; Mara 2000; Krug and Weinberg 2004; Fountain and Slagan 2001).

Historically, strategic planning was first developed by large corporations in the 1960s to help them manage their diversification and plan their production, marketing, and business development. Large multinational corporations used strategic planning to integrate and align their goals and objectives across different continents and countries. Strategic planning was first introduced in public organizations in the early 1970s, and it has been increasingly used since, following the diffusion model described in chapter 1. The growing professional capacity of many local governments in the 1980s and 1990s has undoubtedly furthered its use as well. Nonprofit organizations have also seen growing use of strategic planning. In both sectors, strategic management evolved from strategic planning; whereas the latter focuses on developing and implementing plans, the former focuses on the executive management of issues that are strategic to the organization, and require top level attention because they often cut across departments and commitments from key external stakeholders (Poister and Van Slyke 2002; Maranville 1999). There are now many excellent examples of strategic plans, some of which have been posted on the Internet sites of organizations and jurisdictions.

The growing use of strategic planning has also led to some concern about its effectiveness. In some instances, plans have been developed that saw little follow through, and hence little effectiveness. They gathered dust, causing some cynicism. Sometimes strategic plans were developed in order to satisfy demands from oversight bodies or donors; they were seen as "jumping through hoops" rather than as a genuine commitment to change (Behn 2005b; Mittenthal 2004). Also, when strategic planning is done too often, there may not have been enough change to result in a plan that is markedly different from the previous one. In other instances, top leaders have used strategic planning to communicate their vision to others in a directive, top-down manner without being open to input from others. They have also used it to justify difficult personnel decisions that involved major organizational restructuring. What these examples show is that any new or mature performance improvement tool can and will be misused and used ineffectively. Negative experiences do not invalidate the model; they require understanding of what went wrong and how things can be done better next time.

The purpose of this chapter is to show how strategic planning can be a useful tool of change and improvement. It shows how the conditions for effective change are managed to increase success, and the steps that strategic planning entails. It also examines some other approaches to change, as well as the use of community-based strategic planning. The latter is increasingly important for dealing with regional and other problems requiring coordinated and collective actions by multiple organizations.

Strategic Planning for Organizations

Strategic planning is a process; its purpose is change. Strategic planning processes typically involve the following four phases:

1. a preplanning phase that assesses and establishes the conditions for successful strategic planning,
2. a research phase of fact gathering and consensus building,
3. a design phase in which agreement is reached about specific missions, visions, values, goals, objectives, strategies, timetables, and resources, and
4. an implementation phase during which plans are put into practice.

Each of these phases requires a blend of management, analytical capability, and the development of processes that result in support and commitment from those who are critical to the plan's success.

The Preplanning Phase

In the previous chapter, the following five conditions for success were identified: (1) top or senior management support; (2) a real, urgent need for change (or, crisis); (3) a critical mass of people who support the change; (4) some early and easy successes; and (5) sufficient trust among people involved in the change. The purpose of the preplanning phase is to ensure that conditions are in place for executing a strategic planning process that will produce the necessary plans for change as well as engender commitment to change. Managers should be concerned about plans that are DOA (that is, dead on arrival) and processes that engender little enthusiasm.

The first condition, top management support, is a given when strategic planning is a top management activity, as it often is. However, if elected officials need to vote on the plan, or they or important donors are required to consent to later funding or initiatives, then their needs and priorities will need to be considered. Top managers are apt to conduct initial discussions with these stakeholders to gauge and obtain their support for strategic planning. In nonprofit organizations, obtaining support from board members may also involve conversations about the appropriate roles of the board, executive director, and supporters of the organization. As nonprofit organizations grow, so must the role of the board change from being a working board to becoming one that guides rather than drives the staff initiative (Werther and Berman 2004). Small jurisdictions may face the same problem.

Revisiting the need for top-level support one level lower, department managers who lead strategic planning in their departments will need top management support. They will similarly want to be attuned to the agendas and priorities of their top managers, and develop consensus about the appropriate roles of each.

A typical purpose of strategic planning is to light a fire for change. Sometimes, the targets are managers and departments that have been reluctant to change in the past, but at other times it may be communities or elected officials that have been slow to embrace new activity. In either case, managers must show a clear and urgent need for change. What is so wrong that requires a new course of action? A persuasive case for action must be built. Answers to this question must (1) increase the desirability or inevitability of future changes and (2) decrease the possibility or desirability of continuing the status quo. Benefits of change must be enumerated as well as the costs of not changing. Managers increase understanding of the need for change by developing the rationale and circulating it over several months, internal and external of the organization (recall the rule of three in chapter 3), thereby forcing discussion. This may include evidence of stakeholder dissatisfaction and performance problems. Managers need to be clear about what changes can be made, and what types of contributions or discussions they want.

But trust matters, too. Leaders should show that they are indeed committed to change and follow-through, such as by ensuring resources for plans that may be adopted. Typically, small amounts are already allocated for pilot efforts, providing tangible evidence. Managers will also need to show how to deal with the negative consequences of change: eliminated or changed positions. Often, leaders commit to new positions or exit packages for those who lose their positions. Leaders will want to ensure employees and managers that their needs are being listened to in clear and accountable ways. Rewards can be provided for those who commit themselves to change, providing tangible evidence of benefits to come. Trust needs to be shown in many different ways.

Obtaining a critical mass of support and some early successes are outcomes of strategic planning. When strategic planning involves the entire organization, then the enthusiasm and support of managers and others helps determine who is deemed a supporter, fence sitter, or resister. The 25–50–25 rule applies here as well. Likewise, strategic planning may involve community organizations. Top managers are apt to take their cue from participation, and develop an initial implementation effort that builds support and involves some early, easy successes. Strategic planning requires a cadre of initial supporters, and one that grows over time. This also means thinking ahead about how to deal with those who resist or otherwise fail to support these efforts.

The purpose of the preplanning phase is to assess and increase receptivity to change. The above activities help lay the foundation for subsequent success.

The Research Phase

After the decision has been made to go forward with the strategic planning process, one of the first steps will be the development of a process to gather and analyze information to better understand the environment of the organization and the organization's capabilities. Often, the leader and senior managers have some understanding of the main challenges facing the organization, and how the organization might adapt to these. The purpose of the research phase is to fact-check past and current performance of the organization, gather data of broad trends that are likely to affect it in some way, and research changes and opportunities in the organization's environment and clienteles; good research is about the synthesis of these facts (Coolsen 2000). It is useful to think of different categories of potentially relevant information, and gather as much information as possible within each, from whatever source. The research phase establishes a factual basis for decisions and future discussions, and is guided by the current mission, a sense of what difference the organization is designed to make, urgent reasons for change, and any other considerations that point toward future change.

The research phase often is overseen by a team consisting of top and senior managers. The team that is responsible for the research is typically called a strategic planning committee (SPC) in large organizations. Typically, these managers task analysts to assist them in collecting the above data. External stakeholders are involved, either as members of the SPC or as a separate stakeholder advisory committee, which provides input to the SPC and is a source of knowledge and data about the environment of the organization. Analysts may conduct additional research, such as client or citizen surveys, to better understand emerging needs of their clienteles. Top leaders sometimes personally interview community leaders in order to get their assessment of changing community conditions and their expectations of the agency. Doing so also helps to forge community alliances that can bolster support later. In very large organizations, the analytical work is performed by separate task groups and the SPC may be composed of several different management teams. Doing so broadens participation and increases input.

The above data may be organized in various ways. The first type of analysis identifies past, present, or future critical events. For example, an environmental organization will want to consider changes in federal laws, plants closings, and environmental catastrophes. The second type of data concerns trend analyses. For example, changes in population demographics and economic activity often affect the environment. Both of the above analyses focus on the external environment. A third type focuses on internal strengths and weaknesses of the agency, as well the external opportunities and threats that affect the agency and its community. This is SWOT (strengths, weaknesses, opportunities, threats) analysis. A SWOT analysis is more encompassing than an event and trend analysis, and focuses on agency capabilities for dealing with issues, as well as external factors that are political, economic, social, or technological in nature (that is, PEST). While analysts gather the data, managers will need to think through these matters carefully. Although perfect information is seldom available, what exists should be gathered and brought to their attention. A summary of a SWOT analysis is shown in Table 4.1.

The data collection phase ends with a shared understanding about the problem and its context, the opportunities and threats. Critical issues are identified as those concerning specific results or problems that strategic plans must address and which are often used by others as benchmarks for evaluating success. The data-gathering steps alone do not produce this understanding. Rather, the development of shared understanding is a creative process that involves techniques of brainstorming and reality testing. Brainstorming ensures that problems and issues fully surface and are explored. The knowledge of individual group members is brought to bear. The data are the factual backdrop for these creative processes, and sometimes analyses are further refined and assumptions fact-checked. The development of a shared understanding is often conducted over several meetings. The data collection phase can last from three hours to three months depending on the size of the organization and the complexity of its activities and environment.

The Design Phase

The outcome of the research phase is not only consensus about the facts of an organization and its environment; it also gives focus to the next step, that of formulating the organization's vision for itself. The vision statement is a short, concise, and general statement about what the organization wants to become and achieve in the years ahead. Typically, a vision statement builds on the opportunities and strengths of an organization, while respecting the

Table 4.1

SWOT Analysis and Strategic Issues from a Strategic Plan of a Public Administration Department (Modified)

I. SWOT Analysis

Strengths	The PA Department has a positive approach to serving its students, involvement in professional associations, freedom in decision making, and a sound managerial structure. Classes emphasize hands-on applications that students feel are relevant. The PA program is growing impressively, with an abundance of internships.
Weaknesses	There are three unfilled positions, and high turnover of faculty. The chair is temporary. The faculty should publish more. The department uses too many adjuncts. The student to faculty ratio is high, which increases demands made on faculty. The admission standards are minimal: the perception of an "easy" program complicates efforts to raise standards. Too many meetings. Considerable travel between branch campuses.
Opportunities	The three vacant positions should be filled with research active faculty. Curriculum revisions should further shape the program and provide special tracks. Courses in the proposed Ph.D. program should be made available to Master of Public Administration students.
Threats	Pay discrepancy between faculty members, inadequate space and resources, insufficient student support for teaching and research, funding limits, competing philosophies among faculty, sacrifice of quality for quantity.

II. Selected Strategic Issues

1. Ensure re-accreditation of the M.P.A. program.
2. Provide support for faculty to increase research productivity.
3. Strengthen ties with the community.
4. Increase diversity among faculty.
5. Update or redesign the public administration curriculum.
6. Pursue additional revenues.
7. Retain faculty, reduce high turnover.
8. Start the Ph.D. program.
9. Identify and fulfill new stakeholder needs.

"core" businesses of the organization. Sometimes the original mission is revisited, too. The mission statement is a concise description of the main activities of the organization, their objectives, and the approach toward reaching the objectives. Some organizations only have a mission statement, but many have both a mission statement and a vision statement. For example, below are the mission and vision statements of the Human Resource Department of Buffalo State College (2005):

Mission Statement:
The mission of the Human Resource Management Office is to support and influence the strategic direction of Buffalo State College by providing managers and employees with innovative solutions to organizational and human resource issues. The department exists to provide services which help the college to attract, retain, and reward competent and dedicated faculty and staff who share a commitment to the values of excellence and innovation in teaching, research, and service to students and the community.

Vision Statement:
We aspire to build partnerships with management at all levels of the organization to create a campus culture that values all employees. This culture encourages and rewards exceptional performance and continuous improvement, fosters teamwork, and supports balanced attention to work and personal life issues. We provide services of the highest quality in a cost-effective manner while creating a healthy professional environment that fosters respect for both diverse perspectives and a service orientation.

Do such statements hold water? An important benefit of having such a statement is that it allows the organization to then develop specific goals and programs that further develop the mission and vision. They terminate prior conversation of a philosophical nature about what the organization should be or become—these statements settle those matters. Managers will want to give careful consideration to the process for developing mission and vision statements and ensure that these statements have legitimacy among employee and other groups. For example, managers or members of the SPC might draft a statement, and then conduct a meeting with employees to discuss and further improve it. They might want to eventually post it on their Intranet for further discussion. While mission and vision statements do not guarantee that action plans will result from strategic planning, they do serve a purpose in the strategic planning process.

The next steps are to identify (1) goals that embody the vision of the organization, and for each goal, (2) specific objectives, strategies, and timelines for achieving the objectives and, hence, the goals. This is the strategic plan, a blueprint of the specific actions that the organization plans to take in the years ahead. The strategies should be feasible, and may include budgets, other resources, and timetables. In large organizations, strategic planning task forces of managers, analysts, and employees are created, often to develop objectives and strategies around each separate goal. Lower managers are typically part of this process, because of their expertise with specific strategies, and also because the outcome of this phase should be commitment to the proposed strategies. They participate in the planning activities that will result in new tasks for them. Organizations vary in the extent of lower managers' involvement. Some organizations ask for lower manager's involvement only as needed, whereas others engage in organization-wide planning processes to ensure increased awareness and commitment.

Strategic planning documents show a characteristic ordering of goals, objectives, strategies, and target dates. Goals are general ends that advance the vision in these specific issue areas. Objectives are specific, measurable outcomes that advance goals. Each goal has several objectives, and each objective will have several strategies to help achieve it. Strategic plans typically develop these for each area of the organization's core or main activities. For example, the City of Colorado Springs' Strategic Plan (2000) shows goals developed for six areas: transportation, public safety, infrastructure, citizen services and workforce, economic development, and community development and growth. Within the area of transportation, for example, there is one goal, three objectives, and eight strategies. Some of these are shown below:

Goal: Provide an effective, efficient, affordable, and sustainable transportation network.

Objective 1: Provide funding to develop, implement, and maintain a transportation and bridge system that meets present and future mobility needs.

  Strategy 1.1: Ensure sustainable funding for construction and maintenance through a combination of measures, including ballot initiatives, user fees, grants, state and federal funds, and develop contributions.

  Strategy 1.2: Preserve adequate right of way for all major transportation corridors, including interchanges where required.

  Strategy 1.3: Sustain a service level of "D" or better for major thoroughfares.

Similarly, Objective 2 (with four strategies) and Objective 3 (with two strategies) are presented. Then the next five areas are discussed, each with goals, objectives, and strategies. A second, implementation document develops each of the above strategies by further identifying specific tasks, target dates, and budgets. Managers will want to familiarize themselves with a range of strategic plans in their line of work. Sometimes strategic planning also includes a prioritization of objectives and goals. Although each organization and jurisdiction must develop its own plan—strategic planning is a process—it obviously helps to consider examples from others.

The purpose of the design phase is not only to develop a blueprint but to obtain commitment, too. Managers will want to involve lower managers and employees in the development, and also to have the plan accepted by those who have legitimacy and authority. These are the strategic priorities for the organization in the years ahead, and efforts that support and further them are expected and preferred. For example, managers in nonprofit organizations will likely seek approval from their board of trustees, public managers in local governments will seek approval from their elected councils, state officials will seek approvals form the governor's office, and federal officials will seek approval from appointed executives or those in the Office of Management and Budget (OMB) or the president's office. This is not a substitute for an open development process, but it does help make the strategic plan a fait accompli for those who might see it otherwise.

Implementation

The final step is implementation; strategies are put into action. A singular frustration, and great source of cynicism, is plans that gather dust. Top managers will want to ensure that they identify some "ripe apples" so that they can tout the early successes of the strategic planning effort. The organization may already be undertaking some efforts that can be highlighted as examples of success. Leaders also consider which managers they trust to implement the new plans; the supportive and enthusiastic 25 percent (of the 25–50–25 rule) of managers or units are typically first targeted for major efforts, while de-emphasizing departments in which managers are thought to be resistant to change or incompetent. A bias exists toward some form of earnest inclusion and responsiveness in all phases of the planning process in order to increase the odds of generating a cadre of committed lower managers. Implementation may also lead to creating new partnerships and alliances, which are discussed in chapter 9.

The implementation phase typically lasts a few years. Some objectives are readily accomplished, whereas others take a bit longer. It is common to examine existing strategic plans yearly to ensure that objective and strategies are still on target and that underlying assumptions remain valid. The strategic planning process often is conducted about once every three to five years in many organizations. This, then, is a useful tool for reexamining the need for major shifts and changes.

Finally, strategic planning often is a first step toward addressing other problems, such as inefficient production or delivery processes, inadequate coordination, poor communication within the organization, inconsistent rewards, poor project management, and lack of professionalism. Some problems are identified as such in the strategic planning process, whereas others become evident through implementation. Organizations that do strategic planning often undertake other performance improvement strategies to address these issues in subsequent years. This is yet another reason to ensure that the outcome of strategic planning is commitment by subordinate units to goals and objectives that have been agreed upon.

Community-Based Strategic Planning

A useful variation of strategic planning is to help communities and regions deal with broader, regional problems. Examples include regional economic development, community public safety efforts, environmental protection, regional transportation, education, and other examples as shown in Table 4.2. Many of today's problems are those that no agency or jurisdiction can adequately confront alone; they require close collaboration among public and private organizations. For example, many public safety issues involve local police, schools, neighborhood associations, churches, and parent associations. Community-based strategic planning is also helpful in dealing with problems for which no agency or jurisdiction exists; this is sometimes the case in transportation and environmental protection. It can certainly be argued that regions that are able to effectively address their problems are more likely to gain competitive advantages than those that are not (Blair 2004; Wheeland 2003; Luke 1998; Chrislip and Larson 1996; Bryson and Crosby 2005).

Community-based responses are increasingly used to address the growing complexity of many problems, as well as to better utilize the capabilities of local organizations. In 2003, 74.3 percent of cities with populations over 50,000 agreed or strongly agreed that they frequently participate in community-based planning activities (Berman and Korosec 2005); a few years earlier, in 1997, 52 percent of cities over 50,000 reported that they had used community-based strategic planning during the past twelve months, as had 38 percent of large social service organizations (Berman and West 1998). Community-based strategic planning is also used by state agencies that have decentralized operations in different counties, as well as by some federal agencies and programs that embrace a bottom-up approach to planning that is grounded in local interests and resources. Community-based strategic planning is also used in other countries to assist in economic development, for example.

Community-based strategic planning involves four distinctive phases, similar to those of organizational strategic planning, but it is characterized by some noteworthy differences: community-based strategic plan-

Table 4.2

Examples of Collaborative Leadership

Economic Development
- Local government develops comprehensive economic development strategies together with leaders of area businesses, schools, universities, neighborhood associations, county governments, banks, and community organizations.
- Local government works with area hospitals to create a regional center for biomedical instrument research and manufacturing.
- Banks work with neighborhood associations and governments to provide home improvement loans and to build homes for low-income families.
- City works with insurance companies to ensure coverage for nonprofit vendors.

Human Services
- County welfare agencies work with courts to provide integrated services for child care payments, noncustodial parent involvement in child care, and job skills training for custodial parent.
- Preventive services for poor women (e.g., breast cancer screening, prenatal care).
- Local government works with nonprofit organizations to provide comprehensive care for homeless families and adolescents (e.g., housing assistance to prevent eviction).

Education
- Schools, parents, teachers, and employers collectively identify the educational needs of children.
- National Network of Educational Renewal: Brings universities and school districts together to renew the education of educators.
- School boards work with local governments and planning commissions to reduce overcrowding by requiring growth management impact fees and building lead-time.
- Schools work with police and nonprofit organizations to provide early warning of domestic violence affecting their students.

Public Safety
- Police work with middle schools to teach students to avoid becoming victims.
- Police work with neighborhood associations to provide community-based policing.
- Police work with manufacturers, insurance companies, and shipping companies to reduce auto theft.

ning is a facilitated rather than a directed process, it involves consensual decision making and implementation rather than top-down management, and can involve many more decision makers (10 to 1,200; see Table 4.3). The following discussion is guided by the four phases, while noting important differences between organization-based and community-based strategic planning.

Table 4.3

A Comparison of Traditional and Community-Based Strategic Planning

Traditional strategic planning	Community-based strategic planning
Single organizations	Multiple, "networked" organizations
Involves a few decision makers (typically 1–7)	Involves many stakeholders (10–1,200) who are often the leaders of their organizations
Assumes that goals, objectives, and strategies will be accepted by affected parties	Assumes that stakeholder participation is essential to acceptance and, hence, implementation
Assumes adequate information of threats, opportunities, strengths, and weaknesses by a few participants	Uses many stakeholders to provide needed information about participating organizations and their environments
Can be conducted in two hours to two days, although usually between two days and three months.	Requires three to six months for ensuring awareness and consensus on problems, goals, objectives, strategies, and priorities.
Requires commitment from the top leader.	Requires commitment from the key public and private stakeholders.
Planning leader leads the planning process and develops and decides on new strategy.	Planning leader is facilitative and relies on stakeholders to suggest and accept new options.
Implementation is often top-down, and ensured by hierarchical authority.	Implementation is consensual, and ensured by peer pressure.
Outcomes occur over six-month to five-year period.	Outcomes occur over a two- to five-year period.

Preplanning Phase: Getting Started

Public officials play a leading role in launching community-based strategic planning. Such officials include mayors and governors, as well as chief appointed officials such as state and federal agency directors. Ranking elected officials are prominent in this process because they readily command the legitimacy of dealing with public issues. They also hold forth a credible promise of public support through new policies, programs, or funding in the event that subsequent decision-making efforts lead to action. Sometimes, chief executive officers of prominent nonprofit organizations also lead in initiating community-based activities (Berman and Werther 1996).

As a practical matter, leaders must decide which problems or issues they will address through community-based strategic planning. These decisions often reflect three key considerations. First, issues are more likely to be addressed when they are seen as salient concerns by other citizen groups and organizations. Public support furthers the commitment of leaders. Elected leaders must also feel confident that leaders of other organizations are likely to follow their initiative, and that they have support from their organizations, too. A second condition is that issue areas and potential strategies must be consistent with the priorities and ideologies of elected or self-appointed leaders. Many elected officials enter office with visions of future accomplishments, and issues that are consistent with these visions are more likely to be acted on. Third, elected officials must believe that community-based action is effective. They must feel comfortable with existing models for achieving community-based commitment and decision making. Managers of public and nonprofit organizations can play important roles by bringing to the attention of elected officials these successful practices of community-based planning.

After the decision has been made by a leader to "go forward" with an issue and deal with it through community-based strategic planning, a team of community leaders is created, the strategic planning committee. This is usually done with the assistance of a process facilitator who guides the strategic planning effort. One example of a community-based strategic plan occurred in the city of Hollywood (Florida), population 135,000, in which the author was involved. The driving reason for the strategic planning effort was the city's failure to capture its share of economic growth that was occurring in South Florida. The strategic planning process brought together 34 community leaders in an SPC, representing organizations that had shown a commitment to Hollywood. The group size represented a balance between inclusiveness and manageability, and other community members who wished to participate served on various subcommittees discussed later. Eventually, about 150 persons participated.

Another example concerned the provision of public health services in Nebraska. In the late 1990s, 16 local public health departments provided services to only 22 of the state's 93 counties. Strategic planning was initiated by the Nebraska Department of Health and Human Services to examine and address the need for better public health services. The research phase included a public health stakeholders group (PHSG), which consisted of diverse coalition of local public health departments, medical and hospital associations, community organizations, universities, and representatives of ethnic and other organizations. The PHSG evaluated the effectiveness of the current delivery system, and made recommendations for key objectives that involved health promotion, disease prevention, and medical care (Palm 2005).

One of the very first issues facing SPCs is clarification of the group mandate: On whose authority is the group proceeding? Although public officials often play a leadership role in convening the group, the group itself is an informal network that generally does not fall under any public jurisdiction. The group must create its own mandate. This informal act is furthered when leaders state their organization's commitment to the process. They must indicate their organization is willing to participate and that it will devote resources to the effort. Ground rules are clarified. A frequent concern is that mandates do not bind organizations to participate in recommendations or even to complete the process: such a requirement would scare most organizations away from the table. Group mandates are often very brief in anticipation of further work on mission or vision statements. Mandates often identify the willingness of organizations to cooperate in studying the issue or problem, and to work toward identifying strategies that address it.

Inclusiveness broadens support, but this implies that officials must frequently interact with individuals or organizations against whom some animus exists. Leaders sometimes have concerns about how they will deal with such persons and organizations. In this regard, the constitution of a new group of stakeholders for strategic planning allows for fresh starts. To ensure broad participation, ground rules for decision making usually include that adversaries will have the opportunity to contribute their views. Of concern also is dealing with elected officials. Their participation greatly increases the likelihood that recommendations will be adopted in later public policy settings. Political opponents are usually invited, too. Political opponents often participate in order to be part of the process, to keep tabs on what is happening.

Research Phase

As in organizational planning, strategy development requires a solid factual understanding of the problem. Reports on past, present, or future critical events, trend analyses, and SWOT analyses are prepared. Data are collected about the community and its organizations. Because the planning scope of SPCs is usually large, subcommittees are used to generate understanding for different issues. This also enables other community leaders and interested citizens to participate. Group participation furthers consensus building about the significance of events and trends. The generation of shared knowledge typically requires several meetings over a two- or three-month period. These activities help forge community among otherwise disparate leaders. The data collection and analysis phase of strategic planning often lasts about three to four months.

During the data collection phase, citizen and business surveys are often used to gather further information. These efforts serve a dual purpose, namely, to collect data and to inform citizens about the activities of the group. Managers contribute by ensuring that surveys are conducted in a timely and credible manner. Public support increases the legitimacy of such efforts, whereas the lack of such support sometimes creates obstacles to implementation. To ensure public participation, media representatives are also often invited in order to keep citizens apprised of these activities. These journalists ensure that articles appear about the strategic planning effort. In some cases, public meetings are also used, although these are typically later, in the context of policy adoption by public bodies.

The data collection and consensus-building stage ends with the development of a shared understanding about the problem and its context. As in organizational strategic planning, this is a creative process that involves techniques of brainstorming and reality testing.

Design Phase

Upon acceptance of the SWOT findings and critical issues, the strategic planning committee must identify the critical issues. This is necessary because often more priorities are identified than can be pursued, and also because some critical issues exceed the mandate of the SPC: for example, neighborhood safety is an appropriate concern of neighborhood development, but public safety issues are neither the focus nor the mandate of most local economic development efforts. Identifying these issues is also a first step toward developing a mission statement because it causes the committee to focus the efforts of the group. For example, the Hollywood mission statement states (in abbreviated form): "The mission of the City of Hollywood Strategic Planning Committee is to empower our citizens to adjust to economic change. . . . To accomplish our mission, we will establish new directions which will . . . retain jobs, create an environment that stimulates economic growth, maintain Hollywood's existing tourism industry, rehabilitate neighborhoods and provide effective municipal services."

After formulating the mission statement, new subcommittees or task forces are formed to develop goals, objectives, and strategies that address each critical issue. This allows previous research subcommittees to be reconstituted and to accommodate new participants and gain fresh perspectives. The activity of developing goals, objectives, and strategies is creative, and usually occurs over three or four meetings. During this process, facilitators help participants to focus on goals, objectives, and strategies that are both feasible and within the mandate and mission of the group. Representatives from organizations that are involved in subsequent implementation participate, too. Their perspectives ensure that proposed strategies are reality-based. Likewise, experts are sometimes brought into decision-making processes, for example, to inform of experiences in other communities.

A concern of most planning processes is that plans do not gather dust. Several strategies are commonly used to avoid this problem. First, facilitators often seek commitment for implementation from elected officials, agency heads, and the directors of organizations. This furthers the legitimacy and the marshaling of resources. Second, where practicable, some organizations begin implementation prior to formal adoption. Third, to ensure adoption by elected bodies, elected officials are involved in the planning process. This allows proposals to reflect their views, and hence increase the likelihood of acceptance. Fourth, facilitators discuss barriers to implementation and assess ways in which these barriers are overcome.

The final product of the task forces is a compendium of proposed goals, objectives, strategies, and target dates. These compendia are ultimately adopted by vote by the SPC. Because of the number of objectives, many SPCs rank these in terms of priority. In the Hollywood community-based strategic planning effort, over 125 strategies were developed, each of which is linked to specific goals and objectives.

Implementation

The most important part of strategic planning is the implementation of proposed strategies by implementing organizations. As discussed above, the implementation process often begins prior to formal adoption of proposals. Many proposed actions make good sense, and fall within the existing purview of organizations or managers. There is no need to provide public organizations or managers with new mandates. The implementation process is also furthered by adopting specific start and completion dates for activities. Sometimes the services of the process facilitator are extended to help agencies organize and implement efforts. In other instances, strategic management approaches are used. For example, the previously formed strategic planning committee may become the strategic management committee, overseeing plan implementation, or a strategic management team is created consisting of the city manager, mayor, department heads, and selected staff.

What outcomes does community-based strategic planning produce? The outcomes that result from community-based strategic planning efforts are new commitments from a multitude of actors to work on community problems. First-year results usually include streamlining of procedures and piloting of new services. For example, community colleges improve their planning outcomes through increased interaction with the business community. In the instance of Hollywood, a new public–private partnership was established, and Hollywood has now transformed its downtown area to become a vibrant destination in South Florida. After only a few years, residential areas around downtown Hollywood attracted much new investment and, several years later, Hollywood was considered an up-and-coming, highly desirable area within South Florida. Even if not all 125 strategies were fully implemented, more than enough was done to effectively move the community forward.

Of course, community-based strategic planning is not the only approach to dealing with regional issues. Other approaches include regional summits, working through metropolitan and other planning organizations, and creating new public enterprises. However, each of these has its limitations, and all must deal with the fundamental issues of leadership. For example, regional summits must somehow provide follow-through and implementation, and metropolitan planning organizations may be unwilling to broaden their missions to accommodate new concerns. Public enterprises may not be appropriate for problems that require coordination rather than new service delivery. The ability to address regional problems is indeed one of the foremost challenges of our times.

Other Approaches to Strategic Change

Strategic planning is not the only approach for creating new strategic directions in organizations. Three commonly used alternative approaches are hiring new managers, using mandates and establishing budget incentives and disincentives, and employing quiet or surreptitious strategies. In comparison with strategic planning, these alternatives have the appeal of simplicity, requiring a minimum of management time and effort. However, complications frequently occur.

Replacing Managers

A widely used strategy for change is hiring new top-level managers. Agency directors who wish to steer divisions and programs in new directions may replace existing managers. City councils that are disappointed with current management or policy often replace the city manager or chief administrative officer with one who is more attuned to the orientations of the existing council. New managers are apt to follow the directives of their new superiors.

In practice, this "magic bullet" of hiring seldom works as intended. New managers require commitment, or at least compliance, from subordinates to implement their new programs. They may also need to build ties with stakeholders. Current employees and managers are usually committed to existing programs from which they derive their raison d'etre and their power basis in the organization. New managers must instill a similar sense of urgency about the need for change as described above in strategic planning. They need to provide a rationale for change and find a cadre of managers and employees who are willing to pilot and undertake such efforts. The basis for replacing existing managers is their inability to undertake these necessary processes; the hiring of new managers alone is not enough.

Thus, replacing managers is no sinecure for strategic change. To be successful, new managers will have to build bridges and obtain the commitment for change from others. When new managers fail to do so, significant opposition may result. Although heavy-handed tactics may produce initial successes, long-term loss of cooperation, trust, and, ultimately, leadership, are likely to stifle subsequent performance efforts. The difficulty of making change by replacing managers is seen in the often-unfortunate experiences of business executives who acquire political appointments to run federal agencies "like a business." Quite often, they leave Washington disappointed, unaccustomed to exigencies of collaborative decision making and transparency.

Mandates and Budgets

Another approach to strategic change is to reorder priorities through top-down mandates and budget (dis)incentives. For example, federal mandates may cause cities to adopt new municipal recycling programs. Top managers change budget incentives, which encourage lower managers to pursue efficiency gains, for example, by allowing them to keep a share of cost-savings for a period of time.

The use of mandates and budgets as tools of change is seductive in its hands-off approach. The idea is that organizations pursue incentives that are offered them. But in practice the use of mandates and budgets requires considerable followup and accountability to ensure that units follow the new guidance. When organizations perceive that managers do not follow through, little or no change may result. An example is the federal requirement that cities provide Comprehensive Homelessness Assistance Plans (CHAPs) as a condition for receiving federal funds for homelessness services. Although the intent is to increase community-based efforts and planning in this area, most CHAPs are only a compilation of current efforts. The CHAPs fulfill funding requirements, but do not further the spirit of the intent. A second problem is unintended consequences. The requirement that states get tough on crime has reduced funding for rehabilitation and job training programs in many locales. Instead, more prisons have been built. This, in turn, increases the number of former inmates in society who are unable to support themselves, hence increasing both crime and recidivism.

Such problems with the use of mandates and budgets as tools for strategic change suggest that they are often more involved than advocates expect or intend them to be. Education, coalition building, monitoring, and accountability appear to be necessary, complementary activities when mandates are used. Other organizations must understand how to respond to the mandates and how they will be held accountable. The processes of buy-in described as part of strategic planning occur sooner or later here, too. In the absence of these elements, perhaps most budget and mandate strategies are best used for relatively minor changes that can readily be accomplished within existing means and which do not require new goals.

Quiet Change

Finally, another strategy is to engage in change, but not to inform employees and managers of the change. The purpose is to create initial successes, while precluding the possibility that powerful opponents will thwart initial efforts.

An example is midnight basketball. In many cities, social service agencies recognized that midnight basketball could provide them with access to hard-core, violence-prone youths. They also understood that such programs were likely to generate much public controversy. Thus, initial programs were implemented with very little fanfare and discussion. These programs were successful in reaching certain youths and "keeping them out of trouble." Moreover, they quickly built a support network from community leaders and parents. When midnight basketball gained media and political exposure, the support network in many cities ensured their continuance.

However, other examples have less-fortunate outcomes. The problem with stealth is that at some point it must come into the open. Top leaders and the media may not always understand or embrace these efforts. Thus, the use of quiet or surreptitious strategies is tantamount to postponing the inevitable with regard to building broad-based support for proposed efforts. When such support is not forthcoming, the change effort is often halted.

In Conclusion

This chapter discusses strategic planning as a strategy for shaping the missions of public and nonprofit organizations, and developing new programs and initiatives. Strategic planning involves four steps: preplanning, research, design, and implementation. Each step helps build consensus and moves the organization forward to change. Community-based strategic planning differs from organizational strategic planning in that it typically involves more actors and is a facilitated rather than a directed process. Community-based strategic planning is increasingly recognized as important for addressing regional problems that involve multiple jurisdictions. This chapter also discussed other efforts to instill change such as by replacing managers and issuing directives.

Application Exercises

1. Formulate a process for undertaking strategic planning in your area of interest. What is the need for strategic planning at this time? Which

actors should be involved? How do you apply the steps and proce-
dure discussed here to your process? Which steps would you undertake to ensure that conditions for success are in place?

2. Research examples of strategic plans on the Internet, and obtain examples of planning analyses and PowerPoint presentations.

3. Have you ever been involved in strategic planning? If so, what worked,
and what factors contributed to success? What did not work, and why
not? What could be done to prevent the problem in the future?

4. Identify a problem that would benefit from a regional, community-based
strategic planning approach. Then, define the problem, identify the organizations that should be involved, organizations or their leaders who
could take the lead in pulling these organizations together and the actions of these leaders that would compel these organizations to come
together (preferably by creating win-win situations, rather than using
duress). Discuss the first steps of community-based actions that would
get a community-based strategic planning process going.

5. Research examples of community-based strategic planning. As an
example of an effort to assist in regional data collection and increase
awareness for collective action, visit http://myregion.org.

The Quality Paradigm

The sad truth is that excellence makes people nervous.
—Shana Alexander

The current period in performance improvement is characterized by the emergence of the quality paradigm. Some of principal values of the quality paradigm are heightened customer orientation and improved service quality—providing the right services faster, better, and at lower cost. The name of this period is derived from Total Quality Management (TQM), through which this paradigm was initially implemented. Initial efforts under the name of TQM involved too many different strategies and too many changes, and a consensus was soon reached that TQM should be implemented as separate strategies: customer orientation, process reengineering, empowerment, and benchmarking/performance measurement. Total Quality Management focuses on the systems for producing services and the individual activities of managers or employees within the systems context. Competent people in bad systems produce lower quality than those in high-performance systems. Finally, TQM emphasizes continuous improvement—what was good enough yesterday is insufficient today. New and better services should continuously be developed, and the leader's task is to continuously increase standards for service quality in order to advance these.

The first two strategies, customer orientation and process reengineering, are discussed in this chapter; empowerment is discussed in chapter 7 and performance measurement in chapter 8. Strategies of customer orientation most commonly address unsatisfactory interactions between the agency and its stakeholders (Problem 2) and the need for increased customer orientation, which may reshape existing missions or services (Problem 5). Strategies of process reengineering are used to address problems of inadequately meeting those needs (Problem 1), inefficient service delivery processes (Problem 7), and inadequate coordination (Problem 8).

Early roots of the quality paradigm can be traced to World War II, when wartime production demanded higher levels of performance, reliability, and timeliness. Defective radios, tanks, artillery, and aircraft posed a clear and present danger. During this period, U.S. engineers built on previous, pre-war time-motion studies, quality control practices, and mass production methods to improve quality. After World War II, U.S. manufacturers reverted back to earlier peacetime production practices; many companies considered these methods too costly and unnecessary for consumer goods. Immediately after the war, Divine and Sherman (1948) argued that "Techniques for Controlling Quality" should be used in government, but they were not. The federal government was unreceptive to introducing quality control techniques in its management practices. Some engineers who created higher-quality standards found employment in Japan, to assist with rebuilding its factories during and after the reconstruction period in that country. U.S. quality practices were thus absorbed by Japanese engineers, which further improved these over time.

By the late 1960s and mid-1970s, improvements in Japanese cars and electronics products made them competitive with those of U.S. firms; brands such as SONY, Panasonic, Toshiba, Toyota, and Nissan were introduced to U.S. markets and were readily accepted. These brands soon boasted higher reliability than many U.S. brands, which were quickly losing their appeal. Ford Motor Company, for example, was now being called "Found On the Roadside Dead," or "Fix Or Repair Daily." During this period, quality became defined as conformance to customer preferences for reliability, high performance, low cost, ease of use, and pleasing esthetics. This emphasis on customer needs continues to resonate today. American executives, concerned about their eroding market share, studied these then-Japanese approaches. Many Japanese strategies were adopted by large U.S. multinational manufacturers, especially in automobile and electronics, which faced global competition. The first to be adopted were Quality Circles (groups of employees who study opportunities for process and product improvement), and later TQM in the late 1970s. Then, in the 1980s, TQM-related efforts found diffusion among other large and medium-size manufacturing firms, some service industries, and the federal government. So, in a rather curious way, quality management can be viewed as an American, post–World War II export product that was later significantly improved and reimported into the United States in the late 1970s as TQM.

The quality paradigm follows the diffusion model of performance improvement efforts discussed in chapter 1. TQM was first introduced in the federal government in the late 1980s, and in local government in the early 1990s. The federal government contributed to diffusion of TQM through its prestigious Baldrige Quality Award program, developed in 1987. This award program sets high standards for service quality, customer orientation, vendor relations, strategic planning and leadership, and human resources (U.S. National Institute of Standards and Technology 2005). During the early is period, TQM took public managers by storm, promising new tools and a new way to practice management. It was a hot topic that received much coverage. For example, at the 1993 national conference of the American Society for Public Administration (ASPA) in San Francisco, TQM was all the buzz, and there were numerous sessions on the topic, far more than in the previous year. *Public Administration Review,* the flagship journal of the ASPA, carried an article by Swiss (1992) that became a cornerstone for many articles that followed. Many articles and studies about TQM came about during this period (e.g., Osborne and Gaebler 1992; Kettl and DiIulio 1995; Berman and West 1995).

Since then, various strategies have been implemented and the quality paradigm is now entering the mature stage of development. Some jurisdictions are further along than others, of course. In some other countries, the term "new public management" (NPM) is used to refer to the quality paradigm, while including other strategies such as privatization and some uses of information technology. Heightened attention to these strategies overseas appears to have followed that of the United States by a few years; many countries became involved in these efforts in the late 1990s and beyond (e.g., Lian Kok Fei and Rainey 2003; Torres 2004; Vigoda et al. 2005; Willcocks, Currie, and Jackson 1997; Kettl 2000; Hendriks and Tops 2003). Total Quality Management-based strategies also began to take hold in some nonprofit organizations in the 1990s, and became more widely used around 2000 (Durst and Newell 2001). Among TQM-based strategies, customer service strategies were the first to be widely emphasized, and these are now widely used. This chapter shows where some further improvements are still possible. Process reengineering is also common, especially such applications as one-stop shopping. Performance measurement is in various stages of development; some organizations are just now building adequate capacity, whereas others have fully developed efforts that are well integrated with accountability, performance appraisal, strategic planning, and/or cost accounting efforts. Empowerment and continuous improvement are accepted management concepts and philosophies, but are not always widely used.

The implications for managers are clear: managers need to be familiar with the family of TQM-based strategies. Many of these strategies continue to be subject to further improvement, and managers will want to scan their horizon for ongoing development and improvement of TQM-based strategies.

A New Paradigm

It is useful to consider the quality paradigm as a fundamental critique of traditional top-down management styles. It is no exaggeration to state that the development of many recent management ideas reflects the growing acceptance of these once-radical ideas. As TQM-based strategies are increasingly used, so, too, do our ideas change about what constitutes appropriate management.

The core of values of the quality paradigm reflect early TQM efforts and can be stated as follows: (1) identify, meet, and exceed the needs of customers (and other stakeholders); (2) strive to produce services right the first time (that is, reduce errors that upset stakeholders and cause rework and increased costs); (3) use systematic analysis to evaluate and improve services delivery; and (4) consistently support workers in their efforts to improve quality and meet customer needs (Rosander 1989). The quality paradigm invites managers to think broadly about customer service and needs, and to develop innovative approaches to improve service delivery. The above strategies, customer orientation, process reengineering, continuous improvement, empowerment, and benchmarking/performance measurement, are reflections of these values; they bring one or more of them into practice (Boyne 2002; Osborne and Plastrik 1997).

The type of organization that best embodies and brings forth these values is in some ways radically different from many traditional organizations. This contrast is perhaps best described by comparing the "ideal types" of these organizations. The term "ideal type" refers to a conception of something (here, an organization) in its highest perfection or purest form. In Table 5.1, the column "Traditional Organization" shows the features of a "pure" traditional, rules-driven, top-down, hierarchical organization. The column "Quality-Based Organization" shows the characteristics of such an organization if it strictly and only followed quality paradigm rules and values. The differences are in many ways dramatic.

A fundamental criticism of traditional organizations by early TQM proponents was that the former insufficiently make customer satisfaction a top priority, instead emphasizing budget growth or compliance with the policies and procedures of the organization. Traditional organizations are not necessarily anticustomer, but customer orientation is not a priority. The lack of customer orientation is said to be a cause of citizen alienation in the public sector.

A related criticism of traditional organizations is that their top-down command-and-control structure insufficiently empowers workers to ensure customer satisfaction. In contrast, TQM assumes that frontline workers know more about their customers than managers and are thus in a better position to ensure customer satisfaction in a timely a manner, if empowered to do so. Thus, TQM seeks to empower workers, and sees the role of managers less as bosses and more as coaches who do what they

Table 5.1

A Comparison of a Traditional and a Quality-Based Organization

Traditional organization	Quality-based organization
Hierarchical organizational structure	Flatter structure with empowered work units
Top management planning	Leading autonomous work units
Orientation toward compliance with rules and regulations	Focus on meeting stakeholder needs and outcomes
Centralized command and control	Decentralized planning
"Directing" supervision	"Coaching" supervision
Post-hoc evaluation ("inspection")	Continuous improvement
Training is low priority	Training is a key strategy for continuous improvement
Performance appraisal is individual oriented	Performance appraisal is both team and individual oriented
Separate data systems	Integrated data systems
Workers are the cause of poor performance	Management is responsible

can to help the players succeed. Managers should also be held accountable for the results of their teams.

Further, TQM believes that with modern information technology workers can now assume more responsibility for making decisions; there is less need for middle managers. These implications have led not only to a shorter (or, flatter) pyramid (that is, the reduction of middle management), but the possibility of organization charts that are inverted; they show the supporting role of managers by placing them on the bottom, and the supreme role of customers by placing them on top (Stephens 1999; see Figure 5.1). Employees are supported by managers, and in service of their customers. Another implication is that workers now need a higher skill set, which increases the importance of training and a clear sense of professional responsibility. Workers are far from being mindless souls who carry out orders; they are responsible for ensuring customer satisfaction and producing services with a minimum of error. Outcomes, not efforts, are emphasized.

A final critique stems from the idea of seeking improvement through the

Figure 5.1 **Organization Chart**

Alabama Department of Rehabilitation Services
Customer Support System

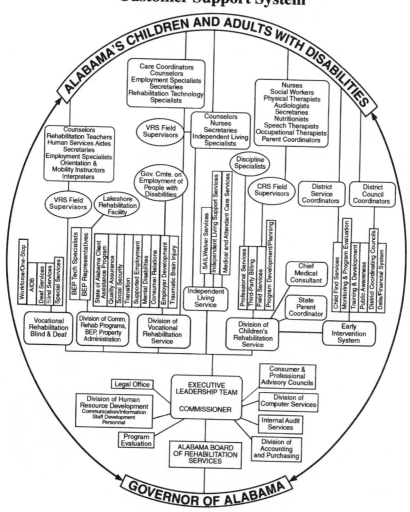

Source: Alabama Department of Rehabilitation Services. Used with permission.

study and change of delivery processes. This stands in contrast with traditional orientations that seek improvement by developing new structures and roles with responsibilities for meeting whatever problem or need has been identified. By contrast, TQM is just as likely to see such additional units and roles as further fragmenting responsibility, and hence a further source of service delivery problems. Rather than creating new units, the analysis of delivery processes often drives TQM-inspired leaders to seek to consolidate rather than expand organizational structures.

These are fundamental critiques, indeed. Of course, no "pure" traditional or TQM organizations exist in the real world as idealized in Table 5.1. Rather, most organizations experience strong, polar tensions as they continuously redefine in which ways, and to what extent, they embrace the items in each column. Although speculative, it might be suggested that most organizations are between 25 to 75 percent TQM based; they have adopted their own, unique mix of some TQM and some traditional items. There are few organizations that are fully traditional or fully quality-based. Yet it is a safe bet that all organizations will adopt more quality-based features in the coming years, because pressures to serve stakeholders in better and new ways are likely to persist, as are pressures to get it right the first time in response to ongoing resource scarcity.

Finally, how is it that emphasis on customers and quality (effectiveness) results in efficiency increases? This very idea has been rejected by U.S. engineers for most of the postwar period. Engineers argued that beyond some point, increases in efficiency result in increased errors as workers try to do more with less resources, or more in too little time. There is only so much additional work that can be done before errors are made. Increased errors imply a drop in quality; hence, efficiency and quality imply a tradeoff. Quality costs—it is never free. By contrast, TQM managers argue that emphases on reducing errors (that is, getting it right the first time, avoiding customer complaints) reduces rework, which in turn reduces the needs for extra resources and time, which in turn increases efficiency. The reduction in errors and getting things right the first time implies increased quality. TQM shows that increasing quality in this way *lowers* costs; quality and efficiency can go hand in hand. A schematic depiction of this argument is shown below ("efficiency" is depicted as O/I, that is, outputs per unit of input; e = number of service or production errors, p = productivity; q = quality):

Traditional Management: $P\uparrow \rightarrow O/I\uparrow \rightarrow I\downarrow \rightarrow e\uparrow \rightarrow Q\downarrow$

TQM Management: $Q\uparrow \rightarrow e\downarrow \rightarrow I\downarrow \rightarrow O/I\uparrow \rightarrow P\uparrow$

Customer Orientation

Ensuring customer satisfaction by increasing customer orientation is among the most basic of TQM principles. Organizations that make customer satisfaction a priority often go through similar stages of customer service. The first stage ensures that customers are treated respectfully and even with friendliness by frontline employees. We call this the "behavioral" or "charm school" approach to customer service. The second stage sets criteria and standards for customer service interactions, and uses behavioral approaches as well as staffing, technology, and work process changes in order to reach higher standards of customer satisfaction. The third stage seeks a deeper understanding of what customer needs are, which in turn shapes which services are provided. It also adopts a more rigorous method of measuring customer satisfaction and assessing customer needs.

It might be observed that this pattern contradicts the logic which states that organizations should first know customer needs (stage 3) before trying to satisfy them with a smile (stage 1). However, the above stages represent a progressive deepening of the customer service experience of organizations. Organizations usually know something about their customer service needs, such as the customers' desire to be treated courteously. They know this, for example, through the anecdotal complaints that they receive, and may assume that all or most customers would also like to be treated this way. Managers seldom go wrong making such basic assumptions, and this therefore warrants the "stage one" efforts.

Stage One: Be Nice!

Not so long ago, many organizations and employees acted in ways that suggested that customers should be pleased that their agency provided them with services of any kind, and in ways that most pleased the agency and its employees. Perhaps some still do so today. Customers were powerless to force change and employees could not get into trouble as long they were going by the book. But customers complained and, as is the legacy of TQM, top management took their concerns seriously. Employees were held accountable for leaving customers satisfied—or at least for not causing them to complain.

The first step in this effort is the obvious: don't be rude and say things that cause them to be upset. This might be called the "charm school" approach. Specifically, the following expectations are typically set for customer-friendly behavior (e.g., Clark 2004; McClendon 1992):

- Be on time
- Always be polite and answer with courtesy and respect

- Follow up on what was said or promised
- Never overpromise, and go the extra mile
- Give options, but don't confuse the customer
- Make eye contact
- See disappointments from the customer's point of view

To achieve this, managers set these standards and implement them through activities such as the following:

1. Provide a training session (often by an external consultant) to increase awareness about common or expected customer service interactions. The training should address situations that are representative of those that workers actually experience.
2. Hold one or more planning/workshop sessions to formulate desired customer service responses to specific problems, such as how to say "no," and deal with unclear or difficult requests in specific areas. These sessions may also suggest some minor workflow adjustments or physical changes to service areas in which interactions occur.
3. Agree on the new customer service interactions and implement the proposed changes.
4. For some weeks, managers closely monitor customer service interactions and conduct exit interviews with clients to assess success. The service experience is discussed with employees and changes are made as needed.
5. To ensure that the new approaches are maintained, managers periodically discuss with workers their customer service efforts. Employees discuss how to resolve new situations. In the beginning, these conversations occur several times weekly, and eventually taper off to biweekly. Expectations are established for performance appraisal. Managers continue to encourage customers to provide feedback and complaints through comment cards, direct hotline, and so on.

Good customer-oriented behavior is especially important when public officials and nonprofit providers are confronted with customer requests that they cannot meet. Some poor responses are "It's against our policy or the law" or "I would like to but I can't," without explaining further or suggesting an alternative course of action. These responses often create anger because customers' expectations of having their problems solved are dashed, ignored, or disrespected. These responses are further aggravated by withdrawn body language and insisting on having the last word. Instead, officials should focus on the underlying problem and reach agreement with the customer on some alternative course of action ("I'm sorry that we can't do that this way, but we can do this. Would that help?"). This approach is especially important when dealing with customers for whom nothing is satisfactory and adequate ("I understand that you feel that way, but . . . "). Training and commitment to being helpful are keys to developing good customer service habits.

It is clear that customer service in public and nonprofit organizations has greatly increased in recent years (Long 2004; Boardman and Vining 2000). Instances of employees being rude have generally declined. Numerous consultants provide customer service training, often targeting problems such as poor phone service, rude or unethical behavior, and so on. Such training often is generic, not tied to a specific service area, and assisted by videos. These activities assist with Step 1 efforts, but are widely regarded as being insufficient; the other steps are needed, too. One barrier to higher customer satisfaction is that some workers are just not "people" people; they are not cut out for frontline, "friendly smile" service interactions. They may have poor social skills (Problem 16). Managers need to know which employees to select for what roles, and recognize that some employees are better suited for other valuable work. Those who are selected for customer service roles must be provided with adequate training, standards, and feedback.

Stage Two: Setting Service Standards

It is natural to take stage one to the next level by considering standards and, if possible, measuring customer service against service standards in some quantifiable way. Most generally, quality standards for service usually concern expectations (meeting or exceeding customer expectations), service performance, conformance to industry or other standards, reliability and dependability, and the timeliness of the service. Of course, managers need to figure out what standards to set for their specific activities.

As an example, many agencies have developed standards for *answering telephone calls* such as answering calls on four rings; giving a time when the person they are calling will be available if they are not available at the time of the call; forwarding their call to the appropriate department if the incorrect department is called first; returning calls within 24 hours; being able to handle calls in several languages; remaining conscientious and aware of callers put on hold; forwarding calls to another staff member when employees are away from their desks, and so on. The point is that without setting and monitoring such standards, quality phone service is unlikely to occur.

Standards can be set for all stakeholder interactions. The process is to (1) identify the aspects of the service, or conditions surrounding the service, for which standards could be set, and (2) determine the standards, informed by industry norms and common sense. This process can involve managers and their employees. Standards can be set for public waiting areas, calls to elected officials, planning activities involving the public, explaining budgets and other technical matters, and so on. Standards for Internet interactions often concern the accuracy of information, timely response to information requests, secure transactions, a promise not to sell or provide e-mail addresses to third parties, a warning by governments about their ability to limit or prevent disclosures of electronic exchanges (sunshine laws and the like), clearly organized websites, and so on.

Organizations distinguish themselves by the standards they set and maintain—or not. Managers need to decide how good they wish their services to be. As a practical matter, different strategies are used for monitoring compliance with standards. Some data can be acquired electronically, such as calculating the length of phone calls or the number and nature of Internet transactions, but much is still done physically, by walking around and observing, perhaps by using a checklist. Employees can share in this task, helping each other. Customer concerns and complaints are another source of important feedback. The adage is that for each customer concern, seven other customers had similar experiences but did not complain. A customer complaint is like the tip of the iceberg; there are more below. Though the scientific basis for this adage is not well established, it does explain why each concern is to be taken seriously.

It is obvious that meeting standards often costs money. Positive considerations for these customer service improvement efforts often come from three sources: (1) top management seeing customer service as priority ("people who interact with us should have a professional experience!"), (2) expenditures that may result in lower service costs later, such as Internet interactions that reduce the need for costlier office visits, and (3) expenditures that allow the agency to meet its strategic goals for providing service to more customers or those in previously under-served areas. The performance improvement proposal in chapter 3 provides a framework for making such a proposal. It is obvious that initiatives that promise cost savings and are aligned with strategic goals are more likely to find positive consideration that those that are not.

Stage Three: Systematic Assessment

A third stage in customer orientation is to reflect in more systematic ways about customer needs, and to collect data about these needs and customer service experiences. Within this third stage, the first step is to fully identify various customer groups: clients, representatives of other organizations, employees of other departments, and so on. The second step is to ask them, in a systematic way, what they expected from customer interactions. Stage three efforts are less common than stage one or two efforts in customer satisfaction.

The first step often leads to some broadening of perspective. For example, a county jail identified as voluntary customers visitors of inmates and their families, judges and other judicial personnel, lawyers, bondsmen, and police officers. Each of these has interactions with the jail, and each of these interactions can be studied. The second step involves asking customer groups what they expect from the organization, what are important areas in need of improvement, and whether they have suggestions for improvement. Customers often have good ideas for improvement. For example, one idea to minimize waiting time in the central booking area was to provide those waiting with a phone number they could call to get an estimate of the approximate release time of inmates. Doing so reduces the number of people waiting in the jail, and provides better service to citizens.

Different strategies exist for soliciting systematic feedback. Focus groups, customer comment cards, and interviews with customers who complain or have a concern are frequently used to solicit ideas for area of improvement. These often provide useful ideas, even if they are not generalizable or do not reflect the concerns of most customers. Systematic surveys are increasingly used that aim to accurately assess the experience of customers as a whole (e.g., Van Ryzin 2004). These often are phone surveys, which use open-ended questions (e.g., "which are three things you like most/least?") as well as a very large number of items with closed-ended responses. Such surveys are further discussed in chapter 8. One result of these systematic efforts often is reflection on which services are provided, and how they are provided. This, then, may result in subsequent process reengineering of existing services.

Process Reengineering

Reengineering examines the entire process of service delivery. Typically, process reengineering (also called "business process reengineering") streamlines delivery processes and thereby reduces the number of units or people that are involved. It daringly takes a blank slate approach, that is, it designs service delivery processes from scratch, rather than trying to incrementally improve them. Reengineering often redefines goals and objectives, and looks at new ways in which people, resources, and technology are best brought together to achieve these new goals and objectives. Of course, existing rationales and solutions are considered as part of the process reengineering design approach. Process reengineering is increasingly common in organizations; first introduced in the mid-1990s (e.g., Hyde 1995; Hammer 1995), it has become a staple of performance improvement strategies and remains useful today (e.g., U.S. General Accounting Office 2005; Hammer and Champy 2001; Daly 2002).

Process reengineering is commonly associated with improving ineffective or inefficient delivery processes (Problem 7). It also addresses coordination problems (Problem 8) by reducing the need for coordination. It should be noted there are two types of reengineering: process-specific and organization-wide. Here, we focus on the former, which is associated with the quality paradigm. By contrast, organization-wide reengineering is associated with massive reorganization efforts in which sometimes entire departments are restructured, assigned different responsibilities, merged with other departments, or eliminated. This type of reengineering is called "restructuring" or "reorganizing," and is associated with traditional management, and is discussed in a subsequent chapter.

The need for process reengineering is deeply rooted in the fundamental critique of traditional organizations discussed earlier. Specifically, it notes that traditional organizations are sometimes more concerned with how many services they deliver than with how well they deliver these services. Rules and procedures are used to justify decisions and departmental autonomy. When this is the raison d'etre, other purposes, such as customer service or service efficiency. become less emphasized. Customers may then be required to conform to inflexible department rules, or have to deal with different offices, each with their own rules. All of this is highly frustrating, and it is the butt of many jokes about poor customer service.

Principles

Process reengineering is guided by several principles. A first and key principle is to organize around outcomes, rather than efforts or departments. The guiding focus is the end, the service goal: What are we trying to achieve? What is an effective and efficient process for doing so? How can we meet or exceed customer expectations? This should be a creative inquiry, stretching the mind beyond how services are currently provided.

A second principle is to minimize the number of times that work is handed off. Errors occur each time that work is handed off: requests for services fall between the cracks of departments and are shuffled between departments, causing delay. Reengineering usually starts with mapping the existing service delivery process, and identifying steps where work is transferred. Process reengineering often leads to cross-training and one-stop shopping as ways to reduce such errors.

A third principle of process reengineering is to eliminate steps that add little or no value. Typically, these are review and inspection steps and are readily identified by mapping the existing process. Process reengineering often asks employees to make their own inspections and review decisions, subject to being accountable for errors and missteps later. The cost of employee errors often is less than the cost of delays due to inspection, which also produce errors.

A fourth principle to ensure timeliness is to speed up the process by conducting steps in parallel fashion when feasible. Traditionally, many steps are done sequentially, but many processes can be done faster in parallel.

A fifth principle is to improve the use and dissemination of information. Information should be provided that speeds up and improves decision making, it should be made available to people when people need it, and it should provide for rapid performance feedback. Many information technology applications have these features, such as Internet services that help citizens apply for permits or jobs online, manage their accounts, and so on. Agency intranet services often also have these features.

Many of these design principles come together in one-stop shopping applications, which have been a popular application of process reengineering. For example, employees are assigned to one person in the human resources department who handles all of their benefit requests. Another example of one-stop shopping may be community-based policing, in which community officers act as case managers for citizen requests. Employees who staff these positions are cross-trained in various disciplines so that they have the knowledge and skills to make a wide range of decisions. They are empowered to make these decisions without further review, so that customers are provided with an immediate response. Requests that exceed the knowledge, competency, and authority of these frontline employees require staff specialists. Although this takes more time, the frontline employees are empowered to seek these opinions and obtain final opinions within a limited time (say, twenty-four hours).

Process flow analysis is an important analytical strategy of process reengineering. It generates understanding of the current process, and establishes benchmarks against which future improvement is measured. Process flow analysis focuses on the number of steps and the time that it takes to complete a process. Figure 5.2 shows the before and after re-engineered processes of travel reimbursement; the symbols in Figure 5.2 describe the steps of each process. This example does not show one-stop shopping, but rather the typical application in which processes are made faster by reducing steps. Specifically, it shows empowerment by the office manager to make certain decisions. Such empowerment may also make the process more accurate (less prone to error), because work is handed off less frequently.

Figure 5.2 **Process Flow Chart**

The Quality Paradigm

ACTIVITY: Travel Reimbursement
OM = Office Manager
BO = Budget Office
AD = Accounting Department

Old Process:

0 > # D @ Staff informs Office Manager
0 > # D @ OM draws up paperwork
0 > # D @ OM sends to Budget Office
0 > # D @ Request waits turn
0 > # D @ BO reviews request
0 > # D @ BO requests more info
0 > # D @ BO sends to OM
0 > # D @ OM requests info from staff
0 > # D @ Staff provides info
0 > # D @ OM redoes paperwork
0 > # D @ OM sends to BO
0 > # D @ BO reviews request
0 > # D @ BO sends to Account. Dept.
0 > # D @ AD reviews request
0 > # D @ AD enters data
0 > # D @ AD waits for pay period
0 > # D @ AD processes request
0 > # D @ AD sends file to OM

New Process:

0 > # D @Staff informs OM
0 > # D @ OM reviews request
0 > # D @ OM asks for more info
0 > # D @ Staff provides info
0 > # D @ OM does paperwork
0 > # D @ OM processes request
0 > # D @ OM enters data

Symbols:		*Comparison:*	Old	New	Difference
0	Operation: Item is acted on	0	8	6	2
>	Movement between offices	>	5	0	5
#	Review or quality control	#	3	1	2
D	Delay or Interruption	D	2	0	2
@	Storage: Item not acted on	@	0	0	0
		Total Steps:	18	7	11

The lack of detailed analysis of process can be a symptom of ineffi-
ciency and waste. The U.S. State Department's review of export license
applications was faulted for lacking procedures to monitor the flow of license applications, lacking guidelines on the length of time review should
take, and lacking systematic checks on the progress of applications (U.S.
General Accounting Office 2005). Though the U.S. General Accounting

Office (GAO) acknowledged that hiring more licensing officers reduced the processing time, the GOA believes that the State Department's review process needs to focus more on a controlled and timely flow of applications. It reached this conclusion after conducting a process flow analysis. The response—to increase the number of inspectors (licensing personnel), rather than to questions the system (process) itself—is a classic response of many traditional organizations.

Process of Reengineering: Implementation.

How do managers successfully design from a blank slate? And get their organizations to implement the design, too? Authors describe the strategy of process reengineering in somewhat different terms. The following is adapted from Linden (1998), who described a four-step "design" process that encompasses steps D through G, which are the unique analytical activities of process reengineering:

A. Assess Readiness
B. Make the Organization Ready for Change
C. Assemble Steering and Design Teams
D. Map the Current Process (Flow Analysis)
E. Establish Desired Outcomes
F. Set a Stretch Objective
G. Design From a Clean Sheet
H. Approve the New Process
I. Create the Implementation Team
J. Implement and Monitor the Pilot Project
K. Implement Full Project
L. Replicate Elsewhere As Appropriate

The first three steps (A through C) and later steps (H through K) relate to the material of chapter 3, "Achieving Success."

Step A: Assess Readiness. The five conditions for successful change are imperative for process reengineering as well, and managers will want to assess the extent that conditions for success are present. Top or senior management support is especially critical, because re-engineered work processes often involve coordination among different departments, and change managers can expect to be challenged by them and others. A strong rationale (urgent need or crisis) is important because the scope of intended change is large. Managers will also want to think about some early successes and using a small group for designing and carrying out initial changes. Preexisting trust is not always present when members come from different departments; team leaders will have to undertake those actions that engender trust and confidence among team members. As regarding the models of large-scale change, in reengineering, the management team is often called a "steering team," and the project team is called the "design" team (and after the design, the "implementation" team).

Step B: Make the Organization Ready for Change. This step involves ensuring that the five conditions for change are in place and setting up a communication structure. It is the nature of many permitting, inspection, registration, tax, and other processes that they involve many people, and so the pilot effort often draws considerable attention. Top managers and others sometimes find themselves frequently communicating about the importance of the change.

Step C: Assemble Steering and Design Teams. The steering team is a management team that is responsible for the service delivery process, and provides the "go-ahead" and support for the design team to develop a new delivery process. Specific duties of the steering team are to provide resources and authority, to explain to the organization the need for the new process, develop and approve the general criteria for the project, and approve recommendations of the design team. The design team consists of a project leader, representatives from each department, and possibly customers (end-users). Design team participants should include a mix of competencies and skills. For example, they should have familiarity with the project, the required technical skills (for example, in information technology), and a few "big picture" thinkers who can challenge the current way of doing business and suggest different approaches to better meet service delivery objectives. Some design teams may have problems getting started, if they are unsure of what they are really expected to do. This problem can be overcome by the steering team approving and clearly communicating the general criteria and purposes of the project, along with timelines.

Step D: Map the Current Process (Workflow Analysis). It is important to develop a shared understanding of the current process, and to establish benchmarks against which future improvement is measured. The key element of workflow analysis is tracking the workflow process(es) by identifying the relevant steps, including decisions, delays, transfers, and (sometimes) cycle times.

Step E: Establish Desired Outcomes. This important step in process reengineering establishes the minimum standards to be met. Previously mentioned tools for identifying stakeholders and their needs apply here also: surveys, focus groups, customer comment cards, and interviews, can all be used. In addition, it may be helpful to study those organizations that have done truly innovative and cutting-edge applications in the area.

Step F: Set a Stretch Objective. This is a very daring step in process reengineering. The goals should clearly exceed customer expectations, not merely meet them. It is one thing to reduce request processing time; it is quite another to cut it by 80 percent, for example. It is one thing to reduce errors and rework, it is quite another to reduce them to practically zero. Of course, the feasibility of meeting such targets (in fact, performance measures) depends on the ability to design relevant processes and on support from the steering team for any implications. An important reason for setting a stretch objective is to ensure that the reengineered process, which will likely to be in place for some years, meets future, rising expectations.

Step G: Design from a Clean Sheet. This is a most creative step in process reengineering, requiring people who can think outside the box. Some blocks to creativity are assumptions or statements by others such as: "they won't buy it," "it can't be done," "why change something that works?" "it's against our policy or rules," "we've never done it that way," "it's too expensive," and "who will deal with the fallout?" Instead, focus on these questions:

> "If you were a customer, what would you like to see?"
> "Which law or rule says we can't do that?"
> "How can we give stakeholders more choices or information?"
> "What if we just cut out this step? It doesn't add much value."
> "How can we do this in less time or effort?"
> "There must be some way to make this happen!"

These questions are designed to get people to look at things in a new light and push them beyond the ways in which they are accustomed to thinking or acting.

Step H: Approve the New Process. The steering team approves (sanctions) the proposed new process and authorizes the implementation.

Step I: Create the Implementation Team. Many people of the design team will also serve on the implementation team (especially the project owner), but some new personnel may be added, perhaps to ensure expertise that had not been anticipated until the new design had been completed. Also, it may include people who are better at implementation than at developing new ideas.

Step J: Implement and Monitor the Pilot Project. All new efforts involve trial and error. It makes sense to try out the new process. Consider a "beta" version—the question is not whether there will be errors to be fixed, but rather when and how they will occur. Even if the new process cannot be done on a small scale, it should be done along side the established, regular process until it performs as intended. At this stage, the steering team closely follows implementation and is available for necessary resources and policy to ensure success.

Step K: Implement Full Project. The new process is likely to require some or even considerable staff training. All of the previous concerns and reasons will be communicated to staff that has hitherto not been involved in the project. A reasonable "getting accustomed" period should be built in, with ample communication and support from top management. Despite best intentions, new problems will surface, and staff needs to be available for addressing them. Appendix 5.1 discusses some continuous improvement techniques that are sometimes useful in tracking performance over time. There is a moment of truth, when the old process is "switched off" and the new process is exclusively used.

Step L: Replicate Elsewhere as Appropriate. Although other departments have different processes, they may share some common features or design issues; they may benefit from the developed expertise or similar, innovative changes. Then, new steering and design teams should be created, benefiting of course from the expertise of people who served on this one.

In Conclusion

The quality paradigm suggests some radically different ways of organizing and delivering services. Some key values of the quality paradigm are to: (1) identify, meet, and exceed the needs of customers (and other stakeholders); (2) strive to produce services right the first time (reduce errors that upset stakeholders and cause rework); (3) use systematic analysis to evaluate and improve services delivery; and (4) consistently support workers in their efforts to improve quality and meet customer needs. The quality paradigm gave birth to new performance improvement strategies: customer orientation, process reengineering, continuous improvement, empowerment, and benchmarking/performance measurement.

This chapter also discusses customer orientation and process reengineering. Customer orientation efforts often are characterized by three distinct stages: being nice, setting and maintaining service standards, and systematically assessing stakeholder needs. The first two stages are far more common than the latter. Process reengineering is a blank slate approach to service design, focusing on ends rather than on improving traditional ways in which services have been provided. Process reengineering uses "stretch objectives" and innovative organizational structures. Both customer service and process reengineering offer numerous improvement possibilities for managers.

Application Exercises

1. Identify a process that involves clients or citizens in your agency. What level of service do they receive? What standards of customer service might be set? How does current customer satisfaction measure up? Develop a program to increase the level of customer service.
2. Search the Internet for "customer service training" to see what companies offer and what topics are often covered.
3. A frequent problem in the public sector is saying "no" to requests, or providing applications with a "denied" response. Show how explaining the reason for a negative response plus giving customers some options for creating a more satisfactory outcome can go a long way to generating customer satisfaction.
4. Develop some ways of getting customer feedback about your services. How can you most effectively use this information?
5. Identify some processes that might be re-engineered. For one of these work processes, develop a process flow chart.
6. Apply steps A through L for implementing your re-engineered process.
7. Which values or practices of TQM do you like? How do they differ from traditional ones? How do they differ from the practices in your current organization? What arguments and steps might be made to advance TQM values or practices in your organization? What counterarguments do you expect, and how will you deal with these?

Appendix 5.1 **Continuous Improvement**

Continuous improvement (CI) is a TQM-related strategy connoting both a philosophy and a set of techniques. As a philosophy, CI is about trying to do better, pushing the standards, and always finding better ways of doing what it is that one is doing—continuous improvement. How much and how fast organizations push is, of course, what distinguishes organizations from each other. Some settle for mediocrity, others do not. At an individual level, CI is also important as a personal performance strategy—some people want to improve themselves more than others.

As a set of techniques, CI is closely associated with the analysis and improvement of production processes. Specifically, CI includes a set of tools that help with (a) tracking performance and errors, and (b) analyzing the sources of variation. Both are precursors to subsequent improvement. Though only varyingly used in connection with service improvement, they nonetheless provide some basic, valid insights. It is very useful to track performance on a periodic (say, daily or weekly) basis, and compare that against some standard. This is shown in the control chart, although any form of tracking is of course useful.

Typically, such an activity leads to questions about circumstances that cause performance to fall below acceptable standards. Sometimes managers want to dig deeply into possible causes of problems. An analytical tool that helps identify causes of incomplete or "wrong" steps is a cause-and-effect or fishbone diagram. This is a brainstorming tool that helps focus on problems of training, people, material, and procedures that cause the faulty work process to occur. The causes of errors are identified on the diagonals such that the resulting figure resembles a fishbone. An example of a fishbone diagram is displayed. It shows that interruptions are one of several causes of long waits.

The next step is then to monitor how frequently these circumstances occur. A common experience is that some causes occur more often or are of greater significance. It is important to direct efforts to those causes that are most important. An analytical technique to help identify such causes is a frequency chart that displays the frequency of each in descending order: thus, frequently occurring causes are readily observed from this chart. These are called "Pareto" charts, named after the Italian economist who noted that in many countries 80 percent of the wealth was held by only 20 percent of the population: likewise, in many work processes few problems often account for the majority of reasons for poor quality.

Whether or not managers want to use any of these tools is, of course, up to them. However, the basic insights about setting standards, tracking performance, and understanding the causes of poor performance are essential to performance improvement.

Figure 5A.1 **Control Chart**

Figure 5A.2 **Fishbone Chart**

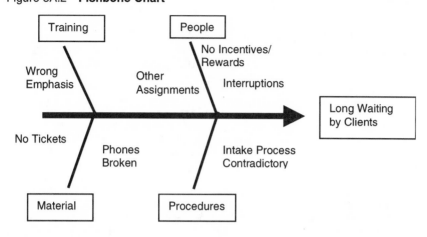

Figure 5A.3 **Pareto Chart**

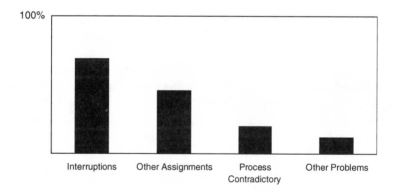

Information Technology

Information technology (IT) applications are ubiquitous in performance improvement. Almost everyone—citizens, clients, employees, managers, representatives of organizations—expects public and nonprofit organizations to have electronic interactions and management. Many people want to use the latest applications. Reasons for the popularity of information technology are easy to see. Information technology improves working with information, sometimes through software programs that are uniquely designed to process or store information in specific ways, thereby making analysis and data retrieval faster and easier. It also increases access to information and improves communication. Citizens and clients are increasingly able to interact online, and through this they gain better and faster access to services. Administrative decisions, too, are based on better and timelier information, and can be faster and with more participants and stakeholders sharing information and perspectives. In short, IT has the potential to help public and nonprofit organizations better serve public needs.

Access to information technology has come a long way in a relatively short time. In 1989, only 15.0 percent of all U.S. households had a computer, compared to more than half (56.5 percent) in 2001—about a decade later (U.S. Census 1989, 2001). Today, presumably even more households have a computer. Among households with total incomes over $50,000 in 2000, 81.7 percent had a computer at home, and almost all school-age children (89.6 percent) had access to a computer at school or home. In 2005, CNN broadcast a series on how the Internet had changed peoples' lives in just a short decade. Today, for many households, having a computer is now almost as ubiquitous as having a television—and it already is a given for most professionals (National Telecommunications and Information Administration 2002).

This chapter addresses the following questions: (1) What are some applications of information technology that increase productivity? (2) What are some strategic issues involved in information technology today? (3) How can information technology best be managed in agencies?

Using information technology for performance improvement relates directly to many performance problems mentioned in chapter 2. Information technology can be used to better meet the needs of target groups (Problem 1), and reduce the number of people who are dissatisfied with the agency (Problem 2). It can provide citizens with access to information about public agencies and programs, and thus reduce the level of apathy (Problem 3). Information technology can make delivery processes more efficient and effective (Problem 7) and improve coordination (Problem 8) and communication (Problem 9). Information technology also helps with project management through improved tracking and monitoring (Problem 12), providing clients with more frequent and informative updates (Problem 13). Finally, information technology is not only an area in which technical skills may be lacking (Problem 15), information technology can also be used to train employees in a variety of technical skills.

IT Applications

Information technology is integrated into our work. Some information technology applications are widespread, and others are at the cutting edge but not yet very common. The use of IT applications is the reflection of past decision making. Managers need to develop a *strategic perspective* about the use of information technology, showing how technology supports their mission. The following are *key questions:*

1. What are the agency's or department's "core businesses" (efforts or programs that support key missions)?
2. What goals and stretch objectives (chapter 5) are set for improving these core businesses?
3. How can information technology assist in reaching these new objectives?

There are many reasons for taking a strategic perspective. First, the missions of departments should always be center stage when thinking about performance improvement. Identifying "core businesses" reinforces the centrality of the mission and provides a focus and justification for IT activities and investments. Second, information technology may be ubiquitous, but it does not come cheap, and investments in information technology tend to be somewhat "sticky" or enduring. Once made, departments have to live with their IT choices for some time. Information technology investments need to be made wisely and surely where they count most. Third, changes in information technology tend to bring about invasive changes that require managers' attention for several months. Some of these changes concern new uses of information technology (e.g., new programs on which users such as staff, clients, and other departments must be trained), and other changes involve altered delivery processes (e.g., process reengineering as a result of new information technology). Fourth, the implementation of information technology is never "glitch free," and addressing things that did not go as expected will certainly also require managers' attention. So, although there are many interesting applications that could be applied to almost any program, the question is which are the really important ones, according to the above questions.

Having established the case for a strategic perspective to IT management, managers will need an overview of IT opportunities in their line of business. What are the possibilities for improving core and other businesses? Most generally, IT helps programs by:

- Increasing the speed, accuracy, and reliability of transactions and operations.
- Reducing the cost of transactions and operations.
- Providing more comprehensive and timely information and services.
- Increasing interactions among stakeholders inside and outside organizations.
- Allowing people to interact from remote locations and in more convenient ways.
- Accessing and linking to data and information from other agencies and programs.

Managers will want to consider where improvements are most needed in their businesses, and whether existing IT applications can provide for these. They will also want to consider opportunities that are provided by new IT applications. This is a creative process of thinking through the possibilities. Information technology solutions may involve new applications in such areas as:

- Communications (Web, e-mail, electronic transactions, cell phone)
- Database applications (including real-time integration of multiple databases, sometimes across departments, agencies, or even jurisdictions)
- Word processing (including publishing and presentation software)
- General data analysis (spreadsheets, statistical software)
- Specialized problem-solving and monitoring software (including artificial intelligence) for different lines of business or concerns

- User-friendly interfaces (including Geographic Information Systems and searchable databases)
- Gadgets and devices that address specific needs (including security cards, wireless data communication, etc.)

As almost everyone knows, basic and ubiquitous applications of information technology include e-mail, word processing, database management, presentation software, desktop publishing, telecommunications applications (voice mail, call forwarding, cell phones, etc). Managers must ensure that they are familiar with recent advances in these areas (for example, voice recognition, remote access, groupware), and ensure that their office's technology in these areas works effectively and reliably. In some cases, standard information technology applications provide effective solutions. For example, some services require a physical presence by a citizen or customer. Rather than waiting in line or in an area, public and nonprofit officials can provide beepers (similar as in restaurants) to customers or call waiting for customers on their cell phones (if they have one). Thus, waiting customers are able to go elsewhere, perhaps to a cafeteria or attend to other business.

Beyond these basic applications are Web-based transactions (such as registering for classes), and increased database integration that provides comprehensive information and allows agencies to provide electronic one-stop shopping. Many areas have seen great increases in the number of useful programs. For example, a local government may provide a one-stop shopping site for prospective home buyers to provide information about past sales, zoning, schools, taxes, building plans, flooding, crime, and a host of other matters, including access to e-government service requests and permit filing applications. The interface is user-friendly, taking full advantage of geographic and visual displays to help the user navigate through a host of useful information. It does not take much imagination to envision this integrated with rating information, such as concerning school quality, as well as other information from citizen satisfaction surveys, insurance ratings, average neighborhood household incomes, shopping and marketing data, and so on. A current frontier is data integration across departments and levels of government, integration that is both "horizontal" and "vertical" in nature. The result is a powerful tool in the hands of citizens, promoting their well-being as well as economic development (Holden, Norris, and Fletcher 2003). Other examples include a tool developed by the U.S. Department of Homeland Security that enables managers of large-capacity stadiums (over 30,000 people) to gauge their vulnerability with regard to information security, physical assets, communication security, and personnel security. This program also makes recommendations for improving security. The possibilities for developing specialized software programs seem endless today.

Nonprofit organizations are also finding an increasing number of uses for information technology. Some applications involve database development that, for example, helps to better track client service utilization and outcomes or the giving activities of sponsors. Other applications include Web sites that increase community interactions and empower clients to seek services and information. Information technology is also used to identify grant opportunities and better manage relations with sponsors by providing them with increased information about the organization's activities and outcomes.

Many fields also have dedicated "gadgets" and devices, such as security cards and readers. At a minimum, managers need to be familiar with the range of applications that are used in their line of work. For example, state-of-the-art IT applications in transportation include electronic toll collections, automatic license plate readers (to identify those violating toll collection and speeding regulations), speed monitoring equipment connected to drivers' license information systems, traffic management systems (for example, to regulate traffic lights and direct traffic), and electronic communications between transportation departments and contractors responsible for maintenance and improvements. Other applications include ramp metering, incidence response systems, travel information systems, and fleet management systems. Higher education applications include handheld devices that allow students to electronically signal to professors in their classroom whether they understand the material, agree or disagree with a stated proposition, and so on.

Different functions in public and nonprofit organizations have different IT applications. The task of managers is to be aware of what is common and state-of-the-art in their fields. Such applications may or may not fit the strategic missions and needs of departments, but it helps to know what is going on. Fortunately, many information technology applications are discussed online, so it is easy to know what is going on.

Strategic IT Issues

Information technology entails several important strategic issues that managers in public and nonprofit organizations must address. The following are some of the most important concerns.

Security

Security remains an important IT issue. Access, data integrity, and the protection of information assets are important; public and nonprofit organizations increasingly rely on their information systems for operations and deci-sion making, and threats to IT systems are subject to increasingly sophisti-cated viruses, hackers, and sabotage. Many organizations have horror stories of stolen computer files, lost data, and compromised systems. In one case, a State of Florida office in Tampa lost a confidential file of AIDS patients in the community, which later surfaced after it had been sold to several people at a nightclub. Following the terrorist attacks on September 11, 2001, some local governments restricted access to information about their critical infra-structure such as sewer, power, and emergency response systems. The fed-eral government, too, became serious about protecting the security of its systems. The Federal Information Security Management Act (FISMA) of 2002 is one of several acts that requires federal agencies to now monitor compliance with IT security standards set by the National Institute of Stan-dards and Technology, obtain security certification for their IT systems, and ensure that contractors follow equivalent procedures for federal data stored on their computers (U.S. Office of Management and Budget 2004).

The security of many personal and small business computer systems is typically limited, involving changing passwords regularly, automatically updating antivirus programs, using firewalls, being wary of e-mail attach-ments and unknown software, establishing physical access controls, keeping software updated, and making regular backups of important files and soft-ware that are then stored in a safe location (Internet Security Alliance 2004). Access to IT systems is often limited through the use of passwords, and site verification and identification devices can be used to further ensure the iden-tity of computer users. Some recent advances in identification use biometric data based on fingerprints and the iris, and in the United Kingdom personal identification cards have been proposed that use biometric data. Beyond these procedures, data encryption strategies protect public and nonprofit organiza-tions from unauthorized eavesdropping over transmission lines. Computer viruses (programs that corrupt other programs and data files), continue to be a main threat to IT systems, and data integrity is further compromised by human error; training users in correct data input and security verification procedures is an important strategy.

The security of public IT systems requires additional vigilance, such as regularly monitoring unauthorized use of IT systems, having support to deal with security incidents, and being familiar with the latest research on new threats and security responses. The federal government has developed exten-sive capacities in these areas. The U.S. Department of Homeland Security, Directorate of Information Analysis and Infrastructure Protection, serves as a focal point for threat assessment, warning, investigation, and response to threats and attacks on critical IT infrastructures. It also helps agencies identify and prioritize critical assets and system interdependencies, detects and responds to Internet events, and coordinates with state and local governments and private and international partner agencies. Because the U.S. Department of Homeland Security was established only after the September 11 attacks, the organization of these responsibilities is subject to considerable change and is likely to be further developed in future years (U.S. Department of Homeland Security 2003). The Federal Bureau of Investigation (FBI), through the Cyber Division, investigates crimes related to unauthorized access into U.S. government and commercial sites.

But security issues cut several ways. While many security systems minimize unauthorized access and use, citizens have the right to know information about them that is kept in the records of public agencies. Individuals must be able to find out which data are in their records, and how these data are used. They have the right to prevent agency use of their information for purposes other than that for which it was originally collected. Agencies must provide citizens access to their files so that they can become familiar with their data. These basic rights, part of the Privacy Act of 1974, have been upheld in subsequent legislation and many court rulings. The act was amended by the Electronic Freedom of Information Act of 1996 (FOIA), which extends disclosure requirements to include information found in electronic records. The FOIA excludes certain categories of records from disclosure, specifically, material related to national security, internal personnel rules and decisions, proprietary business information, inter- and intra-agency predecisional memoranda, information that may affect a person's privacy, and records compiled for law enforcement purposes (U.S. Department of Justice 2005). Some of these latter concerns have been put on a back burner following the September 11 terrorist acts, but it is likely privacy concerns will once again become important in the years ahead.

Governance

During the 1990s, debate started about Internet-based voting, and a few cities have made some experimental progress in this matter. Teledemocracy has its proponents and opponents. Arguments in favor of teledemocracy include the possibility of broader participation through Web-based forums. It also gives people who are handicapped, shy, or have a speech impediment such as stuttering a bias-free, electronic arena in which to express their views. Two prior arguments against teledemocracy are that that it discriminates against those who do not own computers, and that it may stir up uncontrolled discussions. But these concerns have lost currency since voters can still vote in customary ways, and blogs and other forms of electronic expression have become common. Today's main concern is with security to prevent fraud and illegal voting, and in recent years new systems have been pilot-tested in local elections. The focus has shifted from debate about teledemocracy to the narrower concern of e-voting. It would seem that voting from the convenience one's home, workplace, or remote access is just around the corner. The argument seems irresistible that if people can do their banking from home, then why not also their voting? Yet, several lawsuits filed during the 2004 election season show enduring problems with security, vendor selection, and recounts (Electronic Frontier Foundation 2005). It seems likely that as these issues recede, the broader debate about teledemocracy will be rejoined soon in some way.

Information technology is increasingly used to provide citizens with access to decision making. Cable-based local government and C-SPAN channels provide citizens with direct access to public debates and interviews. This helps build citizen trust and confidence in government by increasing transparency and information about government programs and policies. In 2001, a survey of Orange County (Florida) residents found that 42.3 percent of residents watch Orange TV (the area's local government access channel), and that 34.9 percent of respondents state that they have watched a Board of County Commission meeting on Orange TV during the last twelve months (Orange County 2001). By contrast, only 15.1 percent of respondents stated that they had *ever* attended a Board of County Commission meeting. Some local governments are now also planning to make these debates available on their Web sites. This is not only an alternative delivery mechanism, but also allows for convenient archival access. Citizens can search by topic and retrieve not only documents, plans, and other information, but also interviews and commission debates.

Reliability

At present, great strides have been made in making IT systems more reliable. Although IT systems still often "go down," effective backup systems are now more readily in place. Today, data are seldom unrecoverable, lost, or corrupted, and system downtime is now on the order of minutes or a few hours, rather than many hours or even days. Several high-profile cases in the mid-1990s prompted improvements in this area. For example, when air traffic computer systems failed in Miami (Florida) in the mid-1990s, commercial jetliners flew on multiple occasions for several minutes with only voice guidance from traffic controllers. Though no disasters occurred, these events prompted the Federal Aviation Administration to speed up its computer disaster recovery efforts. But the reliability of computer systems, especially in an integrated world, is still far from certain (Brown and Brudney 2004).

Although the causes of IT failures are not always known, many analysts attribute computer failures to the increased complexity of computer systems, software that causes small bugs to come into play, and failures in telecommunication access systems. However, planning now must also consider catastrophic and unrecoverable failures due to natural disasters (hurricanes, earthquakes) and sabotage (U.S. Secret Service 2005). Managers must have backup plans for when their information technology systems are down or unavailable. In some instances, traditional, low-tech (manual and phone-based) operations are adequate to keep functioning at some level for some time. In other instances, no downtime can be tolerated, such as in nuclear power facilities, air traffic control towers, subway and other rail systems, and strategic weapon systems. Managers need to have emergency plans in place.

E-government

In recent years, governments have focused on improving customer/citizen interactions with agencies through improved electronic access to information and services, thereby reducing costs and improving response times. It has also sought to improve access to agencies through one-stop shopping and portals that integrate access. Many citizens are familiar with the federal government's portal, www.FirstGov.gov, and its efforts to get taxpayers to file online. E-government applications often are targeted in one or more of the following ways:

- G2C (government-to-citizen): increasing access to government information, allowing citizens to make or complete service requests online or access their account or other information online;
- G2B (government-to-business): increasing the ability of citizens and businesses to find, view, and comment on rules and regulations; enabling businesses to file taxes online; reducing time to fill out export forms and locate information; reducing time for businesses to file and comply with regulations;
- G2G (government-to-government): decreasing response times for jurisdictions and disciplines to respond to emergency incidents; reducing time to verify birth and death entitlement information; increasing number of grant programs available for electronic application;
- IEE (internal efficiency and effectiveness): increasing availability of training programs; reducing time to process clearance forms; increasing use of e-travel; reducing time for citizens to search for federal jobs; reducing time and overhead costs of purchasing goods and services.

Within the federal government, various act such as the E-Government Act of 2002 help to keep the momentum going. Many governments have adopted a common perspective of what the government and each agency within it do. Common perspectives have been developed around different users groups, such as citizens, businesses, and other governments, as well as federal managers seeking to improve processes and reduce costs. Applications include e-payroll, e-recruitment, e-clearance, e-training, e-grants, e-travel, e-rulemaking, e-authentication, and e-vital. Web sites for different user groups include: Volunteer.gov, Recreation.gov, GovBenefits.gov, BusinessLaw.gov, and GoLearn.gov. A 2003 survey of the Council for Excellence in Government found that 75 percent of e-government users think that e-government makes it easier to get information, and 67 percent like doing transactions with the government online (U.S. Office of Management and Budget 2003; Melitski 2003, 2004; Ho 2002).

Information technology is increasingly used in relationship to the internal management of programs. It can be used to provide more information, in real-time, to program managers. Also, the Government Performance Results Act of 1993 requires agencies to document their performance, and some agencies now provide some of their performance reporting online (Holley, Dufner, and Reed 2004). It is clear that while e-government applications are increasing, agencies and jurisdictions vary in their use of e-government. One can reasonably speculate that this reflects different emphases on IT in agencies, the roles of the chief information officer, and leadership for overcoming parochialism and practices that reinforce agency-centric thinking. One area in which the latter still is sometimes apparent is in linking databases across agencies and programs.

User Support

The explosion of end-user computing has increased the demand for technical services. Many IT units now also assist end-users with their long-term needs for information technology through planning and procurement. This obviously expands the contribution of IT services to the realm of strategically important decisions for managers. Such assistance can be an ad hoc, or a more formalized effort that involves such planning questions as: Are you planning to purchase any new software or hardware in the near future? If so, what? Would you like more information about options? Do you feel that you might benefit from assistance in your purchasing effort? Would you welcome us assisting you in matters concerning your service contract? Would you like us to install your system or software for you? Would you like us to maintain your system or software for you? Such questions not only support end-users in their information technology strategy and acquisition, but also help clarify the role of the IT unit.

Information technology units continue to provide technical assistance. A customary problem is that people who are hired by IT units often have strong technical skills, but deficits in communication and social skills needed to effectively interact with end-users. End-user satisfaction with technical support is of strategic importance, and IT units must plan and evaluate their technical support. Many IT units train their staff to minimize jargon and to be responsive and courteous. Customer service is an important function that can be strengthened through feedback, for example through user surveys that address questions such as:

- How often have you called our office for technical support during the last three months?
- How do you normally contact us (phone, e-mail, written request, or in person)?
- How satisfied are you with our handling of your initial request?
- If we have had to come to your office to examine problems, on average how satisfied are you with the speed with which we did so?
- On average, how satisfied are you with our ability to promptly solve your problems?
- On average, how courteous is our staff?
- In the event that we did not immediately solve your problem, how satisfied are you with the final result? What did you like? What did you not like?
- If there is one thing we could to improve our service, what would that be?

Organizing the IT Function

Information technology requires planning, organizing, staffing, and so on, just as any other function. POSDCORB (described in chapter 1) applies to IT as well. For managers, it is not only, or even primarily, the technology that is the focus, but rather the organization and integration of IT activities with the rest of the organization that is at stake. The basic organization of IT involves:

- The chief information officer (CIO) function
- Central IT units
- Technical and user-support services
- End-users with IT capabilities

Most IT units are headed by IT directors such as Chief Information Officers (CIOs) who reports directly to the head of the organization. This structure ensures technical expertise and the development of IT policies. The specific CIO responsibilities are:

- Developing a comprehensive IT strategy
- Determining policies, procedures, and standards for IT
- Evaluating and acquiring major IT products and systems
- Ensuring coordination among IT units, and between IT and the rest of the organization
- Educating top managers and others about uses and developments in IT
- Staffing and overseeing the general operations of IT programs

Thus, the CIO plays an important role in helping the organization to meet its strategic information technology needs (Chief Information Officers Council 2005).

The central IT unit is responsible for:

- System development
- System operations
- Data management
- Data communications
- Technical support

These responsibilities require separate skills, and large organizations often organize these functions as separate departments within central IT units. Small IT units often combine these responsibilities as part of assignments of individual employees and managers. For example, very small IT units may have one person who is both the CIO and systems development manager, another who does operations and management, and a third staff person who is responsible for both user support and communications.

The structure of separate, central IT units ensures technical expertise and the development of IT policies, but it does not ensure that IT activities are aligned with the needs of user-departments. Indeed, end-users frequently complain about inadequate service by central IT staff. In addition, CIOs often emphasize technical over financial criteria in making their information technology investment plans. The problems and challenges of traditional bureaucracies are revisited upon IT units. Ironically, these bearers of progress must be brought under the same precepts of the quality paradigm as other departments and services—they must be customer friendly and use modern, streamlined delivery and development processes. Some first steps are the use of advisory councils made up of end-users to help bring the voice of users into IT decision-making processes and being held accountable to the head of the agency, which can help provide feedback to ensure a broader perspective, assuming that the agency head has an interest in information technology.

Information technology units depend on vendors for their systems and communications. It has become commonplace to purchase reliable, off-the-shelf systems. Many managers tell horror stories about much-ballyhooed software that failed to perform, or small software firms that failed to provide support beyond the first year. Increasingly, vendor contracts have taken on the character of multiyear partnership agreements because of the need to ensure reliability and adaptations to meet agency needs (see chapter 9). Bid specifications also include attention to the need for emergency support, technology upgrades, the financial security of contractors, and provisions for dealing with escalating costs. Some vendors may have a staff person permanently assigned to a system to quickly address operational problems.

In recent years, the growing decentralization of information technology budgets has caused end-users to increase their expertise in information technology applications as related to their area. End-users increasingly possess sufficient technical knowledge to solve many of their own information technology needs. Increasingly, department heads are held accountable for formulating their own IT strategic plans; they are expected to work with the agency's central IT group, which not only provides information about recent advances but also ensures system integration and connectivity with other departments.

Organizations have made large investments in their information technology. At this point, few seem to question the strategic imperative of information technology. It is obvious that narrow, rate-of-return cost-benefit analyses fail to capture the strategic ends of information technology and its organization. Rather, the assessment of the IT function focuses on broader concerns, such as: (1) the qualifications and leadership of IT managers; (2) whether IT departments have strategic plans that are aligned with end-users (departments); (3) operational plans relating to system development, data management, and communications; (4) quality standards and controls to ensure reliability of data operations and networks, including disaster recovery; (5) security and control procedures; (6) use of modern management tools and strategies (e.g., in procurement); (7) evaluation and capabilities of technical support; and (8) performance appraisal of IT personnel.

Productivity in IT Projects

Finally, we discuss some aspects that may help in managing information technology projects: justifying (selling) the project and understanding success factors.

Selling the Project

Managers who seek new information technology investments will have to make their case for such expenditures. The multifaceted and strategic nature of IT projects suggests that narrow, rate-of-return analyses are not always appropriate. Efficiency analyses are usually only appropriate for investments in operations in which the main purpose is to automate functions that result in cost savings. Examples include such narrow (but important) applications that automate the handling of citizen inquiries. In such cases, personnel savings can be compared against IT costs. However, even in these instances it is often a challenge to assess the full cost of IT investments. Hardware and software often constitute only 25 to 40 percent of total costs. Other costs include training, purchasing, installation, maintenance, conversion, modification, and consulting. A further challenge is to estimate a realistic range of probable outcomes. Nonetheless, research suggests that organizations that set formal targets for returns on such investments are more likely to produce high rates of return.

Strategic and managerial IT investments often aim to improve customer service, enhance decision-making capabilities, and increase employee skills. The evaluation of such projects requires more balanced, multifaceted analysis. Many authors suggest combining a financial perspective with criteria of customer satisfaction, innovation, and performance enhancement, and a strategic perspective that focuses on making core functions competitive. Specifically, the plan for justifying new IT investments might include:

- Contribution to core function
- Performance of proposed investment
- Impact for customers/users: demand, use, access
- Compliance with industry practices
- Compatibility with existing information technology infrastructure
- Impact on organization and program practices
- Pay-off (cost-benefit/effectiveness analysis)
- Alternatives to the proposed investment
- Method of financing/budgeting
- Other considerations (Dawes et al. 2004; *PA Times* 2003)

The above can be brought into line with the performance improvement proposal and five conditions for successful change mentioned in chapter 3. Information technology proposals, like all proposals, require top management support and should respond to urgent needs. It is obvious that IT proposals stand a better a chance when they are consistent with the priorities and agendas of top managers. It is often observed that interest by top managers for IT is an important determinant of how fast agencies move forward in IT. Information technology proposals also need a critical mass, typically unit heads and managers who will use the proposed investment and are proponents of it. There needs to be some early successes so that initial naysayers and skeptics can be persuaded of the capabilities, and perhaps become supporters of the project. And, finally, there needs to be trust in the ability of the CIO or IT director to produce the results in timely, cost-effective, and "friendly" ways that leave others feelings good about the investment. The conditions for change also apply to IT.

Managing the Project: Success Factors

Many studies have examined the characteristics of both failed and successful information technology projects. For example, Pinto and Millet (1999) reviewed such studies and found that although technical problems and limitations are important, other barriers are poor top management support, unmotivated teams, leadership problems, conflicting objectives, and deficient procedures. These findings are replicated in many different settings and for different project phases, and are part of broader and well-established research about project management in general (Schwalbe 2003; Phillips 2004). The findings are now well-known and have remained essentially unchanged for about twenty to thirty years. Management matters. For example, although technical problems can surface at any time, the lack of planning and leadership may cause such problems to be detected late in the project and with inadequate foresight to developing contingency strategies.

Many authors suggest that managers should adopt the following practices. First, IT managers should keep the project mission and specific objectives in the forefront at all times. Projects usually experience myriad pressures that cause delays or changes to specifications. Second, project managers must consult with clients and users early in the process. Their input is key to specifying quality, time, and cost objectives, as well critical user needs that the project must satisfy. It is often very costly to reverse engineer projects in late stages to incorporate user parameters. Third, managers should also stay in touch with clients through the project. Doing so allows for receiving client input and for trying out new ideas or deviations from contract specifications on clients. Involving clients also helps bridge the gap between contract specification and final product.

Fourth, IT managers must ensure that IT technology works, and put their applications through rigorous testing. Many projects involve great creativity to ensure that applications work as contractually agreed. Fifth, managers must set and maintain project parameters. A tendency exists to allow for time and cost "creep" as managers and employees deal with unexpected problems. Managers must insist that despite unanticipated problems, project parameters stay on track. Sixth, managers must select the right people for the team. This involves ensuring their technical competence as well as the ability to work well together. A rule of project management is that any project requiring more than ten people will never get done; when more people are needed, managers should consider using two or more small teams.

Seventh, all projects must have top management support. This helps overcome threats to authority and budget, and may facilitate overcoming bureaucratic red tape. Eighth, managers must anticipate the possibility of failure and deal with it. Managers need a variety of contingency plans to deal with unanticipated complications. For example, key people get sick, small tasks may have to be further subdivided causing potential delays, and key liaisons are transferred.

In Conclusion

Information technology is ubiquitous in performance improvement, and managers will want to take advantage of it. However, IT is neither cheap nor easy to deploy, and it usually involves considerable management planning and involvement. This chapter suggests that managers should (1) be familiar with common and advanced IT applications in their lines of business, (2) identify how they use information technology for their programs, departments, or organizations, and (3) consider strategic issues such as security and governance as described in this chapter. Information technology offers many opportunities to improve performance through e-government, increased access and use of information, improved communications with stakeholders, and improved decision making.

Application Exercises

1. List important information technology applications in your line of work. Include some common ones, as well as five that are cutting edge. How do these applications relate to the information technology objectives mentioned in this chapter?
2. Which stretch objectives (chapter 5) might you set for your program or department? How can information technology help to meet these goals?
3. Develop a proposal to invest in a new information technology. What justifications would you use, and how could these be quantified?

What efficiencies or cost-savings do you project? What strategic or effectiveness justifications would you use?

4. (a) Consider the responsibilities of the CIO and central IT unit. How well are these needs being met in your agency? (b) Consider the role of department heads in formulating an information technology strategic plan for their department. Does such a plan exist in your department?

5. Which issues of IT security, fraud, unauthorized access, and viruses do you face? How well are you protected against the various threats?

6. How reliable are your systems? What would you do if your systems became unavailable for a day? For a week? What would the impact be if all data in one of your programs or subsystems became permanently lost or irretrievable? Are your backups up to date in order to protect yourself against these possibilities? Visit the Web site of the U.S. Computer Emergency Readiness Team and research topics of your interest at www.us-cert.gov.

7

Productivity Through People

What really matters is what you do with what you have.
—Shirley Lord

People are key to performance. When managers and workers are motivated and have appropriate skills, performance targets are accomplished and often exceeded. Challenges on the path to performance are taken in stride and overcome—they are genuinely viewed as learning opportunities. By contrast, when managers and workers are withdrawn and lack adequate skills, performance improvement becomes an exercise in futility whose success is measured in terms of getting by. Strategic planning, for example, might then be viewed as an exercise in paperwork ritual. The management of people, especially their motivation, is viewed by many scholars and practitioners as key to performance improvement.

This chapter examines strategies for raising employee motivation, as well as other strategies for increasing productivity through people, such as empowerment and improving teamwork. The strategy of increasing worker motivation often is based on aligning worker motivations with the needs of the employer. This strategy involves a heightened amount of dialogue and feedback, which also allows for addressing other problems such as insufficient professionalism (Problem 14, in chapter 2) or a lack of willingness to address deficits of a technical (Problem 15) or a social nature (Problem 16). It can also be used to clarify unclear or contradictory communication (Problem 9).

While this chapter focuses on strategies of aligning motivations as a tool to increase performance, not all problems of poor motivation are caused by the above-mentioned problems. Some motivation problems are caused by rules, regulations, or outdated delivery processes that have nothing to do with how employees are treated. Hence, the strategies discussed here are no panacea for incorrectly using process reengineering or information technology, for example. Nonetheless, when employers follow strategies described in this chapter, they increase communication, which can help avoid or deal with some of these problems as well.

Motivation

Empirical data suggests that the level of motivation in the workplace is mixed. Whereas some workers are highly motivated, others are cynical, wary, or only modestly motivated. Managers should expect that their workers vary greatly in their level of motivation. The 25–50–25 rule mentioned in chapter 3 appears to apply here, more or less. In previous research we found that that 29.8 percent of city managers in cities with populations over 50,000 agreed or strongly agreed with the statement that "employees are highly motivated to achieve goals," that 48.8 percent only "somewhat" agreed, and that 21.5 percent disagreed in varying degrees with this statement (West and Berman 1997). Respective data from a sample of directors of large nonprofit social service organizations show that 56.0 percent agreed or strongly agreed that employees are motivated, that 36.0 percent only somewhat agreed, and that 8.0 percent disagreed in varying degrees. The finding that nonprofit employees are more satisfied with their work is consistent with other research (e.g., Light 2002b). Though some people may experience greater or lesser levels of motivation in their units, it is clear that motivation varies.

The variation in workplace motivation reflects some fundamental realities. First, people are motivated by different things, and vary in their ability to find those things in their job. We don't all want the same thing from our jobs, though there are some commonalities. A great boss may be relevant to one person and largely irrelevant to another. Money may be important to one and less motivating for another. A key principle of motivation is that *people are motivated to pursue and satisfy their needs,* and their needs vary. Second, while managers acknowledge the importance of motivating their employees, many managers find the topic of motivation confusing, and their actions do not suggest that they know how to improve motivation or that they make worker motivation a priority. Some managers are dissatisfied with their ability to lead and inspire workers; in fact, some managers succeed quite well at demotivating workers, knowingly or unknowingly.

The strategy of worker motivation is twofold. The first and basic strategy is for managers and their organizations to provide a broad range of conditions in which most employees can find something that significantly satisfies their needs. If we know or make reasonable assumptions about what the needs of most workers are, then organizations can provide a fairly decent work environment by providing these conditions. It will provide some measure of motivation for most employees, and this is seen to be the case in many workplaces. The second and advanced strategy is for employers and employees to discuss, on a one-on-one basis, what each wants from the other, and establish a mutual understanding about the extent that these things can be provided. This understanding is a called a "psychological contract" and it is a pathway to high performance. Employees may not get everything, but more than they would otherwise get. When people express what they want, they have a better chance of getting it. There is truth to the saying: "Be careful what you ask for—you just might get it."

Needs That Motivate

The idea that employees are motivated by pursuing their needs is well-established. Five different groups of needs can be distinguished. First, people have a need for *physical security*. This includes being able to pay for food and shelter, as well as other benefits that provide protection against the loss of this security; health insurance and retirement contributions have become very important motivators for some employees in recent years. Job security is also important, and one reason why some people join the public service. The importance of meeting current and future basic needs is widely recognized. For example, Maslow (1954) identified physiological and safety needs as prerequisites for satisfying other all needs. According to Maslow, people do not focus on other needs, discussed below, until these basic needs are met. While some of the following draws on Maslow, it is important to put these older theories in modern context, as done here. For example, health insurance benefits play a larger role today than they did fifty years ago.

Basic needs are also recognized, albeit cynically, by managers who motivate by threatening employees with the loss of their jobs. However, these fear-based approaches are increasingly in disrepute because they often lead to subsequent demotivation, resentment that is associated with increased litigation and workplace violence, which also affect employee morale; word gets around quickly. So, fear-based motivation is not the best way to motivate workers. Of course, workers should be responsible for their actions and commitments, and hence a certain fear of consequences for failing to live up to these obligations is appropriate. However, fear of irrational, arbitrary, and disproportionate actions is not reasonable, and this causes resentment and demotivation.

A second group of needs focuses on receiving *acknowledgment and recognition* from others. Most people like a compliment, which acknowledges both their contribution and acceptance into the group showing the appreciation. Some people have a stronger need to have their work appreciated, whereas others have a stronger need to feel part of a group. Being acknowledged is an important need for many, and managers make a mistake when they assume that people know that they are appreciated. Managers should say "thank you" at least several times each day. If managers don't show that they care, then why should workers? Many nonprofit employees have a strong need to have their commitment acknowledged, and such needs are also present among older employees who sometimes accept pay cuts to join organizations.

Acknowledgement is also shown with salary raises, bonuses, promotions, and formal recognition. Because managers have little leeway over raises and bonuses, it is important that they take full advantage of nonmonetary rewards. Table 7.1 shows some of these rewards. Not all employees value these alternative rewards and recognitions in equal ways; they may be more meaningful to some than others. Therefore, managers should ascertain from individual workers which nonmonetary recognitions they value most. Rewards matter, but when workers believe that they are being underrewarded, then demotivation sets in. Also, the flipside of managers failing to show appreciation are employees who fail to say that appreciation matters to them. Employees vary in their need for appreciation, and the forms in which that may occur, and so should be willing to give managers reasonable clues that it matters to them. Appreciation is a two-way street.

A third group involves the individual need for *accomplishment, creativity, and growth* by acquiring new knowledge or skills. There is ample evidence that many people in public service join the public sector in order to make a difference, and many people feel good when they are able to make that difference. Some employees also have a strong need for high achievement and creativity. Maslow recognized the creative need as the pinnacle of human motivation, and Nadler and Lawler (1977) also acknowledged the importance of work as its own motivator. Employees with high achievement needs often seek out new challenges and managers need do little more than provide these achievement and growth opportunities. However, managers must be careful of imposing creative challenges on those who do not have this need; difficult goals motivate more than simple goals, but only when the challenge is accepted by workers. Those who do not have this need may experience the accompanying stress as severely demotivating, especially if not accompanied by other, extrinsic rewards.

A fourth group of needs involves the acquisition and use of *power.* McClelland (1985) noted that employees and managers are motivated by power, as well as by affiliation and achievement. People want to make a difference, and power is a means to impact the world around them. Through power, new programs can be created and policies developed. Performance improvement

Table 7.1

Alternative Rewards

Acknowledgment from the organization
Acknowledgment from team members
Acknowledgment from supervisor
Book certificate
Birthday card
Choice assignment
Computer training
Conference travel
Dinner certificate
Extra night stay during travel
Extra office staff support
Job rotation
Flextime
Free transportation for a month
Free parking for a month
Friday off
Gift certificate
Guest of honor
Movie certificate
New computer or printer
New furniture
New software
Office decoration
Personal stationery
Small cash award
Team leader for a week
Theater certificate
Training
Use of an assistant

implies the use of power. For some people, the acquisition of power is itself the end. Managers, lawyers, and politicians often have a strong need for power, hence their pursuit of positions that provide them with it. Power often is accompanied by such prestige symbols as a corner office, personal assistant, choice assignments, titles, and higher salaries. Power is also involved in having some meaningful control over their workplace, such as being able to design one's own work, work environment, or work schedule.

Power can be used toward positive and negative ends—it can be used to build things as well as to destroy things. It can be used to lift people up and also to knock them down. Such negative uses are well documented, and have a highly demotivating impact on workers. Bosses who use power in negative ways often are experienced as narcissistic and inconsiderate bullies who devalue others and praise themselves (Lubit 2004). High-performance organizations often let managers know that they will be scrutinized for their use of power—they are held accountable. By contrast, in mediocre organizations the abusive use of power is often unpunished, and hence continues unabated.

A fifth group involves *other, nonwork needs* that are satisfied through work. Work allows employees to satisfy other needs such as buying a boat, living in a nice house, raising a family, taking vacations, and so on. These are important motivators for many people, and work allows them to pursue these things. A widespread example is to take care of one's family and help them afford a better lifestyle. Many parents are highly committed to raising their children and are motivated to work because of the material benefits that it provides them in raising their family. Many employees and managers also have ego needs that are satisfied by living in an upper-class neighborhood or driving a luxury car. These means, satisfied through work, signal to others that they have made it in the world.

In sum, employees and managers have many different needs. According to Henry (1995), research shows that employees and managers in public and nonprofit organizations have higher needs for achievement and security and somewhat lower needs for acceptance and financial rewards than those in for-profit corporations. While these are useful generalizations, managers and employees will want to focus on their individual needs.

Other Considerations

In addition to the above, Herzberg (1959) noted that while some factors motivate, other conditions often demotivate workers. Specifically, he mentioned rules and regulations and supervisory relations. Good rules and regulations seldom motivate—few people come whistling to work because of their organization's great policies and procedures. But bad rules and regulations do demotivate workers when they get in the way of recognizing workers, allowing them to make a difference in the world, taking on new and challenging assignments, obtaining day care services, pursuing continuing professional education, and meeting other needs they might find important.

Similarly, supervisory relations and peer relations are also thought to have more downside than upside. Poor supervisory relations and peer relations induce significant stress in workers. Workers worry about what might or will happen next, and whether actions and comments are harbingers of bad things to come. Poor peer relations can have similar affects—not knowing who can be trusted or who might be conspiring. By contrast, positive relations seem to be of less importance than meeting other needs identified above.

The role of money as a motivator warrants some discussion. It is more complex than commonly assumed. When people make inadequate income to satisfy their needs, there seems little motivation to go to work, apart from not making matters worse by not going to work at all. Then, the current salary is a demotivator, and the prospect of making more money is a motivator if enough to overcome the current problem of not having enough. But when people make good money, they quickly adjust their expectations to that higher level. Then, the higher level no longer provides much motivation for many people, apart from the fear of losing it. The problem for managers is that the motivational effect for many workers (but not all) soon dissipates after the salary raise is given (i.e., the goal is achieved). The lure of money is only a temporary motivator, and the motivational strategy of offering ever-increasing salaries is untenable for any organization, of course. These problems with money suggest that employers do well to not depend only on money as a motivator. In a broader context, rewards and acknowledgment can be considered as feedback.

Some writers view human motivation as a function of the consequences that employees experience from their behavior. As noted by Skinner (1971), "behavior is shaped and maintained by its consequences." It suggests that needs are largely shaped by positive or negative feedback that individuals receive from their actions. For example, frequent negative feedback often causes some employees to reduce their own needs as way of reducing future disappointments over unrealized needs. This reduces motivation, too; mediocrity is sometimes explained by the presence of punishments for negative behavior and the absence of rewards for positive behavior and accomplishments (Werther, Ruch, and McClure 1986). In short, employees need positive feedback and rewards. It should be noted that although behavioralists sometimes maintain that all needs are a function of social reinforcement, an integrative perspective maintains that humans have needs that exist independent of the feedback that they receive.

Regarding goals, the motivational impact from setting challenging goals quickly becomes complicated when goals are set by managers rather than by employees who freely choose them. Of course, managers are required to set goals. First, managerial goals are more likely to be pursued with high motivation by employees when they are perceived as being aligned with employees' needs in some way—such as for making a difference or receiving some transactional benefit (a reward, acknowledgement, etc.). Second, expectancy theory suggests that even well-aligned goals may still not be much pursued when employees feel that they are unfeasible. Research shows that performance increases as the perceived difficulty of goals increases from low to moderate to challenging, but quickly diminishes when goals are perceived as impossible, the latter causing feelings of resignation (Locke et al. 1990). Employees need the skills and power to achieve what needs to be achieved.

It follows that managers should not set impossible goals, and that they should also suggest strategies for realizing difficult goals. However, excessive guidance diminishes the challenge and may reduce motivation among employees who have a strong need for creativity or achievement.

Motivation is thus affected by many different factors that vary among employees. From the perspective of managers and their organizations, the following constitutes a general climate for worker motivation. If all of the conditions are present, workers will likely find something that motivates them, though some more than others. While the following factors should be present, they do not replace the need for individual dialogue discussed further:

1. Competitive salaries;
2. Relevant benefits that address workers' needs for economic security (today and future) and some nonwork related needs (family, vacation);
3. Meaningful rewards and recognition (and distribute them in equitable ways);
4. Opportunities for challenging (yet, achievable) assignments with further opportunities for learning and skill development;
5. Friendly and cooperative workplace relations;
6. Assignments that allow workers to make a meaningful contribution to society;
7. Feedback that provides both recognition and opportunity for development;
8. Meaningful control over their work environment and resources to do their jobs;
9. Minimized demotivating effects of rules and regulations;
10. Reduction in negative supervisory relationships.

It is indeed easy to see that a work environment with these conditions will provide a significant amount of motivation for many workers.

Psychological Contracts

To go beyond a general climate of motivation indicated by the above ten items, managers will need to know what motivates individual workers, and find some way to provide that to them, perhaps in exchange for increased performance. However, some managers fail to engage their workers in such conversations, and some workers may be hesitant to talk about their needs with managers if not asked to do so. Some workers may feel, for example, that telling managers about their needs is to make them vulnerable to future manipulation.

A valuable tool for increasing productivity through motivation is the *psy-*

chological contract. It is a somewhat new tool, barely mentioned in the 1980s, but increasingly discussed and subject to a growing body of research starting in the mid to late 1990s. People who have used them say that they work, and many students report similar experiences. In 2002, a survey of senior local government managers found that 57.3 percent of respondents reported that in their jurisdiction most supervisors establish psychological contracts with employees, but only 20.7 percent reported that they used processes similar to those described below. Very few managers call them "psychological contracts," but rather use such terms as informal agreement, mutual understanding, and so on (Berman and West 2003; Rousseau 1995). Because of these divergent terminologies and variable uses, it is difficult to empirically assess where the use of psychological contracts might fall on the diffusion S-curve. However, their considerable use, present confusion about their "correct" practices or applications, and a decade-long introductory stage are all consistent with performance improvement efforts that are just beginning the take-off stage.

A psychological contract is defined as an *unwritten understanding about mutual needs, goals, expectations, and procedures.* Psychological contracts go beyond employment contracts, which typically provide agreements about salary, benefits, grievance procedures, and working hours. Although these are important conditions that affect motivation, they do not clarify other conditions that also, and sometimes more strongly, affect worker motivation. Psychological contracts are potentially broad reaching (almost any work-related topic is fair game), but usually limited to those issues that are highly valued by employees and managers. Topics for psychological contracts include support in dealing with child care responsibilities, the frequency and nature of managerial feedback, the possibility of training and acquiring new skills, and so on. Psychological contracts increase motivation by allowing managers to better understand the needs of individual employees, by helping to provide rewards and conditions that address individual needs, and by ensuring a high degree of clarity about roles and expectations.

A good psychological contract is one in which: (1) the important needs of an individual worker are identified; (2) managers explain through dialogue which needs can be met, which cannot, and which can be met in modified form; (3) the manager and worker reach agreement on worker needs that can be met; and (4) the manager agrees to meet these needs if the worker is willing to do those things that are required to meet those needs. These are typically things that the manager wants to get from the worker; (5) the worker and manager agree that a fair balance exists between what the worker will get, and what they are asked to do (a framework for doing this is shown in

Figure 7.1 **Psychological Contract**

	Expect to Get	Expect to Give
Worker		
Supervisor/Others		

Source: As adapted from Osland, Kolb, and Rubin (2000).

Figure 7.1); and (6) the worker and manager agree to periodically, or as often as needed, meet to ensure that the understanding is still in place. Suspected violations of the understanding are causes for further discussion to reach a renewed mutual understanding.

Several factors make a psychological contract effective as a motivational tool: (1) it addresses workers' needs that motivate them; (2) it is perceived as a fair balance between what the worker wants, and what the worker is expected to give (there is no perception of someone trying to take advantage or being taken advantage of); and (3) it has a mechanism for following up, ensuring that the agreement is implemented, and addressing any road bumps ("pinch points") that may occur.

Psychological contracts are easy to establish with subordinates. A manager can go to his or her employee and note that it has been some time since their last conversation, and the manager would like to know how things are going. The manager might ask whether there is anything he or she can do to make the employee's work better. Following the employee's perhaps surprised response, the manager asks whether the employee has anything he or she would like to achieve over the next, say, six months. Then, as items are listed by the employee, the manager explains why something can be met (for example, training or flextime), or cannot be met (much more salary—manager does not have control over that), or can be met in a modified form only (promotion—manager does not have control over that, but can help to through assignments to make the employee more competitive).

Next, the manager informs the employee that the manager has some job-related needs, too. Perhaps some project needs to be completed, or a strategy pilot-tested. In addition, the manager can raise concerns about the performance or skills of the employee. Then, the manager can suggest a meeting of mutual needs, increased performance and commitment to improvement in return for helping the employee to meet some of his or her needs. Perhaps, some employee contributions or improvements are seen as conditions for the manager helping to meet the employee's needs.

After all of the worker's needs and manager's needs from the worker have been agreed upon, the manager summarizes the discussion, and notes that situations and things do change. The door to communication remains open, especially as regarding perceived misunderstanding. Managers should reiterate the psychological contract a few times over the next weeks or months. People sometimes "forget" things or take don't take them seriously unless repeated (recall Berman's rule of three). Also, while it is easier for a manager to initiate a psychological contract with a subordinate, sometimes subordinates can initiate such dialogue with their supervisor or with coworkers. Psychological contracts are also easily established within the first few weeks of employment, before fixed patterns of communication set in.

Teamwork, Feedback, and Other Strategies

Feedback

Through feedback, employees assess their performance. Feedback gives supervisors and others an opportunity to signal their approval or disapproval of employee performance and behavior. Feedback regulates future expectations and intentions. It is also part of a communication process that can be a first step toward identifying and overcoming misunderstandings. Productivity requires that workers receive ongoing feedback about their performance. This not only includes information about corrections that may be needed, but also praise that can sustain or even increase future motivation and performance.

A common error is that managers mistakenly assume that workers receive feedback about their performance from other sources, however, a TQM adage is that few dissatisfied clients express their complaints to service providers, and that they do not always do so to the employees who cause complaints. Feedback should be frequent: A request from one police precinct to provide performance measures on a quarterly rather than a biweekly basis was denied because doing so reduces the number of yearly improvement opportunities from twenty-six to only four. Finally, workers and managers should get feedback from their supervisors, subordinates, clients, and coworkers. Each of these sources has different knowledge about the services that they receive or provide and are able to make valuable contributions to further improvement.

The strategy for providing feedback is straightforward. Managers should:

1. Provide a balanced assessment of employee performance (including both positive and negative aspects);
2. Emphasize the objective nature of service outcomes (some facts are indisputable);

3. Establish their commitment to helping employees achieve positive results;
4. Work collaboratively with employees to develop strategies for improving performance (solutions should not be imposed);
5. Help employees develop their perspective that conditions for success lie within their power to affect;
6. Agree on a timetable for monitoring improvement;
7. Further strategies for support and feedback; and, importantly,
8. Determine future rewards for improvement.

This eight-step approach helps minimize the potentially demotivating effects of negative feedback by depersonalizing outcomes and providing strategies for success. The purpose of feedback is to encourage productive behaviors and arrest unproductive behaviors. Demotivation occurs when employees feel bad about themselves as professionals and fail to develop effective response strategies. So, feedback should help workers develop good responses and, as such, feedback is part of an ongoing effort of developmental improvement. Feedback leads to higher performance than no feedback, but negative feedback, as perceived by workers, suppresses behavior, whereas positive feedback reinforces behavior. For example, impulsive, emotional outbursts of managers caused by an employee's behavior are apt to have negative, demotivating effects on employees. They contain nothing that can be construed as helpful to employees in understanding how the outcome occurred and what can be done to improve it in the future. While such outbursts may induce employees to seek improvement, the resulting resentment is likely to be high as well.

In recent years, a new area for improving and expanding feedback is in emotional intelligence, defined as the competencies that are involved in assessing and managing one's own emotions, as well as recognizing and managing emotions in others and in relationships (Goleman, Boyatzis, and McKee 2002; Cherniss and Goleman 2001). Emotional intelligence involves social skills, such as actively listening and being aware of others' feelings, as well as inspiring and guiding individuals and groups, helping others improve performance, and managing conflict. Feedback is a cornerstone of developing these skills, especially to identify such barriers to effective communication as being impatient, derogatory, or not sufficiently focusing on the relationship. Managers with poor social skills often underestimate the extent and the impact of these deficits.

Empowerment

In recent years, empowerment has become an important performance improvement strategy. Empowerment involves the delegation of decision making to employees while holding them accountable for outcomes. Empowerment is consistent with performance improvement because it allows organizations to respond more quickly and with greater flexibility to client concerns. One-stop shopping centers in government (for example, for permit applications) are examples that use empowerment. It is consistent with the use of psychological contracts, because it suggests increased responsibility for performance and rewards. The basic steps of empowerment are:

1. Deciding what should be delegated, and why;
2. Identifying who should be empowered;
3. Ensuring adequate resources for successfully fulfilling the new tasks and addressing changes in working conditions;
4. Creating a pilot effort (with participation from employees);
5. Monitoring implementation and outcomes; and
6. Making adjustments as needed.

Tasks that lend themselves most to empowerment are those that involve highly differentiated or customized services, customer-intensive relations, complex technologies, and unpredictable service requests. Examples of tasks that require high levels of empowerment are community-based policing, neighborhood casework, building long-term relations with funding agencies, and various business inspection and regulation activities. In these situations, empowerment of employees can help agencies to better accomplish their tasks (e.g., Blanchard 2001; Amar 2002; Plunkett and Fournier 1991).

Empowerment is not without its challenges. Empowerment often is frustrated by unrealistic assumptions and inadequate planning. In order for empowerment to work, workers must be given decision-making authority, information, skills, and rewards that are consistent with their tasks. Managers must ensure these conditions exist prior to empowering. For example, officers involved in community-based policing must be given discretion for handling a broad range of issues. They must be provided with training opportunities to acquire needed skills, information about changes in their neighborhood, and rewards and incentives that reflect goals for community-based policing. Managers must also decide which tasks cannot be delegated, such as those that involve significant legal issues. To test whether these conditions exist, managers should ask employees whether they feel that they have adequate control over their ability to perform well in the manner for which they will be held accountable. Employees should also be asked what, if anything, management can do to help them perform better. In short, the intent to empower and follow through must be present.

Another problem is that while some managers believe that many workers are waiting for empowerment, in practice, some workers prefer the predictability of their current routines and expectations. Introducing empowerment induces anxiety about uncertain demands and rewards (or punishments). Managers must overcome such fear by clearly explaining the rationale for empowerment, as well as steps that are undertaken to ease implementation and ensure fair and positive consequences for employees. Another misconception is that empowerment is tantamount to democracy. It is not. Managers retain important veto powers and determine the rules of the game, even though many decisions involve more worker input. A further myth is that empowerment produces instant results or quick returns. Workers need to be given leeway to discover new approaches for achieving their goals. This is a process of trial and error that requires patience and encouragement by managers, not criticism and micromanagement.

Teamwork

Teams of employees and managers are increasingly used in organizations and are an important productivity improvement strategy. Teams are often used to increase the speed at which things are done, to bring together diverse expertise for dealing with complex, multifaceted problems, to focus organizational resources on specific targets, to increase learning and sharing among group members (thereby increasing future productivity), and to provide a single point of contact for outside stakeholders.

Teamwork is not always easy. Some specific problems are:

1. Confusion about the team's authority and type of team;
2. Inability to generate consensus and support for team goals;
3. Inadequate support from managers or organizations outside the team;
4. Confusion about the team roles of individuals (e.g., Who is the leader? What is expected from this person?);
5. Inadequate vision or expertise among team members or team leaders;
6. Concerns about performance appraisal;
7. Team goals or rewards are not aligned with the needs of team members;
8. Inability of leaders to deal with interpersonal rivalry or immaturity of team members;
9. Inadequate resources and mandates to accomplish team mission.

Effective team building requires that these issues are addressed. This is best done prior to creating the team; for example, by managers who establish clear team goal and objectives, working relations with other departments, and a selection of team members that ensure expertise. Then, the first few meetings of the team are used to lay out the ground rules of the working relationship, clear goals and objectives, timetables for accomplishment, and procedures for dealing with inevitable challenges that will occur. All this lays the foundation for successful teamwork. Specifically, high-performance teams are characterized by:

- A strong sense of shared ownership and commitment to team goals
- Participatory and empowering leadership
- A high degree of open and fearless communication
- Trust among team members
- Emphasis on developing, using, and evaluating new approaches
- Members are focused on time, the task, and quality

It is difficult to assess the productivity of teams, but many observers believe that many teams spend about 30 to 50 percent of their project time on laying the groundwork and agreeing on the work to be done. It often appears that as deadlines loom nearer, teams find sufficient motivation to overcome differences and reach agreements that allow team members to press on. Being aware of this, managers may chose to set rather tight deadlines, and ensure that the above issues are dealt with prior to team formation, or in the early phases of teamwork (e.g., Ephross and Vassil 2005).

Dealing with Difficult People

There are some difficult people in the workplace, for sure. Some people are highly abusive and hostile, who bully and overwhelm others. They don't stop until they get their way. They are inconsiderate of others, and support no one but themselves. Others are indecisive or unresponsive, failing to actively support a project. Sometimes they insist on every detail being worked out in advance, hence slowing everything down to a bare crawl. They say they agree and support, but do nothing. They also support others to avoid discord, even when others are ineffective. Still others are negative or have an opinion about everything, but the opinion does not move the project in the right direction. They, too, are barriers to progress and, if given the chance, will likely doom any project. These are difficult people, indeed.

For the most part, the purpose or consequence of difficult behavior is for a person to gain *control* over others or their work situation. Difficult behavior is a control-and-dominate game. People who are abusive will cause others to more easily agree with them or let them have their way—they are less likely to be challenged. People who are indecisive may control the project pace and even whether or not the project exists. People who are negative or have an opinion may do the same, and try to steer the project in a direction of their choosing, even if it is not a very effective one.

The point of dealing with difficult people is to stop the negative impact that their behaviors have on work and on others—difficult people often provoke negative feelings such as resentment and hate. The first step in dealing with such people is to recognize the situation for what it is. We need to identify the specific actions of difficult people that are problematic. We need to acknowledge our feelings. We need to examine the effectiveness of our initial responses, which may not have produced the best results (Bramson 1981).

For example, it is quite common to wish for the difficult behavior to disappear. It is theoretically possible that through rational discourse difficult people may come to see that their actions are unproductive and that they agree to change some aspect of it. But this is not usually the case. The impulse to act in difficult ways may run very deep, or may reflect learned behavior over many years. Abusive people are just as likely to use such feedback against the person making it, argumentative people are likely to become argumentative in the face of feedback, and indecisive people will take it under advisement with little or no follow up or consequences. In short, the wish that difficult behavior might disappear may not come to pass.

The point of further action, then, is to minimize the impact of difficult behaviors. Productivity is achieved by not damaging it further. The basic strategy is to arrest patterns of interaction with the difficult person through (Lubit 2004):

- Avoidance,
- Setting boundaries, and
- Confronting each difficult behavior in appropriate, controlled, and controlling ways.

Regarding the latter, an indecisive person might be challenged with, "I understand, but we need to move forward now," and a negative person might be told, "I disagree, and believe this will work." People will have to defend themselves against comments by the hostile person, such as by noting that their comments are not helpful, correct, or relevant to getting the job done. Demeaning behavior needs to be exposed as such. We need to confront difficult behavior, and can often do that by focusing on the purpose of the job.

Beyond this, boundaries and avoidance are useful tactics. Boundaries are set by communicating that certain behaviors will not be accepted, such as being addressed in rude ways. Such communication often is verbal; written expressions are typically viewed as first steps towards grievances, formal reprimands, and progressive discipline. To be effective, boundaries need to be consistently maintained by responding to each alleged infraction as described above. Of course, it is not always possible to maintain boundaries. A second tactic is avoidance, which is an important option with abusive bosses. The point is to reduce one's availability for being part of the difficult person's controlling behaviors. This gives peace, and more time to reflect on finding effective responses. While it does not make the problem disappear, it may make it more manageable.

Finally, we should not rule out looking for another job as an appropriate response to dealing with difficult bosses, especially abusive bosses. There is only so much that can be done. The presence of difficult bosses may reflect the management culture, and the employee may want something better. While the new workplace is likely to have difficult people, too, hopefully none is going to be the new boss.

In Conclusion

People are key to performance. When people are motivated and aligned with the goals of the organization, performance targets often are accomplished or exceeded. But people vary in their motivation; the 25–50–25 rule (chapter 3) appears to apply here. To ensure a minimum of motivation, organizations should provide such things as competitive salaries and benefits, meaningful rewards, opportunities for challenging assignments and making a difference, friendly workplace relations, and meaningful feedback. Beyond this, managers increase motivation by creating mutual understandings (psychological contracts) with workers. Through such understandings, workers and employers are better able to align their needs, and provide a structure for discussion when potentially demotivating or unproductive circumstances arise.

This chapter also discusses feedback, empowerment, and teamwork as performance improvement strategies. Constructive, positive feedback can lead to significant improvement. Empowerment involves the delegation of decision making to employees while holding them accountable for outcomes. Empowerment is consistent with productivity improvement because it allows organizations to respond more quickly and with greater flexibility to client concerns. Teams are also used to increase speed and flexibility. Each of these strategies requires the right intent, experience, and proper planning for success.

The chapter concludes with dealing with difficult people. Difficult people are found in most workplaces, and performance strategies often try to minimize their disruptive, negative impact. This chapter identified different types of difficult behaviors, and suggested dealing with difficult behaviors through avoidance, setting boundaries, and confronting each difficult behavior in appropriate and controlling ways.

Application Exercises

1. Identify some ways in which your immediate supervisor has knowingly and unknowingly affected your motivation. Which ways increased your motivation? Which ways decreased your motivation? How would you like to be motivated?

2. Make a psychological contract with someone, preferably a work colleague or someone working under you. Discuss what you want from that person, and what that person is willing to give, what that person expects to get from you, and what you are willing to give in order to ensure that the understanding "works out." Then, make the psychological contract and put it in place for a few weeks. See what it does for you. What happened? Was there improvement in any sense? What might you do differently next time?

3. Think of a specific situation in which you gave feedback. What impact did it have? How can you improve the effectiveness of your feedback?

4. Do you feel adequately empowered? Would you like to have more power (authority)? What responsibilities do you think should come along with that? Are you willing to accept those responsibilities?

5. What is the most common teamwork problem that you experience? How can it be addressed? Can it be avoided?

6. Everyone has some difficult bosses and coworkers. What problems did they present for you? Which strategies worked? Which strategies did not?

8

The Accountability Strategy:
Performance Measurement

Performance measurement is the activity of documenting the activities and accomplishments of programs. It is about showing, for example, how well a school system is teaching children, how well the criminal justice system resolves its cases, how well the military fights war, and how well environmental management protects coastlines, air quality, and endangered species. It is about measuring what programs are really achieving. Many people want to know how public monies are being spent and what they are achieving. Accountability is about providing such information to elected officials, oversight bodies, managers, citizens, and others, and of justifying that the activities and choices that were made were legitimate, effective, and in the public interest. Performance measurement systems provide considerable detail about programs, and the accountability that is provided by public officials often relies on performance measurement, which is presented in reports and at public hearings (Poister 2003; Guajardo and McDonnell 2000; Walters 1998).

It can be argued that performance measurement by itself does not constitute performance improvement—it is an information-gathering strategy. However, the purposes to which this information is put are clearly associated with improving performance (Behn 2005a). First, performance measurement focuses managers' attention on certain specific activities and outcomes. As the saying goes, "what gets measured gets done," and knowing that something will be subject to heightened scrutiny later is apt to make it a priority of sorts today. Second, performance measurement can be used to manage expectations and invite innovation by tying standards to expected outcomes. For example, a standard might be set for the number of applications to be completed, or the average cost of providing some service. The standard might reflect past accomplishment or some benchmark performance. Setting high standards forces agencies to find new, effective ways of reaching their goals, and some organizations periodically ratchet up their standards to ensure ongoing innovation. Third, performance measurement offers opportunities for monitoring and controlling so that agreed upon targets are indeed likely to be met. Senior managers may meet periodically with lower managers to ensure that arrests, emergency response times, truancy rates, and so on are moving toward intended performance goals. This requires that performance measurement is conducted on a real-time or frequent basis. Fourth, performance measurement allows managers to know that in fact they are making a difference. It also allows public agencies and officials to get credit and promote public trust that their programs are in fact accomplishing what they set out to do. Feedback and motivation provide additional motivation for managers and their agencies to attain performance.

These purposes are accomplished by using performance measurement alone or in combination with other performance improvement strategies. Performance measurement is increasingly part of strategic planning; according to Poister and Streib (2005), about half of all municipal strategic plans now use performance measurement to track strategic goals and objectives. Measuring progress toward these targets is also a way of monitoring and tracking. Performance measurement is also part of many budget processes, providing additional information that decision makers find helpful in deciding how to best to allocate public monies. The usefulness of performance measurement information led the Government Accounting Standards Board to experiment with incorporating performance information (called Service Efforts and Accomplishments) over a decade ago (e.g., Government Accounting Standards Board 1994), and local government financial reports now increasingly include such information. Performance measurement is also part of many quality improvement programs and other improvement efforts where outcomes need to be measured, providing opportunities for control and celebration of outcomes.

As regarding the specific performance problems mentioned in chapter 2, performance measurement is especially relevant to reversing the tide of apathy (Problem 3) by giving citizens and others reasons to value public and nonprofit programs. It also provides accountability for funding for agencies, and helps to deal with those who make politics at the expense of the organization (Problem 4) by providing information about important accomplishments. Using methods of data collection for performance measurement can also help ensure that needs of target groups are correctly identified (Problem 1). Performance measurement also helps with the control of program implementation (Problem 12), and brings heightened accountability to managers (Problem 15). It can also bring heightened accountability to employees when performance measures are translated into individual responsibilities and assignments.

Historically, performance measurement has had a long development traceable to program evaluation in the 1960s and 1970s. Program evaluations often are one-time activities that very thoroughly, meeting high scientific standards, assess program outcomes and their impact (Rossi, Lipsey, and Freeman 2004). Examples of program evaluation include very detailed assessments of the Head Start program, crisis response programs, and the success or failure of space technology programs. Key limitations of program evaluation include that they often are quite expensive and they take considerable time to compete; the results may be neither accessible to many programs, nor very timely. For example, program evaluation may require extensive interviews with program participants, perhaps with follow up over several months or years to better understand program impacts. Impacts of drug treatment programs, for example, may not be known for many years.

Throughout the 1970s and 1980s efforts were made to make program evaluation more timely and affordable. During the early 1980s the term "performance measurement" was introduced to denote efforts to provide useful information about government programs by using a limited range of indicators, often drawn from administrative data or surveys of citizen perceptions (e.g., Urban Institute 1980). Though less precise than program evaluation, these indicators were more timely and less costly, while offering a clear improvement over anecdotal assessments by program managers and others. Coincidentally, continuous improvement processes of TQM in large corporations during the 1980s established the idea of having ongoing, real-time measurement systems regarding the quality and efficiency of production and service delivery (Halachmi 1999). Performance measurement gained momentum in the early 1990s (e.g., Wholey and Hatry 1992), and the Government Performance and Results Act of 1993 required federal agencies to establish quantitative performance measures and targets. Around that time, nonprofit organizations were asked by funding agencies such as the United Way to document their outcomes as well (United Way 1996).

Agencies have since been required to submit annual reports that monitor their performance. Though in the mid-1990s this activity was largely experimental (Tigue and Strachota 1994; U.S. General Accounting Office 1997); in recent years it has become institutionalized at different levels of government. Barriers that persisted through the 1990s, such as a lack of data collection or analysis capacity, have been increasingly overcome (Berman and Wang

2000), and the number of indicators used in reported program performance is expanding rapidly. Today, consultants offer comprehensive, tailored software that facilitates tracking and performance reporting, integrated with budgeting and other processes. Performance measurement is clearly well into the takeoff phase of the diffusion cycle discussed in chapter 1.

Parallel with these program-level performance measurement efforts have also been efforts to provide quantitative, descriptive reports about the state of communities, the country, and issue areas. In the 1970s reports were prepared of social indicators to report social conditions, or science indicators to describe the state of the scientific enterprise in the United States. Some of these efforts diminished in the 1980s, but in recent years many communities have created statistical portraits of their condition using indicators of demographic, economic, social, housing, community development, civic engagement, family and children well-being, education, health, and economic development. The World Bank has prepared similar statistical snapshots of countries, for example, focusing on health, mortality, per capita income, military activity, and corruption, and some agencies focus on specific issues that confront them, such as community health. Somewhat differently, balanced scorecards (discussed further), first mentioned in the mid-1990s, combine the broad, descriptive focus with specific management interests by providing a set of key indicators about the organization's financial state, customer/stakeholder satisfaction, efficiency and effectiveness of delivery processes, and activities to promote learning and improvement of the organization (Kaplan and Norton 1992, 1996).

Thus, performance measurement has come a long way. This chapter discusses some of the key concepts and terms of performance measurement, along with examples, as well as issues involved in the implementation and further development of performance measurement systems.

Measures of Performance

The Logic Model

How should performance be measured? Underlying any system of performance measurement is a basic understanding of the process or phenomenon that is being measured. For example, we can't measure our progress at work if we don't know what work activities are expected of us, and the purposes that they serve. Likewise, we can't measure the performance of a program if we don't know what it is supposed to do, and how it is supposed to work. In recent years, a general model for describing what programs are expected to accomplish is called a program "logic model," which has been widely promoted in the public and nonprofit sectors. This model was mentioned in chapter 1, and is shown again here:

This model is perhaps best explained by using an example. A program to reduce a public health threat such as HIV/AIDS or tuberculosis (TB) might aim to achieve this by increasing public awareness, ensuring access to health care and diagnosis, disseminating latest research findings to the medical community, and promoting research of various kinds. All of these are *activities* (services that a program is performing), and the level of each of these activities can be measured. For example, public awareness activities might consist of placing local advertisements and distributing flyers at schools and public places. These can be measured. Activities associated with increasing access might involve contacting health centers and asking them to be open certain hours, using indigent health care funds to treat those without insurance, providing funding or encouraging health centers to engage in outreach activities, and so on. These, too, can be measured. The idea of performance measurement is to define measures and collected data on measures of each of the categories in the logic model.

Outputs are defined as the immediate consequences (or results) of these activities. For example, the immediate consequence or result of activities to increase public awareness is increased awareness by the public. To measure increased awareness by the public, agency officials might conduct a poll of residents, assessing their familiarity with various aspects of these public health threats. Or, more narrowly tied to the agency's specific activities, officials might conduct evaluations of those who attended the outreach functions, or simply count the number of people who attended, assuming that they became more or adequately informed as a result. Likewise, the activity of increasing access to health care facilities might be measured by how many clients these facilities treat, how long the facilities are open, and their potential capacity for treating or diagnosing persons. As these examples show, there is no one best way to define performance measures. Even similar programs may differ because of their unique priorities and circumstances. Obviously, managers need to clearly understand *how* their activities give rise to outputs and outcomes, and thinking through such relationships may cause them to consider new strategies or performance targets (Behn 2005c).

The program logic model also shows outcomes and goals. *Goals* are defined as the ultimate purposes or aims of programs. In this example, the goal is to reduce the threat of public health threats such as HIV/AIDS or TB.

Table 8.1

Summary of Key Terms

Term	Brief definition
Activity	Program services that are performed (also, "workload")
Output	Immediate result or consequence of an activity
Outcome	A measure of goal attainment
Goal	Ultimate and final purpose of a program
Effectiveness	The level of outputs and/or outcomes
Efficiency	The cost to produce a unit of service, defined as the ratio of an output or outcome per cost or input
Labor efficiency	The labor cost to produce a unit of service, defined as the ratio of an output or outcome per unit (e.g., hour) of labor
Workload ratio	Activity per unit of input (e.g., workload per worker)
Benchmark	A standard used to assess the effectiveness or efficiency

Goals reflect and state the public interest in the activity. Goals are also closely tied to the rationale for program activities, of course, and program justifications frequently include facts and arguments that further amplify the rationale or merit of program goals—the ultimate aim of the program. *Outcomes* are defined as the extent that goals are accomplished. Hence, in this case, outcome measures may reflect the incidence of these public health threats, such as the number of cases or percentage of the population with HIV/AIDS or TB. These are relevant measures of goal attainment. Often, outcome measures also focus on aspects that are relevant to specific program activities or goals, such as the incidence of public diseases in specific populations such as teenagers, minorities, adults with at-risk behaviors, the elderly, and perhaps those in certain geographic areas. Thus, outcomes include matters of concern to both the public interest and agency officials. Table 8.1 shows a summary of these definitions.

Relatively new strategies often include some ambiguous or divergent terminology. Some authors do not distinguish between outcomes and goals, and refer to outcomes as goals, and vice versa. There are differences among various handbooks on performance measurement (Center for Accountability and Performance 2001). When the time horizon for goal attainment in public programs is quite long (say, ten to twenty years for research, environmental restoration, or modifying of population eating habits), performance measurement might include an intermediate or midterm outcome category as well, such as outcomes attained after only a few years. The rationale is that such measures show that the program is in fact producing worthwhile results, and also that managers and policymakers are unlikely to want to wait for ten to twenty years before finding empirical evidence of likely program success. Then, the program model is restated as:

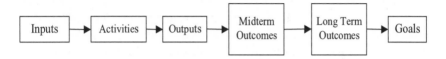

In the above example, which hopefully does not have a very long timeframe, an intermediate outcome might be changes in health behaviors. Then the logic can be stated as: increased awareness (output) → change in behavior (midterm outcome) → infection rates (long term outcome). This shows that both changes in behavior and infection rates are outcomes.

Starting with performance measurement can be overwhelming, and managers often ask for examples. However, each program is unique, and many measures are developed from scratch. There are no canned examples of performance measures that work for every program, even for those that have similar objectives. While some regulatory associations and public agencies mandate the reporting of some measures (e.g., police department have uniform reporting guidelines), these often fail to include those that citizens and others would want to know about. There is no substitute for developing one's own measures. With this in mind, here are some basic questions to get the performance measurement process going:

- By what measures would I like to see this program evaluated?
- Which measures would others likely propose be used?
- Are these measures fair and valid? Should anything be changed or added?
- Which of these measures are outcomes? Considering the program goals, should any other outcome measures be added?
- Which of the measures are outputs rather than activities? Should any additional measures of outputs or activities be added?
- How do these measures compare with those used in other, similar programs?

Answering these questions goes a long way toward getting performance measurement off on the right footing.

Further Measures

Performance measurement often involves some further measures. *Effectiveness* refers to both outcome and output measures; to talk about the effectiveness of a program is to talk about what impact it is having, and hence to specify one or more specific outcome or output measures. Insofar as formulating a five-second media sound bite is important to programs in public arenas, it is useful to think about one or two such measures as the most meaningful indicators of effectiveness. In the example of public health threats, effectiveness measures might be infection rates, the number of people reached by public information efforts, and extended hours for health care screening. These data can be readily strung together to convey the central essence of the program, though these are not the only measures that might be selected for this purpose. Using a limited set of key measures helps bring focus and clarity to programs.

Elected bodies often formulate goals, but frequently leave the "operational" matter of defining effectiveness and outcome measures in large or small extent up to appointed officials. The specific program outcomes are not always fully clear, and program managers then must take an affirmative stand about what their programs are seeking to accomplish on this matter. One strategy is to gather stakeholder input about how the program matters to them, and what they would like to see it accomplish (Holzer and Kang 2004). For example, interviews might be conducted with other managers, community leaders, and program staff, and focus groups conducted with prospective program clients or citizens. Such information helps ensure that important program purposes, stakeholder needs, and operational details are not overlooked, while at the same time ensuring documentation of the decision-making process

Efficiency is defined as the unit cost to produce goods or service. It is calculated as the ratio of outcomes or outputs to inputs (O/I), for example, the number of completed health inspections per health inspector. As there are many different outputs and outcomes that can be used as numerator, and many different measures of inputs that can be used in the denominator, it follows that efficiency measures can be calculated in many different ways. Yet, efficiency measures should be chosen wisely, as they often become a focus of management and oversight concerns. For example, the average cost of health screenings or public mailings may be an important measure affecting decisions about which agency or company should provide these services.

Using efficiency measures for comparison is seldom straightforward and devoid of at least some technical controversy. There are some variations in how efficiency is measured. In its simplest approach, total efficiency requires identifying *all* of the inputs used with producing a given service, such as salaries, overheads, materials, and estimated facility costs. Many disputes between public and private providers, such as in competitive bidding processes, center on whether the other has accurately identified all of the costs associated with providing a given service. If comparison of services is involved, then another challenge is to ensure their equivalency. For example, public services to the entire community may differ from those to selected neighborhoods or clienteles, hence leading to further controversy. These differences also affect comparisons across jurisdictions. It may not be appropriate to compare the cost of mowing grass in the deserts of Arizona to that in the swamps of Florida. Comparisons must be carefully selected for equivalency.

For the above reasons, many efficiency measures are partial measures, and are more commonly used to compare changes over time within agencies. Partial efficiency measures often consider only one source of inputs, such as direct costs or labor costs. For example, the number of health screenings per hour per medical worker is a partial efficiency measure. Such a measure tracked over time is of significant use for assessing improvement efforts within an office, but it may or may not be applicable for comparison with other types of health screenings, or even similar screenings in other settings. When inputs are measures as units of labor, such as in this example, the resulting partial measure is also called labor efficiency. It is common to calculate efficiency indices that assess the development of productivity over time. For example, if in time period 1, 50 units are produced by 60 employees, and in time period 2, 60 units are produced by 55 employees, then the productivity measures for each period are, respectively (50/60=) 0.83 and (60/55=) 1.09 units per employee. The productivity index in period 2 is (1.09/0.83=) 1.31, a significant gain in efficiency.

Although measures of partial labor efficiency are widely used, the measure of marginal efficiency bears mention as well. *Marginal efficiency* is the cost of producing an additional increment of output, for example, the cost of serving an additional client or a larger student population. Marginal efficiency often ignores costs that are essentially fixed (e.g., costs of buildings, staff support, etc.), which do not change when increasing outputs incrementally. Marginal efficiency can be useful when deciding whether or how to expand a service. Another distinction related to the valuation of inputs is the concept of *social* versus *private efficiency.* Most efficiency measures are based on private costs, that is, costs that occur from the perspective of programs of organizations, but inputs can be calculated from the perspective either of society or that of the organization. For example, from society's perspective, building and building maintenance costs should be included in efficiency measures, even when they are not paid for by an agency or program. Likewise, the use of volunteers might be regarded as a free resource for program officials, but from the perspective of society the use of volunteers requires management and oversight time that should be valued, because this time can not be used for other purposes.

Clearly, efficiency can be measured in many different ways. In most areas of public and nonprofit activity, there are few standard, agreed upon ways of measuring efficiency. Many professional organizations do not recommend or mandate the use of specific measures. Thus, organizations must often design their own measures, and in many instances, relevant measures often suggest themselves. For example, parks departments often measure the cost per acre of lawn care or mowing, and police departments often measure the cost per cleared case. Also, in the world of competing top management priorities, improvement proposals that promise efficiency as well as effectiveness gains are likely to be more favorably reviewed than those yielding only effectiveness gains. Hence, proposals for productivity improvement frequently include both effectiveness and efficiency targets. In short, managers do well to choose a few well-considered efficiency measures for their programs.

Workloads are defined as the activity levels of departments and organizations, and workload measures assess activities or strategies, such as the number of classes taught, the number of parks maintained, the number of patrols conducted, the number of fire inspections, and so on. Workloads are often related to inputs, for example, the number of classes taught per teacher, the number of full-time equivalent ground maintenance personnel used per acre of park, the number of patrols per police officer, or the number of officers per patrol. These are *workload ratios.* Although some authors refer to these measures as efficiency or productivity measures, this is technically wrong because they do not measure outcomes. Some examples of workload ratios measures in public safety are the average number of bookings per day, the number of emergency calls received per day, the number of hours spent in court per case, the number of citizen volunteer hours utilized per police unit, the number of minutes per inspection, and the time spent per suspect sketch.

Equity measures are important. Workloads and outcomes are sometimes compared across different target groups, and these measures often have political ramifications. For example, public health agencies may need to show that they serve different neighborhoods in an equal manner. Different treatment rates in minority locations may need to be explained, such as on the basis of disease prevalence. Although it is not always possible to explain equity differences, they should be noted. For example, differentials in student test scores must be explained across gender and race divisions, even though it is not always possible to explain why these differences occur.

Benchmarks are standards, rather than measures of actual performance. Benchmarks exist for outcomes as well as for workload ratios. For example,

Table 8.2

Example Performance Measures

Term	Example
Activity	Inform the public about a health threat, increase access to health care and health screenings, increase amount of research conducted, disseminate health care information to medical community
Output	Percent of population aware of health threat, number of people screened, number of people treated, potential for health care services, research results, type of treatments provided by medical community
Outcome	Incidence of public health threat, by region, demographics, etc.; change at-risk behaviors
Goal	Reduce public health threat
Effectiveness	Any selection of above output or outcome measures
Efficiency	Cost per screening, cost per research hour, cost per dissemination of 1,000 flyers, cost per information seminar
Labor efficiency	Number of completed screenings or treatments per medical worker
Workload ratio	Number of seminars per public health worker, number of patients per medical worker
Benchmark	A standard of the number of screenings, awareness in the population, incidence of at-risk behavior, etc.

a benchmark for fire serve response time is usually 3.5 minutes, and the minimum staffing for trucks and engines is about three firefighters. Standards for parks maintenance are 2.0 to 2.8 hours mowing per acre, and there are many detailed standards for tree, lawn, and weed control. Published standards must be adapted to specific, local conditions. However, for many services no benchmarks are available or published. In these instances, the term benchmark usually refers to an organization's own best practice or that of a comparable organization. Some states provided detailed benchmarks of their performance in the mid-1990s (e.g., Oregon Progress Board 1995, which continues today). Since then, the idea of comparing oneself to a class of "peer" public or nonprofit organizations or programs has gained currency, as well as "aspirant" organizations or programs, which are those that are perceived to be a step above where the organization or program currently is. Even though quantitative comparisons are sometimes problematic and fragmented, awareness of these other organizations and discussions with them often provide insight into improvement opportunities (Ammons 2001). Examples of these concepts are shown in Table 8.2.

Balanced scorecards have become popular in recent years. These provide a snapshot of the organization along important dimensions of it. Some organizations develop balanced report cards that provide a descriptive focus on the organization's financial state, customer/stakeholder satisfaction, efficiency and effectiveness of delivery processes, and activities to promote learning and improvement of the organization. Balanced scorecards provide an overall perspective on an organization or department, rather than any specific program. Balanced scorecards provide a way to compare departments within organizations, and can be used to further common foci such as customer satisfaction, reducing rework, increasing efficiency, and so on. They are driven by the agency's mission, which is used to identify key targets within each of the four areas. Balanced scorecards are now used by many public organizations, such as the Department of Energy, as well as by nonprofit organizations (Niven 2003). Their effectiveness is driven by many of the same concerns already mentioned, such as measuring the right things, measuring things in valid ways, having top leadership support, broad involvement, effective communication, and reinforcing incentives (Barkdoll and Kamensky 2005).

Beyond balanced scorecards, various report cards compare organizations with each other. For example, the Maxwell School of Citizenship and Public Affairs conducted a government performance project that compared federal, state, and local government organizations based on performance measures in areas such as financial management, human resources management, and information technology management (Government Performance Project 2003). The idea of comparing organizations across common metrics has gained increased currency and is now used in many other settings, too (Organization for Economic Cooperation and Development 2002; Coe 2003).

Implementation and Further Issues

Implementing Performance Measurement Systems

The implementation of performance measurement in organizations is usually a gradually unfolding process. Organizations often build the capacity for gathering and analyzing data, and frequently involve only a few measures. In time, new measures are added, and the ability to collect and analyze data becomes more efficient. New uses for performance measurement are found, and some measures are replaced by better ones.

Steps for implementing performance measurement follow the conditions and strategies described in chapter 3. Top leaders need to show that they are serious about performance measurement. This typically involves allocating resources for the development of performance measures in the various departments, including training and expertise, and making the use of performance measurement an expectation. Top managers also show how performance has been used to improve program performance and accountability. Often, a group of committed supporters is found for initial efforts, which are dubbed "experimental." Trust often is a concern in implementing performance measurement, as it raises fears and concerns about new standards for accountability. These fears and concerns are addressed one at a time.

At this point in time, many organizations are contemplating how to expand their current performance measurement efforts. Though initial efforts have been undertaken, further expansion and uses are sought (U.S. General Accounting Office 2001). Often, performance measurement in public organizations is implemented through their budget office and in the budgeting process. Some jurisdictions may pursue the balanced scorecard approach or any other variant that provides an aggregation of data at the department, organization, or jurisdiction-wide level; such data often already exist as part of the budgeting process. Other jurisdictions may attempt to expand the range of financial measures as proposed by the Government Accounting Standards Board, or use other program measures. This often involves investing in the IT capacity to produce these data. One variation is an emphasis on cost-based accounting, which also includes improvement in efficiency measures. Whatever directions are chosen in future years, it is likely that the conditions for successful change will play a role in ensuring their successful implementation.

As in other change efforts, proponents of performance measurement will need to show that their expenditures for more data are justified (Julnes 2004). Being "data rich but information poor" is a problem to be avoided. Managers will need to show how performance data are being used for improving their decisions, why these data are indispensable, and why the costs of acquiring these data are justifiable. This is not dissimilar from the strategic question posed in chapter 6, namely, how investments in information technology support the core businesses of organizations. Here, the question posed is how investments in performance measurement support the core management purposes of managers. What are managers trying to accomplish for the organization? How does performance measurement aid them? It is useful to revisit the purposes stated at the beginning of this chapter. The development of performance measurement will go faster as managers find new purposes for these data.

Perhaps the ultimate vision for performance measurement is a real-time, comprehensive system that provides managers with information about what their departments are doing, what results are being produced, and what resources are being used to that end. Such information allows managers to make many decisions, and increases their ability to monitor what is going on. This vision is not yet reality at this writing, but some organizations are making strides. One barrier, however, is yet to be overcome in many jurisdictions, namely, the ability to gather valid and timely customer or citizen feedback data. This is discussed below.

Data Sources

Performance measurement requires the collection of data. The remaining part of this chapter discusses some practical issues pertaining to the availability and quality of data.

Administrative Records. Organizations frequently produce a plethora of information in the course of managing programs. Administrative data includes information on (1) staffing levels and qualifications, (2) budgets (program, indirect costs, etc.), (3) level of services provided, (4) maintenance, repair, and other activities, and (5) complaints, requests, and compliments. In addition, data from client files may provide information on (6) client backgrounds, needs, and utilization of services. For example, to know what the most common problem is in parks, managers can examine supervisory and inspection reports about park maintenance. In these reports, managers can examine events (e.g., broken benches), as well words and phrases (e.g., things vandalized). Such events can also be examined over time or across different neighborhoods.

It is obvious that performance measurement is greatly aided by the use of information technology. The electronic recording of these data aids in the tabulation of performance information. When the data are entered in real-time, and easily extracted, then weekly or monthly performance reporting becomes possible. In recent years, several companies have developed software for performance measurement; one can readily envision employees or supervisors entering performance data into such software programs, which are integrated with budgeting and other software, and having such data later analyzed by supervisors, managers, and others. These data can also be entered from hand-held devices by employees in the field, which is useful for regulatory inspectors or social services personnel, and which is already being done by many law enforcement agencies.

Administrative data most frequently concerns workload measures and workload ratios; they are often based on traditional management control systems to ensure that people show up, that jobs get done, and that monies are accounted for. For example, workload data are frequently available from work logs and other administrative records (e.g., billing). These data are also readily transformed into workload ratios, for example, caseloads per worker. If standards exist for workloads, then such data are useful to determine whether these standards are being met. Although administrative data seldom capture the full range of outputs that managers and others might be interested in, these data often can be increased to do so. For example, administrative data might capture the number of inspections, but not those that are successfully concluded. Inspectors can be asked to provide this information, too. Administrative data might capture the number of awareness seminars provided by public health officials, but not the number of people who attended, or their satisfaction with the seminar. With some additional effort, these data can be captured, too. In short, managers usually need to decide what information they need, and then ensure that it is captured.

Using administrative data for performance measurement also highlights some quality problems with these data. Such problems often are less pertinent to traditional uses than when used for performance measurement. Problems include: (1) missing or incomplete data; (2) data that are available only in highly aggregated form; (3) data definitions that have changed over time and cannot be compared; (4) data that cannot be linked to particular events or clients; (5) data that are confidential; and (6) data that are inaccurate. The extent of these problems varies, of course; performance measurement often includes efforts to ensure that data are as accurate, reliable, and valid as possible. Administrative data seldom includes much outcome data. For example, the incidence of infectious disease is typically compiled from other sources such as hospital or Centers for Disease Control reports. Transportation departments may or may not track the use of bicyclists on their bicycle lanes and trails. Outcome measures typically require data from other sources, and perhaps even additional data collection activities, such as surveys.

Surveys. Surveys are used to obtain information about citizen needs and client satisfaction in public and nonprofit organizations (e.g., Tetrault 2004). Heightened interest in citizen and client perceptions of the quality of services is clearly the legacy of TQM, in which such perceptions are viewed as important measures of service quality. While the idea of using surveys for obtaining citizen feedback goes back to the early 1970s and before (e.g., Webb and Hatry 1973), the challenge continues to be obtaining such information in sufficiently valid, timely, and affordable ways. While the purpose here is not to provide a primer on surveys (see, e.g., Miller and Kobayashi 2000), some pertinent observations can be made.

First, asking questions in biased ways reduces credibility and is to be avoided; many people are familiar with the problem of biased questions, which are now readily detected. (Table 8.3 provides some examples of bi-

Table 8.3

Problems in Survey Questions

Sample survey questions

Questions should be clear

Question: "What do you think of recycling?"

Problem: The verb "thinking" is unclear.

Better: "Do you believe that your community should increase or decrease its household recycling efforts, or that its current level of recycling efforts should stay the same?"

Questions should avoid double-barreled responses

Question: "Please state your level of agreement with the following statement: the city should turn garbage collection over to the private sector and spend the savings from that on keeping the streets cleaner."

Problem: These are two questions, namely, about privatization and spending.

Better: Ask questions separately.

Questions should be relevant

Question: "Should the city increase funding for the midnight basketball program?"

Problem: Most respondents are unlikely to possess requisite information to respond.

Better: Ask respondents whether gang activities are a problem.

Questions should avoid biasing words

Question: "To what extent do you approve of welfare programs?"

Problem: "Welfare" has negative connotations.

Better: "To what extent do you approve of providing assistance to the poor?"

Questions should avoid negatives

Question: "Please state your level of agreement with the following statement: the United States should not recognize Cuba."

Problem: Some respondents will read over "not." This will cause confusion.

Better: "Please state your level of agreement with the following statement: the United States should recognize Cuba."

ased questions.) Experienced survey researchers avoid this problem by asking questions as unbiased, short statements, and requiring responses on a balanced, closed-ended scale. For example, a person might be provided with a statement such as "The inspection was conducted in a professional manner," to which a respondent is asked to reply with strongly agree, agree, disagree, strongly disagree, or don't know. This is but one example. The format of many survey questions is that of a series of short, concise statements with consistent, closed-ended responses that lend themselves to asking many questions in a short timeframe.

Second, the far greater problem is obtaining a reasonably representative sample of program clients or citizens. A sample based on clients who greatly favor a program or policy is not going to provide a valid measure of customer satisfaction, of course. Voluntary surveys such as customer comment cards that are found on counters are invalid; they typically reflect those with strong positive or negative opinions, and are seldom generalizable to all program clients. This is also why the testimony of those who show up in public meetings is considered to be not generalizable. Further, a very low response rate for a survey also creates doubt; if only 2 percent respond to a survey, it is clear that even minor differences of opinion among the 98 percent who did not respond would greatly alter the results. This is why mass mailings such as inserts that are part of utility bills are considered invalid; the response rate is very low.

Agreement exists that the best way to sample is to randomly select a relatively small sample from among a group of program clients or citizens, and to seek the highest possible response rate from that sample. Citizen surveys usually produce between 200 and 800 completed responses. Because response rates in phone surveys are reported at about 15 to 35 percent, samples of about 800 to 6,000 potential respondents are required. Inaccuracies in sampling lists, such as invalid phone numbers and ineligible respondents, require these lists to be even larger. The effort to conduct citizen surveys is thus considerable; moderately sized survey projects often entail about 15,000 to 40,000 phone calls, as some numbers are dialed and contacted many times. Surveys are therefore somewhat expensive; at present, the cost per completed phone interview is about $25 to $50. By asking questions as a series of statements, phone surveys are able to gather an extensive amount of information. Some surveys consist of 35 to 70 statements, and some include open-ended responses, as well, which are captured with support of voice recognition software. Mail surveys are somewhat cheaper, but the need for multiple mailings makes data collection a lengthy process.

It is unclear how this situation can be changed. The ultimate solution may well be the development of geographic lists of e-mail addresses, similar to traditional phonebooks. Perhaps cities or counties at some future time will request this information from all residents, or those that use certain services. As more and more people have e-mail addresses, the biases in such lists will become manageable. Performance measurement is about developing useful information, not perfect information. Also, if biases can be known, supplemental sampling by phone could be used.

Another problem is that managers may not have a list of program clients. When a sufficiently large percentage of the population is familiar with a program or service, then questions about that service can be asked as part of a general citizen survey. But when services are used by only a small part of the population, such as walk-in clinics, then a different strategy is needed.

In this instance, random days and times should be selected throughout the year, and a random sample of (or possibly all) users surveyed during these periods. This will typically involve on-the-spot surveying of clients.

Focus Groups. The purpose of focus groups is to generate a better understanding of program or client needs. While they do not provide information that is representative, focus groups do provide information about the range of concerns about which information should be collected. Thus, they are usually done prior to conducting surveys. Focus groups involve semi-structured, in-depth, group discussions; this technique was pioneered by companies in their marketing efforts. It is generally recommended that focus groups are homogenous, that is, that group members are selected from the same target group. This is because different target groups are likely to have different experiences, needs, and views. Different populations may also inhibit and drown each other out.

A typical use of focus groups is the following. A parks program operates and maintains park grounds and provides a full range of services and programs for park users. Services and programs include various sports events, educational programs, and collaboration with the local human services department that sponsors self-help and social services in the park grounds. The parks program wants to better understand how the neighborhood community utilizes its activities, which activities should be discontinued, and which should be increased. Because this is an exploratory question, the parks program decided to use focus groups. A generalizable neighborhood survey or needs assessment might be used later. Some typical questions that might be asked of focus group members are:

- Which services did you use? Why?
- How satisfied are you with these services? Specifically, how do these services help to meet your needs?
- Do you have any suggestions for further improvement?
- Which services would you like to see added? Here are some new activities that have been recently suggested: Are there any that you would use? Why or why not?
- The park has certain regulations. We would like to know which you are familiar with.
- Did you have any contact with park officials while visiting the park? If so, which ones? What happened when you approached them? Did you get the information or service you requested? Were officials friendly?

Moderators should be impartial and assist focus group members to fully explore all matters that they have agreed to. Thus, moderators often need to steer discussions back to original agendas; focus groups are not meandering conversations. Moderators are usually assisted by a note-taker, who records comments of participants.

Other Approaches. Experts are used when objective, factual data are insufficient to make judgments about program outcomes and activities, or when the assessment of such data requires the judgment of experts. Some examples in which expert judgment might be used are the maintenance of landfills, analysis of medical records (e.g., treatment of patients), the quality of a higher-education program, and the use of management techniques. Experts should only be used when it is likely that their recommendations will be acted on. A criterion for accepting expert judgment is that it is shared by other experts, therefore program evaluation always uses a range (or panel) of experts. Typically, no less than three experts are consulted.

Trained observers are used to evaluate the condition of facilities (e.g., parks, public restrooms, public housing, nursing homes, beach maintenance, street cleanliness, and so on), as well as events (pickpockets, unauthorized ticket sales, etc.). Trained observers provide unobtrusive observation. The steps in undertaking trained observations are (1) deciding what is to be observed (e.g., street cleanliness); (2) deciding the dimensions of that which is to be observed (working order, paint, weeds, repair, etc.); (3) developing a standardized rating scale. (Usually, only three or four levels are used: for example, something is no problem, a limited problem, or a widespread problem, with each carefully defined.); (4) training and supervision of raters (trainee and trainers should agree 90 percent of the time; (5) performing rating; and (6) using random resampling to determine the accuracy of ratings.

Role-playing is a form of observer-based rating whereby observers pose as clients. Such observers are usually unknown to employees, although many do identify such "ghost" clients. The use of observers allows for spot-checks of service quality. Sometimes, actors are matched with regard to race, gender, or age in order to observe patterns of differential treatment. An example of matched role-playing is the use of minority actors who pose as homebuyers. This is done to detect discrimination in home buying or real estate services by comparing services provided to majority and minority clients. Matched role-playing is also used to detect bias in job hiring.

Role-playing involves several considerations. First, the transactions to be sampled must be clearly determined. Second, the number of cases must be decided upon. Fifteen is usually sufficient to bring about legal action, but larger samples are needed to substantiate incidences of discrimination. Third, the training and practice of observers must be carefully monitored: all actors should act consistently.

In Conclusion

This chapter examined the use of performance measurement, which has gained increased acceptance and is now increasingly common. Performance measurement is used to determine levels of activity, outputs, and outcomes. These measures, in turn, are used to develop measures of effectiveness, efficiency, and workloads. This chapter also discussed benchmarking and the use of balanced scorecards. Performance measurement is poised for further development, aided by information technology applications. This chapter also discussed a variety of data collection approaches for performance measurement, including administrative records, surveys, focus groups, and the use of experts and raters. A problem continues to be the development of citizen-based outcome information through surveys, which continue to be costly at this time. Performance measurement requires careful attention to the purposes to which it is put.

Application Exercises

1. Develop performance measures for a program of your choice. Develop measures of (1) activities, (2) outputs, (3) outcomes, and (4) efficiency. Be sure to state the program goals, and consider the questions posed in this chapter to get the performance measurement effort going.
2. Identify sources for collecting the above data. Is it easy or difficult to gather such information?
3. Consider some different purposes for using these data. Which purposes are most important for you? How does the purpose affect the choice of performance measure?
4. Examine a range of published output measures, and debate whether they are really accomplishments rather than activities.
5. Surf the Internet for examples of performance measurement. Note how many are associated with budgeting. Also, visit the home page of the Government Accounting Standards Board (GASB). Finally, examine which companies offer consulting services in performance measurement for public and nonprofit organizations, and examine what they offer.
6. Surf the Internet for examples of balanced scorecards. Also, examine other types of report cards such as the Government Performance Project, the World Bank Governance Indicators, or any of the many examples of community indicators in different parts of the country or in your state.

9

Rethinking the Organization

The early part of the twenty-first century is seeing new, evolving thinking about organizational innovation and uses of organizational forms. All organizations must change over time, as circumstances and needs change. The previous chapters highlighted how demands for cost-effective and customer-oriented services led to making work processes more efficient and effective in the 1990s. But other circumstances to which organizations must respond are regional and other problems that may lie beyond the abilities or scope of existing public-sector organizations. Another feature is that today many capable private sector organizations exist that can provide alternatives to public sector provision of services. Indeed, organizations can choose to rely on other organizations for implementing their policies and providing services, rather than doing that themselves. They can also choose to work together in making policies and providing services. New organizations can also be created to deal with specific problems such as transportation or the environment. It is time to rethink how society organizes itself for the various tasks that it faces.

This chapter looks at four performance improvement strategies that rethink the nature of organization: privatization, partnering, realignment, and the use of special districts and authorities. Privatization is the contracting out of policy implementation and service delivery to private organizations. Doing so allows organizations to avoid responsibility for producing services while enjoying the benefits of reasonably low costs through increased competition among providers. Partnerships (also called coalitions, alliances, or networks) bring organizations together in new ways. Many modern problems of safety, education, and development require such collaboration. Partnerships can be very effective, but they also require considerable management.

Realignment (also called reorganization or restructuring) helps organizations to refocus their resources and efforts. This is also part of bringing new

Table 9.1

Organizational Choices		*Structure*	
		Temporary/Fluid	Permanent
Responsibility for task	Within an existing organization	Privatization, Ad-hoc Arrangements	Realignment
	Not within an existing organization	Partnerships & Coalitions	Special Districts & Authorities

missions into reality. Realignment helps streamline activities and reduce costs by shedding old functions, reducing the number of departments, and eliminating middle management positions. Special districts and authorities are also increasingly used, to address problems of transportation, environmental management, and economic development in innovative ways. They are created to bring resolution to problems that individual organizations or jurisdictions cannot adequately address.

Clearly, today's managers face a range of organizational options. The strategies serve different purposes, and organizations do well to take full advantage of these alternative forms. Managers are increasingly adept at using these strategies in creative ways. However, the range of options can appear overwhelming and a bit disjointed. Current theoretical thinking about these choices is indeed ill-developed. Table 9.1 shows how these choices are related to each other, and the conditions under which they might be considered. Two key conditions are (1) whether responsibility for a new activity can rest with an existing organization or requires something outside it, and (2) whether the structure for providing the activity is intended to be enduring (and therefore institutional) or more temporary and fluid in nature.

For example, realignment and the creation of special districts or authorities are usually intended as permanent solutions; they provide or reshape stable, institutional structures under which activities occur. By contrast, privatization contracts, partnerships, and coalitions are usually quite fluid. They sometimes are time-limited—by the duration of a problem, rebid dates on contracts, or heightened risk of governance or management failure—and their tasks, if carried out successfully, are sometimes absorbed by the permanent organization. This is not to say that all partnerships are short-lived; some exist for several decades (some problems are enduring and partnerships well-managed). Nor are realignments necessarily long-lived; but the intent to have fluid or more permanent decisions at the beginning of the process is clear. Table 9.1 also shows "ad-hoc structures" as a way of organizing for temporary activities. These include temporary committees or working groups that often are used for short-term purposes. While these are not discussed here, they are a staple of management.

Some partnerships and coalitions involve a few organizations, whereas others involve many at different levels, such as for Homeland Security or those involving the United Way. It should be noted that some privatization contracts are called "partnerships," and some partnerships are in fact organizations (e.g., membership associations). Such usage requires that managers look beyond the terminology in use, and focus on their actual intents and purposes.

Thinking about organization inevitably raises broad, fundamental questions. What is an organization? By what criteria can organizational effectiveness be assessed? Organizations are structures for bringing people, resources, and technology together for the purposes of achieving goals and objectives. The main purposes of organizations are to (1) focus the people, resources, and technology on the mission, (2) provide a management and governance structure for directing and controlling those activities, (3) help maintain and develop capabilities and expertise essential to the mission, and (4) provide a structure for responding to unforeseen challenges and needs as they arise. Different circumstances and needs may lead managers to adopt different organizational forms, but all can be assessed by how well they achieve these fundamental purposes of organization. As these criteria show, we should not try to evaluate organizational forms based only on the extent that they efficiently and effectively assist in accomplishing mission objectives. While these are important criteria, so, too, are matters of governance: Who participates in making which decisions, and with what measure of accountability, are also important matters.

The strategies that are discussed here help address many problems noted in chapter 2. Generally, as regarding implementation, they may increase the effectiveness or efficiency of service delivery (Problem 7). The use of partnerships may also improve coordination (Problem 8), though working with additional organizations also increases the challenge of coordination. Many of these strategies also affect decision making, and thus may help better meet the needs of target groups (Problem 1), ensure that the agency mission is relevant to society's needs (Problem 5), and that the mission is being pursued (Problem 6).

Partnerships

The term "partnership" is often used with a variety of different meanings. Some authors use it philosophically or ideologically to refer to the *roles* of different sectors of society. For example, some refer to the partnership between nonprofit organizations and the federal government in providing for the poor. This is a tacit understanding among leaders about shared responsibilities, specifically, that the federal government provides funding for services provided by charitable organizations. This understanding, or set of values, shapes policy decisions about the delivery of social services and the relationship among sectors.

By contrast, other authors use the term narrowly to refer to *a family of contractual arrangements that involve joint responsibilities for decision making and implementation.* This chapter adopts this latter definition. Typical examples are partnerships among government and nonprofit organizations to create collective food banks, partnerships among local governments to protect area wildlife and its environment, and collaborations among nonprofit organizations to promote their services. Partnerships are very common; they are a mature and well-diffused improvement strategy that is used by many organizations (Berman and West 1998). Some partnerships are established as tax-exempt, nonprofit organizations. In each instance, decision making and implementation is collective in some aspects. Partnerships require considerable forethought about the roles of each partner. By contrast, contracting for services, subsidization, and privatization are usually not considered partnerships, because they involve very little joint decision making. However, a tendency exists to expand joint decision making in these areas as this results in better outcomes.

Through partnerships, organizations extend their capabilities and build mechanisms for joint decision making and cooperation. Partnerships are consistent with building network organizations, that is, organizations that are connected by serving a common purpose. Network organizations are attractive because they require relatively few investments or new organizations, and are built on the largely existing capabilities of members. The downside is that the governance of networks can be complex and that individual organizations have limited control over decisions, which some may desire. The duration of networks can be unstable, and there is thus uncertainty about future capabilities (Hudson 2004; Teisman and Klijn 2002; Shaw 2003; Mulroy 2003; Stephen Osborne 2000).

Purposes of Partnerships

Partnerships fulfill different purposes. Some of the most common purposes involve: (1) coordination, (2) policy formulation, (3) funding, and (4) joint service delivery. Many partnerships involve multiple purposes, although some focus on a single purpose. Some partnerships involve only public or private organizations, whereas others involve public and private organizations.

Coordination. Many public and nonprofit organizations engage in local coalitions, networks, forums, and similar organizations that provide members with a means to coordinate their services. For example, local hospitals have teamed up with schools, churches, and nonprofit providers to ensure that populations such as pregnant women and infants receive necessary services. Health insurers and federal programs are eager to provide these services, which prevent more costly services later. Homelessness services are a particularly good example of the need for coordination, because homeless populations are very diverse—involving mentally disabled adults, female-headed families, substance abusers, handicapped persons, and so on—which require comprehensive services that involve health, employment, and housing. Local homelessness coalitions of public and private providers are increasingly common, which provide coordination for food supplies, emergency shelter needs (blankets, sleeping cots, food, and water), primary health care services (including diagnosis of tuberculosis, AIDS/HIV), legal aid, long-term health care (assisted living programs, medical and mental health rehabilitation, family counseling), supplemental income assistance, affordable housing programs, drug and alcohol treatment programs, and so on (Bridgman 2003; Berman 1996). Other examples include coalitions that provide for common needs. For example, the Florida Respite Coalition provides families and caregivers with a single point of entry within their communities to access support and information for respite care services across the lifespan. Community groups also use partnerships to coordinate their activities and interests (e.g., Nicholls 2003), and recently jurisdictions have coordinated their regional emergency preparedness efforts to ensure effective responses to crisis incidents and smooth population evacuations. Education systems typically need substantial coordination with local governments, public safety, recreation, and nonprofit organizations to meet the educational needs of students.

Coordination helps organizations to collectively provide more comprehensive services without increasing their expenditures or diluting their areas of expertise. To succeed, coordination partnerships such as coalitions and networks often require one or more committed leaders who can maintain the informal, voluntary nature of coordination. These leaders must be able to resist efforts by individual members to engage in policy making that would force upon organizations decisions that they are unwilling to accept, or decision-making authority that they are unwilling to transfer to those outside their organization. Such actions are divisive and often lead to distrust and animosity among organizations. Leaders of networks must maintain the raison d'etre of coordination and engage in collective decision making that prevents individual members from either abandoning the partnership or forcing their views upon it.

Policy making. Some partnerships are designed to engage in collective decision making among organizations. Sometimes the purpose of these partnerships is also to influence public opinion. The areas of such partnership are often those of the "common good," such as environmental, planning, or technology development issues. Such partnerships vary considerably in the degree to which decision-making responsibility is delegated from individual organizations to partnerships. For example, local governments around the Tampa Bay, Florida, area formed a partnership whose purpose is to set policy for protecting wildlife and estuaries. Such planning bodies usually have advisory status and decisions require ratification by individual members. Consensus often is difficult to reach but can be facilitated by incentives of federal funding or benefits from collective actions. By contrast, partnerships that engage in implementation are frequently delegated considerable policymaking responsibilities. For example, some years ago a public–private partnership was created for developing advanced semiconductor manufacturing technology. Because its members had been struggling to develop state-of-the-art semiconductor manufacturing technology, broad discretion was given to the consortium for defining appropriate technology projects. Similarly, consortia and partnerships have been formed in recent years to develop new space, automotive, and health technologies (e.g., Simmons 2003).

Joint Service Delivery. Some partnerships provide joint services. For example, the Department of Energy (DOE) is developing new technologies in collaboration with private companies for cleaning up the DOE's contaminated sites. Both public and private organizations participate in the hope of developing technologies that can be used in other areas as well. They not only coordinate their activities, but work together in the delivery of services. Partnerships are also created between law enforcement agencies and neighborhood associations to increase monitoring. Law enforcement personnel frequently assist neighborhood activists and business owners in organizing efforts to better protect their property and increase public safety.

Many orchestras team up with large corporations to promote their concert series, as well as to increase the community involvement of both organizations. For example, some years ago EDS Corp. teamed up with the Detroit Symphony Orchestra (DSO). EDS not only sponsored the advertising of the DSO, but also provided it with full range of information technology and support for fund-raising, financial management, and marketing services. Arts organizations also team up with neighborhood organizations to increase their exposure into neighborhoods, as well as increase access by residents to art. American Express undertook a major advertising campaign whereby it donated five cents to nonprofit organizations every time one of their members used their American Express credit card. The campaign provided funding for nonprofit organizations and increased use of the card. Such co-marketing arrangements are now increasingly common.

Funding. Other partnerships are financially oriented. These are often found in economic development and housing. In these areas, public and private organizations join together to finance activity that neither can separately afford. In many cities, affordable housing involves financial partnerships of local developers, banks, and local, state, and federal agencies. In these partnerships, local governments often borrow money (through bonds) to undertake infrastructure improvements, which is repaid through higher taxes. They also provide tax incentives for businesses such as supermarkets to locate in these areas. State and federal governments provide subsidies to enable affordable housing. Local developers borrow money to build the houses, which is repaid when the homes are sold or through property management. Such funding collaboration can be quite complex and requires considerable trust and persistence. Some of these partnerships involve special authorities, discussed further.

In recent years, nonprofit organizations are also playing an important intermediary role in financing the acquisition of land for conservation. These are private lands of great natural value that are acquired by federal and state governments for protection. The problem is that state agencies are often slow to react to opportunities for acquisition. These opportunities occur for different reasons, such as the death or bankruptcy of landowners. In these instances, nonprofit organizations such as the Nature Conservancy and the Trust for Public Land provide seed money or bridge loans that enable public agencies to buy the land for conservation.

The list of purposes served by coordination is large and growing, and many agencies are increasing their coordination partnerships. Managers with entrepreneurial instincts have found this a rich approach in recent years for developing and leading new initiatives. It is easy to see opportunities for new partnerships. As experience with coordination increases, the cadre of managers who are effective partnership managers is increasing, and common practices are slowly but surely coming into existence.

Making Partnerships Work

Each partnership is different and unique. Yet, histories of partnerships suggest the following characteristics that make partnerships successful. By and large, many of these are consistent with t he five conditions for change mentioned earlier in chapter 3.

Create Win-Win Situations. Successful partnerships create win-win situations for its members. As voluntary associations, they would otherwise not form. However, partnerships are seldom the only vehicle for organizations to satisfy their needs, and it is important that the extent to which individual needs are satisfied is sufficient. Members must be willing to continue the partnership after it is formed and in place. There must be a sense of parity and flexibility to ensure that benefits are fair, proportional to the effort that individual members put into partnership efforts, and continuously relevant to the missions of organizations. Thus, the win-win strategies that are articulated must be periodically revisited and updated, and members must be sensitive and willing to accommodate the changing needs of organizations. Successful partnerships often plan for ongoing negotiation.

Significant Interest. Partnerships work best when all parties have a significant commitment to their success. They cannot be an afterthought. For example, the DOE routinely negotiates partnerships for the commercial development of its technology, which includes microelectronics, software, and materials research. Such negotiations often involve important legal matters of royalties and liabilities. However, when these contracts were first introduced, DOE lawyers did not view them as very important and therefore they did not receive high priority. Until this was changed, their lack of interest caused delays that reduced the interest of firms. Partnerships often work best when they are perceived as central to the mission of all parties. There must be significant interest on all sides. When some partners do not have much commitment, enthusiasm eventually wanes and the commitment to maintaining win-win situations diminishes.

Anticipate Change. Partnerships are often formed to deal with sudden changes in the environment. For example, health care coalitions often respond to sudden public health changes, such as rises in teenage pregnancy, infectious diseases, and malnutrition. Uncertainty in the environment affects ongoing partnerships, as well. Successful partnerships anticipate environmental contingencies and they develop plans for how this will affect the partnership. In the above example, health care partnerships often plan for further increases in community need, new grant programs for which its members might apply, mergers and changes in its membership, and scarcity or sudden increases in the cost of treatment. The ability to cope with change is a characteristic of successful partnerships. Although partnerships are open-ended, some partnerships plan for their demise when the conditions that give rise to them cease to exist.

Develop and Maintain Clear Roles and Responsibilities. Partnerships build on the diversity of strengths of its members: Different members bring different abilities to partnerships. Well-functioning partnerships require that partners fulfill their commitments. Members must be clear about each other's roles and responsibilities, and establish clear procedures for both formal and informal communication. Timetables, staffing, funding, and liabilities are typically important issues. Staffing involves a considerable commitment on the part of partners, and members are sometimes concerned that other organizations will not commit their best people or that they do not have access to decision makers within their organizations. Liabilities are also an important concern. For example, in technology partnerships, a common clause is that members are individually responsible for any litigation that results from the use of technology developed by partnerships; the absence of such a clause would make the risk to other partners unacceptable. Similar issues occur in financial partnerships. Members must be indemnified from the risk that other partners default on their obligations. Such issues must be identified and resolved.

Skilled Leadership. Successful partnerships have leaders who are skilled in negotiating, compromising, and above all, accomplishing. Leaders know how to balance different interests while maintaining the commitment of partners. Leaders emphasize the importance of building trusting relations among members. This is especially important when members have a history of rivalry or antagonistic relations. For example, leaders of nonprofit organizations sometimes have competitive relations with each other that results from competition for grants, funding, or membership. Such feelings of suspicion must be overcome, at least for the purpose of obtaining the goals that are set for the partnership.

Successful partnerships often involve organizations that have a past history of successful participation in partnerships. Such organizations are familiar with the processes and items of negotiation, and they have a clear view of what is possible and how much effort is involved in making partnerships work. They are especially attuned to the reality of different styles and cultures of organizations. Private leaders know that government organizations have lengthy approval processes and they allow more time for obtaining the commitment and participation of public organizations. They may even have to lobby for their participation to elected officials. Private leaders of small, collaborative nonprofit organizations know that larger organizations have a more bureaucratic culture, and that for-profit organizations are strongly attuned to the bottom line. Leadership is needed to bridge these differences and to create mutual understanding and commitment to the shared purposes of partnerships. Table 9.2 shows some additional considerations for managing the negotiation of partnerships.

Table 9.2

Managing Negotiations

Establishing partnerships involves negotiation. Negotiations must be constructive, geared toward creating a mutually satisfying partnership. They must neither be hard and antagonistic, as if negotiating with an adversary, nor overly soft and compromising, which may cause one's own goals to be inadequately accomplished.

1. Prepare
   Organizations sometimes fail to prepare adequately for negotiating partnerships. Organizations must know what they want from the proposed partnership, and identify concerns that they wish to negotiate. Arguments must be developed that are likely to be persuasive to others. They must do some background investigation on other organizations, and anticipate goals and conditions that other organizations may be seeking, as well as conditions that may cause other organizations to forgo seeking a partnership. Developing a "best alternative solution" also strengthens the negotiation position, and protects organizations from getting involved in activities that have too little return.

2. Set Deadlines and Timetables
   The purpose of partnerships is accomplishment, and it is a particularly bad indication when negotiations drag on. To ensure expediency, organizations should agree on a timetable for completing their negotiations.

3. Develop Trust
   A purpose of negotiation is to build a healthy relationship for subsequent joint activities. Negotiations often start in the absence of trust. There are many things that managers can do to get relations off to a good start. Volunteering to do paperwork and organizing meetings are ways of showing commitment and demonstrating dependability. Being understanding about the needs of other organizations and working toward satisfying these needs also builds trust. Relationships are also furthered by being accepting of people, even when there is disagreement with their position on issues.

4. Focus on Areas of Agreement
   Partnerships are built on foundations of agreement, not disagreement. Managers must create a climate for exploring options of mutual gain. Criteria should be agreed upon to evaluate the success of joint efforts. Goals are emphasized so that they can inspire action. In the process of finding areas of agreement, managers maintain a climate of openness in which members feel free to pursue whatever issues they might have.

5. Handle Disagreements Tactfully
   The tone and style with which disagreements are dealt can determine the outcome of negotiations. An important strategy is to respond to positions by identifying interests. It is important to be able to see such interests from someone else's perspective. This helps to avoid the hardening of mutually exclusive positions. When people disagree on positions, communication stops, coalitions build, perceptions are distorted, and the climate of cooperation rapidly deteriorates. However, when negotiators focus on interests that are served by positions, it may be possible to identify alternative solutions that serve such interests equally well or better.

6. Summarize Agreements and Move Forward
   During negotiations a variety of different problems and solutions are bantered around. Frequent summaries help keep people on the same page and moving in the same direction. It is also an opportunity to identify any new uncertainties and misunderstandings. Agreements help keep the process moving forward, and are useful in dealing with obstacles that may lie ahead.

Special Districts and Authorities

Special districts and authorities are public organizations that operate with substantial autonomy. They are commonly created to deal with such tasks as water and flood management, natural resources management and conservation, road development (e.g., toll roads), airports and harbors, public health (including hospitals), fire protection, economic and community development, parks and recreation, mass transit, libraries, and education. Unlike partnerships, these are intended as enduring entities. The distinction between special districts and authorities is largely legal; in special districts, oversight and regulation are provided by their governing boards, whereas authorities are subject to some oversight and regulation by another, independent government. In practice, both enjoy substantial independence in their policy making and implementation. State governments often provide the legislation that enables their creation.

The existence of these entities is not new, but the public sector is increasingly making more creative use of them. The number of special districts increased from 21,200 in 1967 to about 35,300 in 2002. By contrast, the number of municipalities and townships remained constant during this period, at about 35,000. Many special districts are quite small; only 1,400 are classified by the U.S. Census Department as having revenues greater than $10 million, or debts greater than $20 million; these organizations represent about 88 percent of outstanding debts, and 82 percent of them have more than seventy-five employees (U.S. Census Bureau 1997, 2002). So, some special districts are large, but most are quite small.

Special districts and authorities allow public organizations to create new entities to provide a service that they themselves may be reluctant or unable to undertake. Typically, special districts and authorities obtain revenues from user fees, bonds, or special purposes taxes that are collected through local tax bills. Sometimes states agencies, aided by local jurisdictions or federal grants, provide start-up funding that helps these districts to begin operations and develop essential infrastructure. As one example, the Orlando-Orange County Expressway Authority was created by the State of Florida to develop a toll-based transportation network for that region. Tolls are used as the revenue-generating mechanism that allows this authority to borrow money through bonds and thereby expand and maintain this infrastructure. The road structure encompasses several counties. Without this authority, it is unlikely that the counties could have joined together to collectively finance and manage this road system; the federal government no longer funds major beltway and highway projects, and it is questionable whether such a large debt (about $1 billion) and investment would have been feasible in state politics, competing against other major regions. Water management districts often operate in a similar way, drawing revenues from water and sewer fees in order to finance bonds from which further infrastructure investments are made. Airport authorities also use fees and taxes to finance their bonds and operations.

A rather different example is provided by improvement districts, which are used to promote, for example, business development in urban and downtown areas. Additional taxes or fees are collected at the local level, within the improvement district, and turned over to the board of an improvement district, which dispenses these funds in ways that it sees fit as consistent with its mission to improve some area. Improvements are made in public safety, marketing, beautification, parking and transit, and redevelopment of blighted properties, for example. Such boards may consist of public and private leaders, such as merchants who pay additional taxes or fees that go to the improvement districts (Mitchell 2001). There are many economic and neighborhood redevelopment examples that use these structures successfully. This also shows that activities need not involve costly infrastructure or development efforts; they can focus on service provision, too.

It does not take much imagination to envision such structures for resolving a host of regional and other problems that beset many areas. The structure has been readily adapted to deal with regional problems of the environment, public health, and economic development. It is interesting to speculate how they might be used for other purposes, such as education, arts, crime, and drugs, and fostering healthy lifestyles and well-being. The seemingly "absurd" idea of today is easily the hot ticket of tomorrow when pursued by managers and leaders who have vision and ability. Indeed, it may well be argued that the attractiveness and development of regions is in large measure a function of their ability to address their cross-cutting jurisdictional challenges, and to put in place new organizations and infrastructures that promote the development of their regions in unique and innovative ways.

Special districts and authorities have been an underresearched topic that is getting new consideration. Very little is known about their performance. Certainly, there are many examples of highly effective organizations. Anecdotally, those that are successful tend to be very professionally managed, embracing many state-of-the-art concepts and leading their regions by adopting innovative visions. Also, little is known about the factors that cause them to come into existence. Why are some regions more reluctant to use them than others? Do the five conditions of change apply here, too? It may be that the feasibility of identifying and implementing new "ripe apples" using special districts and authorities has not yet been sufficiently argued by community leaders; the idea is as yet at the initial stages, and the critical mass of leadership is yet to be created. Certainly, the urgency of many unresolved regional and community problems persists.

One concern, however, is with limited trust. These organizations are not subject to the accountability of popular electoral politics, though a recent study of large special districts shows that most do use a variety of methods to ensure accountability and many are well managed (Beitsch 2005). Some existing agencies and community leaders fear additional, competing organizations. Board appointments vary in their balance of political favoritism, community diversity, and the representation of relevant interests. Such concerns are typical of new innovations; "reservations" often are worked out only in the face of successful practices elsewhere that become models for others. It seems probable that in future years public managers will find increasingly innovative ways to adopt special districts and authorities for dealing with pressing problems that existing organizations and partnerships have been unable to resolve. Somewhere, some visionary leader will soon find new innovative uses for this old and growing tool.

Privatization

In recent years, privatization and contracting have received renewed interest as tools of productivity improvement. Neither privatization nor contracting involves much joint decision making and implementation, and neither is considered a partnership. Both privatization and contracting help organizations to reduce costs and improve their services by requiring them to compete.

The original purpose of privatization was to reduce of the role of government. During the 1980s, the Reagan administration used privatization to reduce federal regulation of airlines, banking, and other industries, as well as increase support charitable organizations that provided social services. These efforts aimed to increase efficiency, but they seldom produced the gains that were hoped for. For example, banking deregulation led to uncontrolled risk-taking and resulted in costly public bailouts of failed savings and loan institutions. Reducing welfare funding for nonprofit social service organization increased the number of homeless persons and families; private giving did not sufficiently pick up the slack. Although these ideological approaches to privatization have been debunked, the search continues for ways of making public services more effective and efficient, and in using privatization in an accountable way (Johnston 1996).

In recent years, privatization has come to mean competition by private organizations for public services. This strategy is widely used, and is a staple of management (Berman and West 1998). The argument is made that if the private sector is more efficient, it should be able to beat out public agencies in competition for service delivery. Typical municipal service areas that are subject to increased competition from private sector providers are garbage collection, grass mowing and park maintenance, printing services, fleet operations, building security, snow removal, programs for the elderly, legal services, testing teacher competence, moving services, and employee training. The key feature is competition for services. It should be noted that privatization concerns service delivery, not policy making. Courts have consistently ruled that public organizations cannot abandon their responsibilities for policy making and oversight. For example, public hospitals cannot contract out policy making for indigent care and public health, but they can contract out services in these areas. Under privatization, service standards are set by public organizations.

Increasingly, at all levels of government, contractors argue that they are able to run government operations more efficiently than governments. Some private contractors seek to run road systems, and in some parts of the country they have obtained concessions to run tolls roads. Interestingly, these private providers then compete with transportation authorities and special districts, either as potential or actual providers. In other examples, government operations are set as franchise funds, thereby dependent on receipts from private and public organizations in order to sustain their operations (Callahan, 2003). A somewhat less common use of privatization is contracting for management tasks. In recent years, the St. Louis and New Orleans school boards have hired a private sector management firm to reorganize their systems, consolidating schools and reducing administrative staff. The rationale for hiring an outside firm is that it "provides cover for decisions that few local officials would savor . . . the other things you are buying is the ability of these people to leave town" (*Times Picayune* 2005). The cutback management firm is, of course, subject to policy making and oversight by the school board.

Many public organizations find that they make substantial savings through privatization (Savas 1999). Examples include using for-profit photocopying services, cleaning and maintenance, and trash collection. However, opening up services for competitive bidding does not always result in private provision: public agencies routinely beat out private organizations. One reason in the area of professional services is that top managers and contracted specialists often command much higher salaries in the private sector. Legal services are increasingly being contracted-in by hiring lawyers as public employees; only exceptional or specialized legal needs are contracted out. The threat of losing jobs also forces public employees to develop new approaches to provide cheaper and better services, and many organizations have avoided privatization by improving their services. Some public organizations that lost their services regained service delivery in subsequent years by making improvements and winning out in subsequent bids: this is reverse privatization.

One concern is also that private organizations underbid public organizations in order to obtain the contract, but increase prices substantially in subsequent years. This occurs in part because of unrealistic projections, a lack of alternative private providers in many locales, and disbanding public organizations as a result of privatization. Examples of rapid fee increases are found in some garbage services, cable television services, privatized prison operations, and architectural services. The concern is that privatization is replacing public monopolies with private monopolies. To avoid this situation, many cities *privatize no more than one quarter* of their service effort during any contracting period. This enables public organizations to rebid in subsequent years, and it ensures competition for private providers.

Privatization also involves risks that should be estimated (Lawther 2004). Public organizations must evaluate the risk of service disruption, poor performance, and legal and financial liability. Although these risks are often small, they must be considered and incorporated in negotiations with vendors. Privatization contracts sometimes initially fail to specify standards for service performance and penalties for underperformance. In this regard, one city experienced dramatic dissatisfaction with its newly privatized garbage collection service, but because it had failed to negotiate penalties for underperformance, the city had very little leverage to increase the contractor's performance short of litigation and threat of nonrenewal. Garbage and other private contractors have learned the lesson to positively respond to government exigencies, or face adverse negotiations in subsequent contract negotiation.

The notion of privatization-as-competition can be increased to allow other public agencies to compete for public contracts. This practice is adopted in some European countries, where local governments can compete with provinces—which are the equivalent of U.S. state governments—for maintenance of state parks, roads, or the printing needs of state agencies. Not much has been written about this in the United States. Some U.S. agencies use a system of "franchise funds" to increase competition; some administrative and other services are required to charge their public sector customers a fee for their services, which is used to support their operations. This places them in competition with private sector providers.

Very little is written about nonprofit organizations competing successfully for public sector contracts. Many nonprofit organizations have favorable cost structures due to their use of volunteers. There is also very little known about subcontracting by nonprofits, the equivalent of contracting out by the public sector. One suspects that smaller organizations routinely contract for information, accounting, and cleaning services, but that very large nonprofit organizations sometimes have in-house departments that fulfill such operations that could be contracted out.

Realignment

Realignment (also called reorganization or restructuring) is a staple of management. Many organizations find it necessary to reconsider their purposes. Such efforts are strategic in nature, reflecting decisions about core missions, different client groups, and needs that public and nonprofit organizations aim to satisfy. After initial strategic decisions have been made, organizations must adapt their structures to align them with their new or reconfigured purposes. This is obviously a necessary but often difficult and painful process for those involved. This section discusses some of the principal ways in which restructuring occurs, and its impact on employees.

Consolidating Departments

Over time, many organizations increase the number of departments and divisions. This reflects the continuing addition of new tasks and purposes, and some municipal governments have over thirty departments. Such a large number of departments complicates communication and oversight. In this situation, reorganizations often aim to reduce the number of such departments by merging some of them with other units. Focusing on priorities also brings to light activities that are no longer central, and these are often folded into existing structures. By consolidating departments, organizations benefit from streamlining budgetary processes and by taking advantage of economies of scale in administrative services. It provides organizations with opportunities for cutting back and eliminating unnecessary positions, demoting officials, changing the composition of senior management teams, and altering review and advisory committees. Consolidating departments is also a vehicle for increasing the role of other departments in decision making.

Decentralization

Decentralization is a process of empowering lower managers and field offices that provide services directly to clients. The rationale for delegating decision-making authority and accountability is that units that are closer to their clients have better knowledge of their customers' needs and, when given the means, are better able to provide than centralized offices. In addition, decentralization reduces the need for middle managers whose purpose is to aggregate and analyze information, make recommendations, and provide coordination. Such functions slow down decision making and add to service costs. Computer technologies enable lower-level managers to access the same information and make appropriate decisions.

One challenge of decentralization is to avoid duplication of administrative services and the need for increased coordination. To this end, decentralized units are encouraged to use privatization and competition strategies when needed. They are also given strict ceilings on such expenditures. Another challenge of decentralization is to prevent the perversion and corruption of intentions. Segal (1997) describes how the devolution of power in the New York City public school system created opportunities for corruption. Decentralization led to the creation of school boards in each of thirty-one districts, which were intended to hold principals and other school officials accountable according to the needs of the districts. Instead, the newly elected school board officials used their power to influence hiring and contracting decisions in favor of friends, family, and business partners. Bribery became rampant in some school districts and, in a few instances, sexual favors were exchanged, as well. Segal blames the lack of safeguards to avoid corruption for this perverse outcome. Decentralization requires effective work units as well as policies and oversight to ensure that lower units achieve what they are tasked to do.

Downsizing

Periodically, organizations go through episodes of downsizing. During the 1990s, the federal government reduced about 20 percent of its workforce, though contractors for the federal government increased their employment by about the same number of jobs (Light 2003). Many state governments have also reduced their staff sizes. The purpose of downsizing is often to reduce expenditures *and* improve the alignment of organizations. Organizations try to improve their positioning for future years, and many organizations grow over time in ways that are not directly related to their purposes. Across-the-board cuts do not address the need for realignment and are therefore much criticized. However, in some instances across-the-board cuts are followed up in subsequent years with targeted growth and spending, which helps organizations grow in ways that are most needed. While this addresses some alignment problems, the effective pace of such change is often very slow.

To ensure that organizations are well positioned to meet future challenges, many authors recommend taking a strategic approach to downsizing. The strategic approach is a blank-slate approach that first addresses goals that organizations seek to pursue in future years, and second, redeploys organizational units and personnel to best meet these goals. In this way, downsizing is seen as organizational redesign. This simple approach is complicated, of course, by the fact that missions are not totally malleable, for example, many public and nonprofit organizations have core missions and stakeholders that must be targeted and that cannot be abandoned. Moreover, the redeployment of staff raises significant issues of layoffs, loss of morale, and litigation. Workforce reductions are hurtful for employees and often demoralize those who are left (Olsen, Seymour, and Weaver 2004; Ban 1997). Indeed, many for-profit organizations experience significant declines in productivity after reorganization and downsizing, which is often attributed to lower morale of remaining workers. Downsizing does not always produce productivity gains.

The redeployment of human resources is perhaps the most critical issue in downsizing. Some large for-profit organizations resolve the redeployment issue by dismissing all employees and requiring each employee to reapply for specific, new positions. The loss of staff morale is to some extent managed by consistently and persistently communicating management's intent and involving employees and managers in decision making. Many employees and managers participate in their own downsizing, in part because it allows them to better position themselves in subsequent hiring. Also, the 25–50–25 rule, described in chapter 3, suggests that many employees will see value in the realignment. Communication, participation, goal setting, and emphasis of competency and purpose over organizational politics are widely viewed as keys to successful downsizing. Managers spend considerable effort communicating the need for downsizing. Organizations further reduce the loss of morale by operating according to a swift time schedule and providing employees who remain with adequate training and team building for their new jobs. They must also deal with fears of remaining employees that they might be the next casualties of downsizing.

Downsizing requires a strategy for minimizing employee pain (and hence litigation). Public and nonprofit organizations can sometimes avoid total layoff and selective rehiring by using other strategies of reducing overtime, providing furloughs, getting employees to accept cuts in pay, job sharing, converting full-time to part-time positions, encouraging early retirement, and using hiring freezes to promote staff reduction by natural attrition. These strategies reduce the speed of downsizing, but unlike the environments of many for-profit organizations, the pace of change in the environments of many public organizations is somewhat slower, which may justify a less-radical strategy. Of course, a problem with lengthier downsizing processes is that morale may suffer for a longer period and that managers will need to make ongoing efforts to communicate and ensure participation in downsizing efforts. Table 9.3 shows a checklist for downsizing.

Although the emphasis in downsizing should be on the remaining em-

Table 9.3

Checklist for Downsizing

The following is consistent with the framework discussed in chapter 2.

I. External Stakeholders
- Which groups of external stakeholders does the new mission aim to satisfy? Will the organization be able to adequately meet the needs of each group? By what measure will we assess stakeholder satisfaction after the downsizing?
- Will the new organization be able to deliver world-class services? What strategy is in place for continuous improvement?
- Will the new organization draw adequate support from external stakeholders? What strategy is in place to ensure stakeholder support?

II. Organization
- Is the new mission clear and consistent with the needs of external stakeholders?
- Are all responsibilities identified to accomplish the mission? Is support provided for those units that have this responsibility?
- Are all responsibilities assigned? How will units be held accountable for their results? How will performance be measured?
- Are decision-making structures consistent with the focus of the new organization? Are new advisory groups needed?
- Are units using the most cost-effective form of organizing for fulfilling their responsibilities? Are they using contracting and partnering strategies?
- Have managers of reorganized units developed a structure for clear communication and accountability? How will they deal with mal-performance?

III. Employees
- Are we using strategies to avoid lay-offs such as early/phased retirement, buyouts, natural attrition, relocation/reassignment, and part-time/job sharing?
- Are employees adequately and repeatedly informed about the need for downsizing? Do they know when and how it will occur? Did we get their (union) input in the development of downsizing procedures? Are salary reductions an option for avoiding lay-offs?
- Are we using fair procedures for selecting those who will be laid off?
- Are we giving maximum assistance to those who will be laid off: job search assistance, financial assistance, psychological counseling, support in meeting family needs (e.g., continuation of health insurance, day care, other benefits)?
- Are we giving maximum support to remaining workers to help adjust to their new situation and increased job insecurity? Is training provided for new job skills? Are managers trained to deal with adjustment issues? Will a survey be undertaken to identify new employee needs?

IV. Projects and Programs
- Which operations are affected by the downsizing? How are they affected? Do we have a strategy for deciding which projects and program will receive additional funding to deal with the effects of downsizing?
- Are timetables and resources reevaluated for feasibility of existing projects and programs?
- How does the downsizing affect existing investment plans for technology?

ployees, managers nevertheless spend considerable efforts in dealing with layoffs. The cost of termination and severance pay is many times more than the cost of helping workers to find employment in other organizations (White 2003). Job bridging (or outplacement) is the activity of helping employees to classify their skills, identify vacancies, and prepare them to succeed in job interviews, while providing counseling for dealing with life and family issues. Job bridging can be an effective response for dealing with employment, financial, and emotional concerns caused by layoffs. Many organizations are moving toward outplacement strategies. In general, both remaining and separating employees feel better when assistance is available to deal with these various issues.

In Conclusion

Managers are increasingly creative and adept at developing new organizational forms for accomplishing their purposes. Partnerships are increasingly used to improve the capabilities of organizations and address myriad regional or community problems. Partnerships are used for coordination, policymaking, funding, and joint service delivery. Special districts and authorities are used for service delivery, infrastructure development, and community redevelopment. They provide "permanent" approaches for these problems. Privatization is used to manage costs and services by increasing competition. Realignment is used to restructure an organization so as to better match its resources and activities to new missions. As new problems are addressed, it is likely that new forms will arise and that old ones will be adapted in creative ways.

Application Exercises

1. Imagine how a partnership or coalition of organizations in your area could help your program. What should the partnership be doing? What are its goals? How can the partnership be most efficiently managed? What resources are required? What sources are available for this funding? Are there any grant opportunities? What challenges do you foresee?
2. Identify some examples of special districts and authorities. How effective are they? What do they do? How large is their budget? Research them on the Internet.
3. Think of how a special district or authority could help your community or state address a critical problem.
4. Identify some examples of privatization. What works? What doesn't

work? What aspects of your organization could be contracted out? Should it be contracted out? Why, or why not?

5. Consider the problems of privatization mentioned in the text. Explain why some privatization contracts might resemble partnership agreements.

6. Imagine that you must downsize a substantial part of your unit. How will you do this? What problems do you foresee, and how will you deal with them? How will you deal with resisters and low performers? How will you deal with employees that are critical to your success?

Oldies but Goodies

Some well-established, time-tested strategies exist to increase performance, improve efficiency and manage projects. Through cost savings, efficiency improvements, and effective project management, organizations are able to better meet peak demands, improve their staffing, execute projects on time and within budgets, and find new ways to save money. Doing so allows them to build more roads per tax dollar, serve more clients per staff person, oversee more inmates with less staff, and manage organizations with lower overhead costs. Though these strategies were developed in past eras, they continue to find productive use; they are "oldies but goodies." Managers should decide which ones are useful for them. While these strategies predate the more recent, quality-based philosophies, they can be used as part of those strategies, too. Stakeholders expect organizations to perform efficiently and effectively, and that includes the use of these tools.

Many of these strategies focus on efficiency and project management. The former involves both cost savings and strategies of optimizing resource allocation, which can be viewed as an approach to ensuring efficient service delivery (noted as Problem 7 in chapter 2). Project management strategies are designed to ensure adequate planning, promote effective execution, and client satisfaction with project outcomes. (These are mentioned as Problems 11, 12, and 13 in chapter 2.) While these strategies do not alter organizational missions or affect strategic decisions about, for example, privatization or realignment, they do help organizations and their programs and projects to run better and more efficiently.

Decreasing Costs, Raising Revenues

The analysis of costs is an important subject in productivity. Recalling that efficiency is defined as the ratio of outcomes to inputs, one way to increase efficiency is to reduce costs and another is to substitute expensive resources with less costly ones. The challenge is doing so while maintaining outcomes.

Using Volunteers, Interns, and Clients

Personnel costs often constitute over 60 percent of program expenditures, and the use of volunteers, interns, and clients in service delivery reduces personnel costs. A distinctive characteristic of nonprofit organizations is their use of volunteers as ushers in museums, as caregivers in hospitals, as coordinators for local chapters of the humane society, and so on. Many governments, too, use volunteers. For example, libraries and parks services have active volunteer programs, and police departments, too, are using volunteers for clerical tasks, victim assistance, surveillance, and graffiti eradication. It estimated that about eighty to ninety million Americans donate their time each year for volunteer activities, providing about sixteen billion hours with an estimated market value of about two hundred billion dollars. About 44 percent of adults state that they have volunteered during the past year. Volunteers work on average about 3.6 hours per week. About three-quarters of all volunteered time is spent in organizations; of this, about 70 percent of these volunteer efforts are undertaken in nonprofit organizations, and about 25 percent in the public sector, mainly local governments (Brudney 2004a, 2004b; Independent Sector 2001).

The use of volunteers requires a careful management plan. Organizations should have cogent reasons for using volunteers: cost-substitution is a key reason, but other goals include building bridges with community groups, obtaining access to skilled support, and increasing service delivery by using volunteers to leverage current funds. Volunteers are often used for tasks that are incidental or performed periodically rather than those that are undertaken frequently or daily. Because they are not paid, volunteers often have other commitments and they are seldom available for tasks that must be performed on a continual basis. Typical activities for which volunteers might be used are activities that require either very low skills or skills that are not found within the organization. For example, people require relatively few skills and little training to be ushers or support staff in social or community events. Professionals also volunteer their services, such as lawyers who donate their services to local coalitions for the homeless, or builders who donate their professional expertise to Habitat for the Humanity projects.

Volunteers must be budgeted for; they are not a free resource. Volunteers often require considerable recruitment, training, and development as well as resolution of cost reimbursement and liability issues. In some nonprofits, such as the Peace Corps or AmeriCorps, volunteers receive nonsalary benefits. Volunteers also require training and orientation about organizational workplace policies (such as regarding sexual harassment and use of property), evaluation and grievance procedures, and benefits and absenteeism policies, as applicable. Recruiting volunteers also requires considerable effort. Although some organizations have a plethora of people who want to volunteer their time, in many instances staff must be appointed to obtain the right volunteers. People are more likely to volunteer when they are asked to do so. Once accepted, management must find meaningful tasks or risk that they will leave the organization. Directive and punitive management styles may cause volunteers to quit, and should be avoided. Volunteers must also receive feedback regarding their efforts (demonstrating that their contributions are taken seriously), and be guided to help them improve when necessary. Thus, volunteers are indeed not a free resource (Little 1999; Gazley and Brudney 2005; Handy and Srinivasan 2004).

A second strategy for reducing labor costs is using interns. Interns differ from volunteers in that they are typically seeking an opportunity to prove themselves, to obtain a quality learning experience, and to improve their marketability at the end of the internship. Many seek to be hired by the organization that is providing them with the internship opportunity. Internships are also different from volunteerism in that they are closed-ended commitments. Organizations benefit from interns because they are inexpensive (requiring a small stipend or no compensation at all), usually highly motivated, skilled (albeit inexperienced), and because they provide organizations with an opportunity to carefully observe a candidate without making employment commitments. However, organizations misuse interns when they fail to support their learning and employment objectives, such as when they are given only menial tasks and are not offered any prospect of employment.

Organizations can also involve their program clients in service delivery, perhaps as volunteers or in some other capacity. Finally, organizations also use temporary workers to fulfill emergency needs. Such workers are seldom cheap, but they do eliminate the need for hiring full-time staff who might be underutilized in subsequent periods. They also allow employers an opportunity to better screen employees before hiring them. A variety of other strategies include using part-time employees (who may require fewer benefits) and staff that is on loan from other agencies, organizations, or units.

Audit, Audit, Audit

Employee Compensation and Benefits. Total compensation includes salary, health care benefits, tuition reimbursement, retirement contributions, vacation and sick leave, and child/elder care support, as well as performance

Table 10.1

Lease/Buy Analysis Involving a Photocopier (in dollars)

Annual cost to lease: (373.69 × 12 months =)	4,484.28
Annual maintenance cost (190.00 × 12 months =)	2,280.00
Annualized purchase cost (purchase price of 3,040, 3 years in service, 10% interest, and no salvage value =)[1]	1,222.88
Annual savings from purchasing	981.40
Total, 3-year savings from purchasing (3 × 981.40 =)	2,944.20

Note: [1]The annualized cost is calculated as the purchase prices times $[i*(1+i)^n]/[(1+i)^{n-1}]$, whereby i = interest rate and n = number of periods. For $i = 10$ percent and $n = 3$, the factor is 0.402. This formula coverts a single payment to an annual cost. The annualized cost is also calculated on most hand calculators that perform financial operations. In this case, the future value is zero, the present value is 3,040, the interest is 10 percent and the number of periods is three: the computer calculates the required payment.

incentives and other bonuses. It has proven quite hard to control these costs in recent years. Some organizations have cut back on health care benefits, requiring employees to pay larger out of pocket expenses. Even so, health care expenditures continue to rise. Some public and nonprofit organizations find it profitable to use benefit consultants who monitor health insurance trends and identify less costly alternatives. Organizations can also review their tuition and continuing education program benefits. Many organizations now limit total tuition reimbursement, thereby discouraging the use of more costly private universities. Training and travel benefits have also been reduced in many years, but they remain popular for retaining well-qualified employees. Organizations also encourage hiring recent graduates rather than more expensive experienced staff. Cost reduction practices are also more difficult in public organizations that have collective bargaining practices (Cayer 1997; *Nonprofit Business Advisor* 2004).

Rents. Many office leases contain clauses that cause lease payments to increase over time. Managers should periodically review lease costs based on a comparative analysis of similar properties in the area. Managers should also familiarize themselves with local regulations that may exempt landlords from part of their real estate taxes when a significant part of a building is occupied by a nonprofit organization. Nonprofit organizations should consider ownership rather than office rental. Since nonprofit organizations are unable to raise money by issuing equity investments, real estate is an important asset against which business loans can be secured.

Equipment. Organizations must often choose between leasing or buying office equipment and furniture. These decisions require careful analysis, especially because leasing and maintenance terms change over time. Table 10.1 displays a lease/buy analysis involving a photocopier. Despite these cost-savings from purchasing, continuing increases in service contracts and improvements in leasing terms (such as providing new-model machines each year) may make leases more attractive. Lease terms frequently change and managers need to periodically review previous lease/buy decisions.

Organizations should also consider the full life-cost of equipment, rather than the bid or purchase price. Computers, for example, are an increasingly important equipment cost, with an average life span of only a few years. The full life-cost of equipment includes such factors as (1) the expected lifetime and salvage value, (2) maintenance and repair costs, (3) energy costs (which often exceed the purchase price of such items as light bulbs, motors, and cooling devices), and (4) failure costs, that is, the impact of equipment failure on other items and operations. When full costs are figured into the acquisition decision, the purchase price is sometimes not the determining factor.

Operating Expenses. Energy, phone, and mailing costs are substantial in many public and nonprofit organizations. Managers frequently audit these costs and achieve many cost savings. First, many local utilities now provide free energy audits and may be able to suggest savings on current equipment. Second, phone companies often change their rate structures, and periodic research may suggest advantages from changing long distance services, cellular carriers, and Internet access providers. Third, many public and nonprofit organizations reduce their mailing expenditures by using bulk mail and postcards. They also use mail meters and companies that specialize in providing targeted mailing lists. Fourth, costs can also be reduced by borrowing or pooling resources with other organizations, such as warehousing and transportation services. Fifth, computer costs are increasingly important. Although many organizations employ in-house technicians to provide support, others are finding cost-effective ways to contract and pool this resource. Sixth, organizations need to review their insurance coverage and costs. For example, general liability insurance covers most bodily injury and property damage claims, but managers must ensure that such insurance includes volunteers, too. Board and directors insurance protects board members against the consequences of litigation filed against their organization. Umbrella insurance fills gaps in coverage, such as lawsuits that involve various forms of wrongdoing. The lack of adequate insurance is a major liability that can offset potential savings. The insurance market is very volatile; many property insurance rates went up following the terrorist attacks in 2001, and were coming back down as of this writing. Periodic reexamination of rates and coverage can provide substantial cost savings.

Raising Revenues

Three frequent alternative revenue strategies are (1) fundraising, (2) enterprising (including fees for service and licensing), and (3) obtaining grants. By seeking alternative revenues, public and nonprofit organizations increase the leverage (or efficiency) of traditional income sources.

Fundraising. In social service organizations, private donations often constitute 20 to 40 percent of total revenue, and many nonprofit organizations have well-developed fundraising programs. Successful fundraising efforts help meet the matching requirements of funding agencies and often signal that the organization and its programs are well-understood and accepted in a community. By contrast, unsuccessful fundraising efforts imply that programs and services have little support in the community. Although organizations undertake fundraising to increase their revenue, successful fundraising is usually premised on the ability of organizations to satisfy important donor values and needs. Donors then give to show these values. For example, university presidents spend considerable time explaining the purpose and relationship of their institution to community and business needs. Donors usually start by giving small amounts and as they become more comfortable with the organization's accomplishments they may make larger gifts.

Fundraising involves a broad range of activities. Activities such as mass mailings or telethons often result in many small gifts. Most such pledges are under $100, but some are larger. The efficiency of telethons depends in large measure on the extent that individuals have given in prior years: it is less costly to obtain pledges from these individuals than to obtain new pledges. A strategic reason for conducting telethons is the recruitment of future donors. The fundraising cost per dollar raised through mail and phone campaigns is often close to the break-even point for time donors, but much less for repeat mail and phone donors, hence justifying the cost of acquiring first-time donors. Special events such as galas often target donors who have given before at previous special events or in telethons. Those who are good prospects for $100 to $1,000 donations are targeted. Annual galas are often followed by capital campaigns and other special fundraising projects. These help accommodate a large number of donors. Large gifts are usually made to organizations with which donors have long-term relations or affinity. Such individuals are identified and attended to by organizational leaders. The cost of special events and large gifts is about $.20–$.50 per dollar raised, and many social service organizations that raise $160,000 annually can expect to receive 60 percent of their total donations from gifts that are greater than $500 (Farb 2004; Fogal 2004; Keegan 1994; Miller 2002).

In sum, fundraising requires considerable leadership, management, and coordination. Leaders must set annual goals, develop a vision for donors, and commit resources to a range of fundraising efforts. Fundraising is a long-term strategy.

Enterprising. Public and nonprofit organizations are increasingly engaged in new forms of enterprising. Fee-for-service arrangements are increasingly common in the public sector (e.g., passport or license applications), but many organizations also raise money through cause-related marketing and licensing. As discussed in chapter 9, many arts organizations market themselves through large corporations that pay for advertisements and often contribute large donations. In other instances, organizations license their names or logos for commercial products, or engage in sales of merchandise—universities and museums are well-known examples. It is important to note that although nonprofit organizations are generally exempt from taxation, they may be taxed for profits that the Internal Revenue Service deems are derived from unrelated business. This is also the case when public and nonprofit organizations engage in business partnerships or develop revenue-raising subsidiaries (Boschee 2001; Villeneuve-Smith 2004).

Grants. Grants remain a key source of funding for nonprofit organizations. They are also becoming increasingly important for many state and local governments as they attempt to meet rising demands with stagnant revenues. Many public agencies have recruited grant writers, similar to nonprofit profit organizations. Because many grants and contracts are payments for specific services or accomplishments, the credibility of nonprofit agencies to perform is key to successfully obtaining grants. Successful leaders often engage in visible community leadership and continuing dialogue with grant agencies, often through the advocacy of their board members. Such dialogue helps both sides better understand each other's needs, and frequently, results in requests for proposals (RFPs) that are tailored to specific capabilities (duBose, 2005; Miller, 2002).

Increasing Efficiency

Whereas the above strategies aim to reduce costs and make traditional revenue sources stretch further, other strategies aim to increase the efficiency of resources. These strategies are variously called industrial engineering, operations research, and management science. As discussed in chapter 1, these approaches were first developed in the early 1900s as principles of scientific management and industrial engineering, and were further developed as operations research (OR) during World War II and thereafter for solving a variety of defense and business problems related to inventory, scheduling, and transportation efficiency. Some approaches were later also applied to complex social problems, such as studies that evaluate the impact of pollution, population growth, resource scarcity, and other conditions relating to the global ecosystem and human survival. Many of these approaches are no longer new, but they continue to find application, such as workflow analysis in reengineering (chapter 5). Many applications require the use of computers for simulation and estimation.

Task Analysis

Many efficiency techniques were first developed to deal with factory work processes in the early 1900s. Researchers studied in great detail the tasks that workers performed. From these early studies principles were derived for increasing the efficiency of repetitive work processes. Some important principles of work design are that (Patricia Haynes 1980):

- Work should be conveniently located within an arc of forearm motions.
- Work tools should be easy to find and within range.
- Disparate tasks should be combined into separate lots.
- Distractions should be minimized.
- Motion patterns should be varied to reduce muscle stress.
- Good working conditions should be maintained (good lighting, minimal noise, etc.).
- Employees should avoid lifting heavy objects: they should slide them instead.
- Employees should avoid physical exertion, for example, by minimizing upper arm motions.

These basic principles are still applicable today. For example, employees should have printers conveniently located without having to leave their work area; frequently used files should be well-organized and kept within range; different jobs should be done at different times (e.g., do travel vouchers only twice each week); lighting should be adequate; and employees should avoid injury by taking sensible precautions such as using movers to move heavy objects and adopting good work posture. Often, workers are well aware of inefficiencies that affect them and they welcome improvements.

Another problem is that employees frequently travel to central photocopiers, filing cabinets, and other spaces. Two main strategies for minimizing travel time are (1) bringing destinations and those who frequent them most often closer together and (2) bundling activities that involve travel so that these activities require fewer trips. Although the cost of office travel is usually minimal for individual employees, the aggregate cost is often significant. For example, many offices have only one photocopier per floor. Assume that the average, one-way travel time between workstations and the photocopier is twenty seconds. When twenty-five people travel to the copier on average five times each day, the total travel time is $(25 * 5 * 20 * 2 =)$ 5,000 seconds or 1.39 hours per day. This is equivalent to $(1.39 * 5 * 52 =)$ 361 hours per year, or about $6,498 per floor per year (assuming about $18.00 per hour average, total compensation per worker). This cost is greater than the annual lease price calculated above! In many offices, a small number of people use the machine most, for example, assistants and office managers. Savings are possible by relocating the photocopiers closer to them. These savings are further increased by moving machines away from extremely disadvantageous locations such as corner offices.

Other travel examples involve the location of nurses' stations in hospitals and trips to equipment storage sheds. Of particular interest is the increased use of case management systems in large hospitals. When nurses or social workers are assigned to inpatients, they must follow them through different units that they traverse: intake, surgery, postsurgery, various floors such as oncology and infectious diseases, and rehabilitation. In large, campus-style hospital complexes, this requires considerable travel time, including waiting for elevators. The above calculations are then used to assess the cost of such proposed care. Also important is travel time to outside offices. Organizations increasingly use dispatchers to coordinate employee travel for health inspections, police patrols, park repair and maintenance activities, and social service home visits. By coordinating the travel needs of different employees, it often is possible to diminish this expense.

Task analysis usually involves repetitive tasks. The efficiency of repetitive, multitask jobs is also increased by using process reengineering (chapter 5). However, these techniques are seldom used for nonrepetitive tasks because the cost of analysis seldom justifies the efficiency gains. The efficiency of nonrepetitive tasks can be increased in other ways, such as project management, discussed further.

Staffing Analysis

Work staffing is often an important productivity issue. When employees are assigned to several unrelated tasks, they may be unable to sufficiently focus on each task and thus commit errors or fail to meet expectations for quality (P. Haynes 1980). When several employees are assigned to do the same task, they may get in each other's way: this increases the need for coordination and the management of personal style differences. When employees are assigned to do tasks that lesser qualified employees could

Table 10.2

Staffing Analysis

Marketing Department: Museum

Activity	Total	Director	Staff1	Staff2	Staff3	Assistant
Fund-raising						
Direct mail	8.0	0.5	0.5			7.0
Special events	15.0	3.0	6.0	3.0		3.0
Patrons	3.0	0.5	2.5			
Corporate	6.0			6.0		
Survey						
Visitors	4.0					4.0
Citizens, Other	0.0					
Graphics						
Design	4.0			4.0		
Production	5.0			4.0		1.0
Media relations						
Promotion	14.0		5.0		9.0	
Advertisement	8.5		5.5		2.0	1.0
Database						
List management	5.5		0.5			5.0
Education	2.0			2.0		
Other	16.0	15.0	1.0			
Leave	4.0	2.0		2.0		
Total Staff	95.0	21.0	21.0	21.0	11.0	21.0

Note: Estimated days per month (21 working days).

perform, efficiency suffers because tasks can be accomplished more cheaply. Staffing analysis provides objective data for addressing these issues. Although it seldom conclusively "proves" the existence of such problems, it does help structure discussion.

The first step of staffing analysis is to identify jobs that units need to fulfill. For example, museum marketing and public relations departments undertake regular mailings to a wide range of patrons about upcoming events. They also conduct special fundraising events, such as pre-opening shows of exhibitions or special, black-tie gala performances of opera and other performing arts stars. In addition, they conduct surveys of visitors and are responsible for the design and distribution of posters and advertisements of upcoming events. These tasks are identified, as shown in Table 10.2.

The second step is to identify employees who are involved in these jobs and to identify the amount of time that each person spends on these jobs, that is, a distribution of time for each activity in which they are involved. Such data are not usually available, unless staff is accustomed to filling out detailed work/time reports. Rather, such data are estimated through conversations with staff. These data are entered in a staffing analysis table. The third step is to determine how much time is spent by the collective unit on each job.

At this point, several potential problems of staffing may be identified. First, it may become apparent that some tasks do not have the involvement of those who should be involved. For example, from Table 10.2, it is apparent that no staff persons are involved with the survey effort; is the assistant appropriately qualified to undertake the survey? If so few people are involved, how well are the data being used? Second, tasks with which many persons have limited involvement might be a concern, especially those that might be better conducted by a few persons who focus on this activity. For example, maintaining client records is often best undertaken by a limited number of staff in order to avoid data entry errors. Third, excessive dependence on individual employees is also a problem. For example, when client records are maintained by only a single person, the absence of that person could frustrate many other operations. Fourth, staffing analysis can also be used to identify tasks that are inadequately being pursued. Table 10.2 shows that very little effort is undertaken to inform the community about the museum through education.

A dynamic form of staffing analysis is *demand analysis.* Many public and nonprofit organizations face service demands and workloads that vary by time of day, day of the week, month of the year, or by location. For example, student enrollment applications peak between December and March, patient care requires more nursing services in the early morning than any other part of the day, and police calls are often geographically concentrated in poorer parts of cities. These variations in service demand frequently cause high levels of employee stress and customer complaints. Uneven service demand is principally dealt with through three strategies: (1) reallocating staff to ensure that staffing levels meet peak demands, (2) requiring clients to schedule appointments with staff at specific times, locations, or dates when service demands are low and staff are available, and (3) using information technology and mail-in strategies to reduce the need for face-to-face or telephone interactions. In its simplest form, demand analysis only requires measuring the level of service demand at different hours, days, months, or locations. A bar chart of service demand is made of people who ask for services. Managers are often surprised to find that the volume of peak hour demand is as high as it is, and providing these data is an important step toward creating awareness about the magnitude of the problem. Although some managers resist addressing uneven demands because they fear that it will require additional overtime or hiring, the purpose of demand analysis is to resolve such problems through the above strategies.

Efficiency Analysis

The purpose of efficiency or optimization analysis is to increase the cost-effectiveness of services. For example, orchestras calculate the efficiency of recruiting new season subscribers and patrons, police departments calculate the efficiency of obtaining convictions and the value of confiscated properties, and hospitals examine the cost of settling litigation. Efficiency analyses are used to evaluate as well as help determine courses of action. For example, when deciding how many additional marketing letters to mail out, a museum can examine its previous returns to estimate a breakeven point for sending out more (see Box 10.1).

Efficiency analysis is related to cost-benefit and cost-effectiveness analysis. Cost-benefit analyses are quite comprehensive and are sometimes requested when proposing new investments or initiatives (Gramlich 1997). Different cost-benefit applications such as those in social services, environmental management, and road construction have different standards and conventions for measuring costs and benefits. For example, benefits are often undervalued in social service programs because quality-of-life increases are hard to quantify in dollars. Although policymakers often look to cost-benefit and cost-effectiveness studies to provide a "bottom line," such studies often are controversial because (1) it is seldom to possible to identify and quantify all direct and indirect costs and benefits and (2) the decision to undertake activities includes other values such as effectiveness and equity. Thus, cost-benefit analysis is usually only one tool in the game of obtaining approval. Perhaps the greatest utility of such studies is the systematic identification of all costs and benefits, and an initial assessment of whether, under conservative estimates, estimable benefits are likely to be greater than estimable costs. What-if analysis is often issued to help defuse concerns about the robustness of data and assumptions by examining the effects of different assumptions.

Efficiency analysis can also be used to take distributional considerations into account. For example, assume that data are available about park maintenance costs, utilization rates, and area incomes. Assume furthermore that the parks department is experiencing a budget shortfall and cost savings must be made. Efficiency analysis can suggest a way of distributing the budget shortfall so that high-usage parks and those in low-income areas suffer least. After accounting for critical maintenance activities, the remaining shortfall is budgeted according to the weighted sum of priorities, as shown here:

Box 10.1

Efficiency Analysis

There are many different ways to perform efficiency analyses. Most follow the following steps: (1) identify costs and activities or outcomes, (2) estimate the efficiency of the entire activity or outcome, (3) estimate the efficiency of incremental increases of activities or outcomes, and (4) evaluate the impact of varying one or more assumptions in the analysis.

For example, assume that an orchestra has a 3 percent ticket sales rate for 2,000 direct mailings to patrons. On average, each ticket sale nets $20.00 and the costs for the first 2,000 mailings are 31 cents postage and 10 cents printing for each mailing, a one-time charge of $350.00 for off-set costs, and eight hours of professional staff time at $12.50 per hour (some volunteers are used, too). An easy calculation shows that it is cost effective to undertake the mailing: revenues are (0.03 * 2,000 * $20) = $1,200, which exceeds costs of ($0.37 * 2,000 + $350 + 8 * $12.50) = $1,190. This is about break even, and 60 tickets are sold.

The advantage of using a spreadsheet for doing these calculations is that it is easier to do what-if calculations. For example, what if the director wants to know the impact on revenues of increasing average tickets prices to $25? Then, total revenues are (0.03 * 2,000 * $25) = $1,500, and net profits are $310, assuming the same 3 percent ticket sale rate. Using bulk mail further improves these results. Applying a $0.16 bulk mail rate for nonprofits (better rates are available), costs are ($0.16 * 2,000 + $350 + 8 * $12.50) = $770, and net revenues (profits) are now $730. Further what-if analyses can be undertaken to determine breakeven rates, the number of tickets sales that maximize net revenues, and the impact of price elasticity, for example, assuming a lower than 3 percent yield on ticket sales per 1,000 mailings.

	Use ranking	Area income	Total ranking	Share of shortfall
	(1 = high)	(1 = lowest)		
Park North	1	3	4	4/20 = 20%
Park South	2	1	3	3/20 = 15%
Park East	4	4	8	8/20 = 40%
Park West	3	2	5	5/20 = 25%
			20	

Of course, in practice actual use and income data might be used. Also, what-if analysis might be used by adding a third criterion, or by weighting the criteria. For example, if park usage is rated twice as much as area income, the relative budget shortfall allocations of the four parks become, respectively, 17 percent, 17 percent, 40 percent, and 27 percent. These are very small differences in comparison to those above.

Site location is a frequent problem in public organizations. For example, fire stations often must find the best location that minimizes emergency response time, and parks departments must identify the best central storage and maintenance facility that minimizes travel time. Although sophisticated computer programs are available for this purpose, one hand-calculation method is the *grid method*. First, managers identify the map coordinates of each location to which trips are made and the "horizontal" and "vertical" distances are noted. Second, managers multiply these distances by the frequency of trips to each location. For example, if the coordinates of a location are (2,3) and three tips are taken to this location, the respective values are 6 (horizontal) and 9 (vertical). Alternatively, managers can identify the number of clients served at each location. Third, all of the horizontal distances are added and divided by the total number of trips. Vertical distances are treated likewise. The resulting set of coordinates is the site location that minimizes travel. These calculations are shown below:

Site	X	Y	Number of Trips	Weighted X	Weighted Y
A	1	4	5	5	20
B	2	2	4	8	8
C	4	3	1	4	3
D	5	1	6	30	6
E	1	1	2	2	2
Total			18	49	39

Ideal X coordinate (49/18 =) 2.7
Ideal Y coordinate (39/18 =) 2.2

Other tools for increasing the efficiency of resource allocation include the family of linear programming tools. For example, linear programming can be used to address such problems as the allocation of jet fighters or FedEx aircraft to most efficiently accomplish the necessary travel, taking into account the cost of fuel and such requirements as mail and firepower being delivered within given timeframes. Data envelopment analysis (DEA) compares the relative performance of different units where multiple input and output measures exist (Nyhan and Martin 1999). Queuing models are used to calculate the wait time of clients and to optimize service desk staffing (Stokey and Zeckhauser 1978). Inventory models similarly optimize stock-

ing levels, taking into account variation in use and the time and cost of re-
plenishing stocks.

Project Management

Project management is another well-established area of performance management. Developed from experiences with managing major, expensive defense and construction projects, managers continue to find many project
management tools and insights useful regardless of where they work or the
size of their projects (Marion Haynes 1989; Meredith and Mantel 2003; Verma
1996; Ammons 2002).

Projects often go through different phases: (1) a project definition phase;
(2) a project planning phase; (3) a project implementation or execution phase;
and (4) a project wrap-up or completion phase. Together, these four phases
are referred to as the project lifecycle. Many managers recognize the unique
characteristics and challenges of these phases. It is quite a common experience for the implementation phase to consume about 70 to 90 percent of the
total project effort, but to last only about 30 to 40 percent of the total project
duration time. This reflects rather long lead times that project definition and
planning may require. The project life cycle is shown in Figure 10.1.

Project Definition. This phase focuses on *what, why, and how* things are
to be done. Rationales, methods, and budgets need to be developed, explained,
and justified. Project parameters need to be determined. Background research
must be conducted. Whatever it is that a manager wants to do, there needs to
be agreement. If contractors have to be hired, then approvals may be needed
for the bidding or sole-source contracting grant process. All of this takes
time—several weeks or years, depending on the size of the project and the
numbers of actors or agencies that may be involved. Once the project has
been advertised, the selection of bids and negotiation with the successful
vendor can easily take another few weeks to several months. Getting projects
underway is a time-consuming process that provides an opportunity to think
clearly about what should be accomplished, how that should be done, and
how unexpected obstacles might affect project goals.

Key parts of project definition are: (1) goals and specifications, (2) costs
and other resources, and (3) time. Goals and specifications concern what
will be accomplished. This is based on a clear understanding of their clients'
or agency's needs to ensure that project specifications meet those needs. Typically, different specifications have different costs, and so decisions need to
be made about what can be achieved. Specification is also grounded in a firm
understanding of delivery or manufacturing processes—what is possible, and
how standards are likely to change over time. Whatever is constructed or

Figure 10.1 **Project Life Cycle**

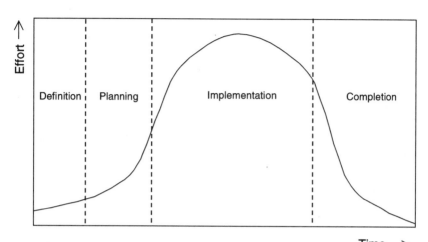

produced must not become obsolete before it scheduled to be terminated at some future date. Managers also examine ways of minimizing costs; there may be more cost-effective ways of working than those presented by their vendors. Costs may also be affected by project time—delays can cause additional costs, and so thinking about ways to minimize delays will factor into project definition, too.

Clearly, the focus on goals, specifications, costs, and time raises many considerations. Project definition involves finding the right balance among them, and doing so in ways that generate commitment from key stakeholders and clients. Idea generation, such as through brainstorming, is usually part of project planning, and it is common to pilot-test or market research the concept in some way, if practical. The result is a preliminary agreement about the project that then is further refined in the planning stage.

Project Planning. The project planning phase focuses on lining up resources and developing a timeline and management control system for ensuring that projects goals, costs, and times are met. It also involves clarifying and further operationalizing project goals and specifications, which may involve further contract negotiation. Clients are involved in this stage so that they can understand the need for any changes.

The project planning phase often starts with developing a chart or list of all the different tasks that will need to be done. If the project is a new fighter jet, the number of tasks will be numerous, in the thousands. If the project is to implement a new IT system, the number of tasks will be smaller, but still numerous. The purpose of identifying all of the tasks is to identify, for each

Figure 10.2 **Gantt Chart**

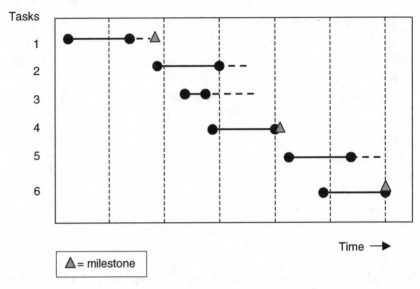

and in detail, required objectives, specifications, costs, and time. This avoids surprises later, and facilitates thinking about the sequencing of tasks. Complex projects benefit from displaying tasks on a tree-and-branch or organizational chart; less-complex projects might suffice with a simple listing.

After all of the tasks have been identified, the next step is to determine the sequencing of tasks. Some tasks must proceed before others. Some tasks can be done in parallel. The basic tool for displaying this is the Gantt chart, shown in Figure 10.2. These charts are named after Henry Laurence Gantt (1861–1919), a mechanical engineer and management consultant who first used these. The dashed lines show possible slack time.

The Gantt chart is critical to estimating and controlling project time. For example, Gantt charts can be used to develop or validate milestones, that is, critical events in the completion of projects. Milestones measure project progress, and often are the basis for distributing payments to contractors. Gantt charts require that managers carefully identify which activities must be completed before others can proceed. A more sophisticated form of Gantt chart is a PERT chart (Program Evaluation and Review Technique), which identifies the sequencing of those activities that are most critical to keeping the project on time (Ammons 2002).

Another use of the task list is to estimate costs. Project planning typically includes a budget of the costs of each task. Typical budget categories are: labor, materials and supplies, equipment use and depreciation, administration and project oversight, and overheads. Profits may be added as a separate category, or built into the above costs.

The task lists can also be used for two further purposes: clarifying goals and specifications, and assigning responsibilities for completion. The former helps to remind those later in the process of decisions about quality that have been made, and which might be forgotten in the heat of making decisions about tasks in the field. The latter, assigning responsibilities, is essential for bringing the plan into action. It gets others thinking about what they need to do, and how they will do it—within budget, on time, and according to specification.

Project planning results in a detailed understanding of how the project is expected to unfold. A useful summary task list can be made which shows, for each task, when it is to begin, when it is expected to end, how much it is budgeted for, key specification standards, who has been assigned lead responsibility for it (and other key personnel), and the availability of other planning documents:

Summary Task List

Task	Begin Date	End Date	Goals and Specifications	Lead Manager	Budget	Major Milestones	Planning Documents	Comments
1								
2								
3								
. . .								
57								

Project Implementation. Project implementation is about controlling performance. One task is to ensure that critical standards, deadlines, and resource availability have been understood by those with responsibilities for executing for one or more tasks. Critical documents that help managers maintain control are milestone charts, periodic progress reports by groups working on tasks, and budget and time charts that compare actual progress with expected or planned progress. Supervisors are asked to plan ahead and ensure that they have the right tools and resources for the next stage of the project. Inspection reports verify that timetables and quality standards have been met.

Typically, pressures exist to deviate from plans, yet the task of the manager is to keep the plan going and avoid or minimize renegotiation of project goals. Managers become adept at finding innovative ways of satisfying specification and meeting goals when things did not go exactly as foreseen. Communication is the name of the game; a climate is needed in which employees and supervisors can freely discuss what is needed to get the job done. The psychological contract technique discussed in chapter 7 can be applied here, to reach agreement between managers and supervisors about what each expects from the other. The implementation phase also provides ample opportunity for practicing conflict and negotiation skills discussed in chapter 9.

Project Completion. There is more than meets the eye when trying to complete a project. Final reports and products need to be provided to the client and sometimes oversight boards and other stakeholders. Seldom is the project wrapped up immediately; some "results" may need to be field tested. Typically, resources and project expertise are kept on hand to deal with final modifications that may be needed. The wrap-up phase can last from several weeks to several months or years.

A useful purpose of project completion is also to take stock of what has been learned and what can be done differently or better next time. What were some unexpected problems that might be anticipated next? What problems were unresolved and should be addressed in the near future? In this way, the project gives rise to future improvement efforts.

In Conclusion

A wide range of proven, time-tested strategies exist for increasing the efficiency of public and nonprofit organizations. These include strategies to reduce costs by using volunteers, interns, and clients, and auditing expenses of rent, equipment, fringe benefits, and others. Alternative revenue-enhancing strategies were also discussed, as well as various industrial engineering and operations research strategies. Project management was discussed, along with various techniques that are used to plan for projects and keep them on track. The art is to meet project goals and specifications on time and within budget. Numerous examples of these strategies were provided with regard to public and nonprofit organizations.

Application Exercises

1. Identify four ways to reduce costs in your program without affecting program effectiveness. What uses can volunteers and interns serve?
2. Find a way to apply tasks analysis or efficiency analysis to your program.

3. Identify the four phases of project management, and how they relate to your next project. What key challenges do each of the four phases imply for your project? How will you address them?

4. Develop a summary task list for your next project. How can it be modified to better suit your needs? Consider other analytical techniques and graphs that can help you.

5. Reflect on your use of psychological contracts for project management. How might that have helped you in the past? How can it help you in the future?

6. Research the Internet for software to design charts for project management and other performance purposes. One such site is (no endorsement implied): www.smartdraw.com, which includes many examples of charts discussed in this chapter.

Epilogue

This book makes the case that performance matters. Strategies of performance improvement help public and nonprofit organizations face their changing environments, heightened demands for service, constrained budgets, increased expectations of accountability transparency, and a workforce that requires a wide range of motivational strategies, for example. The strategies of performance improvement constitute a distinctive body of professional knowledge and practice that slowly but surely diffuses throughout society. The strategies are used because they are helpful, assisting organizations to formulate new purposes, and go about in new, productive ways. There are many challenges. As society is quick to identify new problems, so the development of new performance strategies is all but certain. The new practice of yesterday, quality paradigm, has become the expectation of today. The new practice of today is likely to become the expectation of tomorrow.

What is the future of performance improvement? What is a manager to do next? The future of performance improvement is likely to see new strategies, as well managers becoming increasingly adept at bringing about change in their organizations. The tendency is for organizations and their managers that can improve to do better and accomplish more; those that cannot fall further behind.

One area in which new strategies may emerge are those that deal with urgent problems that lie outside the scope of any jurisdiction, or that require jurisdictions to work together. Many such problems concern the environment, transportation, health and well-being, education, and public safety, which often top local polls. The model of community-based strategic planning is one approach toward dealing with them, but there are others, too. The governance of communities is not a new topic, but models of effective change need to be articulated with greater precision and clarity. The present interest in networks needs to be matched with interest in other approaches. We need to bring the same level of understanding and clarity about organizational change discussed in chapter 3 to that of community change and development.

One approach is to see further innovation in the use of special districts and authorities. Society needs new structures to meet the regional challenges discussed above. Networks are important but limited in their ability to manage long-term commitments that involve substantial capital outlays and obligations. It is not too far-fetched to suggest that a special district or authority might be created to manage environmental management programs, or after-school programs. Special districts or authorities might even be created for to promote investment in "well-being" for citizens, promoting not only top notch spas and workout facilities, but also retreats with programs for mental well-being and awareness, and family-oriented recreation opportunities. The concept of special districts and authorities for managing urban problems is ill-developed, yet ripe for innovation.

The future of performance improvement is also likely to see further progress on the existing family of quality improvement strategies. The availability of performance measurement on an instant, real-time basis is not yet reality, for example. A great need also exists for geographic list of e-mail addresses. While no such e-mail "phonebooks" exist, local governments could make it beneficial for households to provide their e-mail addresses to local governments, for example, for billing or public safety purposes (e.g., alerts). The ability to capture such e-mail addresses provides new opportunities for customer service and citizen input, such as through surveys. The potential of geographic information systems (GIS) systems is still untapped, though they are being used in some communities. Better-integrated data would allow citizens to see the plans for their community in far greater detail, including real-time information on traffic and crime patterns. Finally, it is to be hoped that further use of psychological contracts will increase openness and reduce the number of truly execrable managers, while providing increased opportunities for employees and managers to make a difference.

The previous edition of this book ventured the guess that ethics might be brought into productivity improvement. The reason, quite simply, is that the strategies must be infused with proper values and commitments if they are to be done well. The codes of ethics of many professional associations, including the American Society for Public Administration, note such values as "striving for professional excellence," and "promoting the public interest," both of which are consistent with what is now understood as the culture of high-performance organizations. Since then, ethics has indeed become more important and emphasized, but the level of ethics commitment and training is still thin, and largely undocumented. It is unclear how ethics training, for example, results in changed behavior. It is also clear that people who profess a strong commitment to ethics do not always behave in ethical ways. All of this does not mean that the business of promoting ethics is futile—the evidence is quite to the contrary that moral examples and personal commitment matter. But it does mean that, as a society, we are still trying to figure out how we can best make ethical action take hold. More work is likely to happen in the area of strengthening the value commitments of organizational members, and success at this endeavor will increase commitment to performance, as well.

What is a manager to do next? Managers need to decide for themselves what difference they want to make, where they stand on the matter of providing public service and realizing the possibilities and responsibilities of their office. The diffusion curve of performance improvement implies that many strategies exist that are not always currently used. The opportunities are there for those who want to take them. Some years ago, Stephen Covey (1989) wrote a book titled *Seven Habits of Highly Effective People,* which encourages people to seize the day by being proactive, positive, competent, and empathetic in their interactions with others. Managers who live these habits will find themselves naturally drawn toward performance improvement because it provides tools for making the differences they seek. And by practicing these strategies, they will become better at using them. In so doing, they develop unique skills that, as shown in chapter 1, help advance their communities as well as their own careers.

In the end, performance improvement is an invitation for doing the right thing, in the right way, for the right reasons. It is the opportunity to commit for making a difference.

References

Abramson, Mark A., and Paul R. Lawrence, eds. 2001. *Transforming Organizations.* Lanham, MD: Rowman and Littlefield.

Alison, Michael J., and Jude Kaye. 2005. *Strategic Planning for Nonprofit Organizations.* 2nd ed. New York: Wiley.

Amar, A.D. 2002. *Managing Knowledge Workers: Unleashing Innovation and Productivity.* Westport, CT: Quorum Books.

Ammons, David N. 2001. *Municipal Benchmarks: Assessing Local Performance and Establishing Community Standards.* Thousand Oaks, CA: Sage.

———. 2002. *Tools for Decision-Making.* Washington, DC: CQ Press.

———. 2004. "Productivity Barriers in the Public Sector." In Holzer and Lee 2004, 139–64. New York: Marcel Dekker.

Argyris, Chris. 1990. *Organizational Defenses.* New York: Allyn and Bacon.

Ban, Carolyn. 1997. "The Challenges of Cutback Management." In *Public Personnel Management,* ed. Carolyn Ban and Norma M. Riccucci, 269–80. New York: Longman.

Barber, Bernard B. 1983. *The Logic and Limits of Trust.* New Brunswick, NJ: Rutgers University Press.

Bardach, Eugene. 2000. *A Practical Guide for Policy Analysis: The Eightfold Path to More Effective Problem Solving.* 2nd ed. New York: Seven Bridges Press.

Barkdoll, Gerald, and John Kamensky. 2005. "Key Factors That Make a Balanced Scorecard Successful." *PA Times* 28 (5). www.aspanet.org/scriptcontent/Custom/PAT_Current/print/2005–07aspatimes2.html (accessed August 15, 2005).

Beccerra, Manuel F., and Anil K. Gupta. 1999. "Trust Within the Organization: Integrating the Trust Literature with Agency Theory and Transaction Costs Economics." *Public Administration Quarterly* 23 (2): 177–204.

Behn, Robert D. 2004. "The Psychological Barriers to Performance Management: Or Why Isn't Everyone Jumping on the Performance-Management Bandwagon?" *Public Performance & Management Review* 26 (1): 5–26.

Behn, Robert D. 1995. "The Big Questions of Public Management." *Public Administration Review* 55 (4): 313–25.

———. 2005a. "The Accountability Dilemma." *Public Management Report* 2 (7): 1–2.

———. 2005b. "Hoop Jumping." *Public Management Report* 2 (9): 1–2.

———. 2005c. "Operational Theories." *Public Management Report* 2 (11): 1–2.

Beitsch, Owen M. 2005. *Democratic Voices Speaking Loudly: Does Public Participation Yield Accountability in Special Purpose Governments?* Ph.D. dissertation, University of Central Florida.

Berman, Evan M. 1996. "Local Government and Community-Based Strategies: Evidence from a National Survey of a Social Problem." *American Review of Public Administration* 26 (1): 71–91.

Berman, Evan, and Ronnie Korosec. 2005. "Planning to Coordinate and Coordinating the Plan: Evidence from Local Governments." *American Review of Public Administration* 35 (4): 380–401.

———. 2003. "Customer Service." In *Encyclopedia of Public Administration and Public Policy,* ed. Jack Rabin et al., 294–98. New York: Marcel Dekker.

Berman, Evan M., and Xiaohu Wang. 2000. "Performance Measurement in U.S. Counties: Capacity for Reform." *Public Administration Review* 60 (5): 409–20.

Berman, Evan M., and William B. Werther. 1996. "Broad-Based Consensus Building." *International Journal of Public Sector Management* 9 (3): 61–72.

Berman, Evan M., and Jonathan P. West. 1995. "Municipal Commitment to Total Quality Management: A Survey of Recent Progress." *Public Administration Review* 55 (1): 57–66.

———. 1997. Unpublished data. Some results reported in Berman and West (1999).

———. 1998. "Productivity Enhancement Efforts in Public and Nonprofit Organizations." *Public Productivity & Management Review* 22 (2): 207–19.

———. 1999. "Career Risk and Reward from Productivity." *Public Personnel Management* 28 (2): 453–71.

———. 2003. "Psychological Contracts in Local Government: A Preliminary Survey." *Review of Public Personnel Administration* 23 (4): 267–85.

Bhatta, Gambhir. 2001. "Enabling the Cream to Rise to the Top: A Cross-Jurisdictional Comparison of Competencies for Senior Managers in the Public Sector." *Public Performance & Management Review* 25 (2): 194–207.

Blair, Robert B. 2004. "Public Participation and Community Development: The Role of Strategic Planning." *Public Administration Quarterly* 28 (1): 102–48.

Blanchard, Ken. 2001. *Empowerment Takes More Than a Minute.* San Francisco: Berrett-Koehler.

Boardman, Anthony E., and Aidan R. Vining. 2000. "Using Service-Customer Matrices in Strategic Analysis of Nonprofits." *Nonprofit Management & Leadership* 10 (4): 397–421.

Boschee, Jerr. 2001. *The Social Enterprise Sourcebook.* Minneapolis, MN: Northland.

Bouckaert, Geert. 1990. "The History of the Productivity Movement." *Public Productivity and Management Review* 3 (1): 53–89.

Bowman, James S., Jonathan P. West, Evan M. Berman, and Monty Van Wart. 2004. *The Professional Edge: Competencies for Public Service.* New York: M.E. Sharpe.

Boyne, George A. 2002. "Total Quality Management and Performance." *Public Performance & Management Review* 26 (2): 111–32.

Bramson, Robert M. 1981. *Coping with Difficult People.* Garden City, NY: Doubleday.

Brescia, William. 2004. "Planned Change at the Center on Philanthropy: The CLER Model." *Nonprofit Management & Leadership* 14 (3): 343–58.

Bridgman, Rae. 2003. "Bridging Public-Private Partnerships in a Case Study of Housing and Employment Training for Homeless Youth." *Canadian Journal of Urban Research* 12 (2): 205–31.

Brown, Mary B., and Jeffrey L. Brudney. 2004. "Achieving Advanced Electronic Government Services." *Public Performance & Management Review* 28 (1): 96–113.

Brudney, Jeffrey L. 2004a. "Designing and Managing Volunteer Programs." In Herman 2004, 310–45. San Francisco: Jossey-Bass.

———. 2004b. "Volunteers in State Government: Involvement, Management, and Benefits." *Nonprofit & Voluntary Sector Quarterly* 29 (1): 111–31.

Bryson, John, and Barbara C. Crosby. 2005. *Leadership for the Common Good.* 2nd ed. San Francisco: Jossey-Bass.

Bryson, John M. 2004. *Strategic Planning for Public and Nonprofit Organizations: A Guide to Strengthening and Sustaining Organizational Achievement.* San Francisco: Jossey-Bass.

Bryson, John M., and Farnum K. Alston. 2004. *Creating and Implementing Your Strategic Plan: A Workbook for Public and Nonprofit Organizations.* 2nd ed. New York: Wiley.

Buffalo State College. 2005. Mission and Vision Statements. Buffalo, NY: Human Resource Department. www.buffalostate.edu/offices/hr/missionvision.asp (accessed July 7, 2005).

Caiden, Gerald E. 1991. "What Really Is Public Maladministration?" *Public Administration Review* 51 (6): 486–93.

Callahan, John J. 2003. "Franchise Funds in the Federal Government: Ending the Monopoly in Service Provision." In *New Ways of Doing Business,* ed. Mark A. Abramson and Ann M. Kieffaber, 49–82. Lanham, MD: Rowman and Littlefield.

Caravalho, George A. 2004. "Your First Year on the Job: Conceptualizing New Directions." *Public Management* 86 (4): 8–12.

Cayer, N. Joseph. 1997. "Issues in Compensation and Benefits." In *Public Personnel Management,* ed. Carolyn Ban and Norma Riccucci, 221–36. New York: Longman.

Center for Accountability and Performance. 2001. *Performance Measurement Concepts and Techniques Workbook.* Washington, DC: American Society for Public Administration.

Cherniss, Cary, and Daniel Goleman. 2001. *The Emotionally Intelligent Workplace.* San Francisco: Jossey-Bass.

Chief Information Officers Council. 2005. *Best Practices.* www.cio.gov/ (accessed July 5, 2005). Washington, DC: CIO.

Chrislip, David D., and Carl E. Larson. 1996. *Collaborative Leadership: How Citizens and Civic Leaders Can Make a Difference.* San Francisco: Jossey-Bass.

City of Colorado Springs. 2000. *Strategic Plan: Direction 2000.* Colorado Springs, CO: City of Colorado Springs. www.springsgov.com/units/strategicplan/Direction2000SP.pdf (accessed July 7, 2005).

Clark, Doug. 2004. "Customer Service: Back to Basics Is Better." *Public Management* 86 (11): 6–9.

Coe, Charles K. 2003. "A Report Card on Report Cards." *Public Performance & Management Review* 27 (2): 53–76.

Coolsen, Peter. 2000. "What Nonprofit Organizations Need Are More Left-Handed Planners." *Nonprofit World* 18 (2): 29–32.

Cooper, Terry L. 1998. *The Responsible Administrator.* San Francisco: Jossey-Bass.

Covey, Stephen R. 1989. *Seven Habits of Highly Effective People.* New York: Simon and Schuster.

———. 1992. *Principle-Centered Leadership.* New York: Simon and Schuster.

Daly, John W. 2002. "Implications of Organizational Climate and Ethical Leadership on Reengineering in Municipal Government." *Public Administration Quarterly* 29 (1/2): 198–218.

Dawes, Sharon S., Theresa A. Pardo, Stephanie Simon, Anthony M. Cresswell, Mark F. LaVigne, David F. Andersen, and Peter A. Bloniarz. 2004. *Making Smart IT Choices: Understanding Value and Risk in Government IT Investments.* Albany, NY: Center for Technology in Government. www.ctg.albany.edu/publications/guides/smartit2/ (accessed July 5, 2005).

de Vries, Kets M., and Denny Miller. 1984. *The Neurotic Organization.* San Francisco: Jossey-Bass.

Divine, William R., and Harvey Sherman. 1948. "A Technique for Controlling Quality." *Public Administration Review* 8 (Spring): 110–13.

Drucker, Peter F. 1990. *Managing the Nonprofit Organization.* New York: Harper Business.

duBose, Mike. 2005. *Developing Successful Grants.* Columbia, SC: Research Associates.

Durst, Samantha L., and Charldean Newell. 2001. "The Who, Why, and How of Reinvention in Nonprofit Organizations." *Nonprofit Management & Leadership* 11 (4): 443–58.

Electronic Frontier Foundation. 2005. E-voting. www.eff.org/Activism/E-voting/ (accessed July 5, 2005).

Ephross, Paul H., and Thomas V. Vassil. 2005. *Groups That Work: Structure and Process.* New York: Columbia University Press.

Farb, Carolyn. 2004. *The Fine Art of Fundraising: Secrets for Successful Volunteers.* Cincinnati, OH: Emmis.

Fisher, Roger, and William L. Ury. 1981. *Getting to Yes.* New York: Penguin.

Fogal, Robert E. 2004. "Designing and Managing the Fundraising Program." In Herman 2004, 419–34. San Francisco: Jossey-Bass.

Fountain, Dave, and Jim Slagan. 2001. "Strategic Planning: Equally Important for the Smaller Community." *Public Management* 83 (9): 22–26.

Fournies, Ferdinand F. 1999. *Why Employees Don't Do What They Are Supposed to Do.* 2nd ed. New York: McGraw-Hill.

Garrett, Terence M. 2004. "Whither Challenger, Wither Columbia: Management Decision Making and the Knowledge Analytic." *American Review of Public Administration* 34 (4): 389–403.

Gazley, Beth, and Jeffrey L. Brudney. 2005. "Volunteer Involvement in Local Government after September 11: The Continuing Question of Capacity." *Public Administration Review* 65 (2): 131–43.

Gilliland, Martha W. 2004. "Leading a Public University: Lessons Learned in Choosing the Possibility of Quantum Results Rather than Incremental Improvement." *Public Administration Review* 64 (3): 372–78.

Goldsmith, Stephen, and William D. Eggers. 2004. *Governing by Network.* Washington, DC: Brookings Institution Press.

Goleman, Daniel. 1995. *Emotional Intelligence.* New York: Bantam Books.

Goleman, Daniel, Richard Boyatzis, and Annie McKee. 2002. *Primal Leadership: Learning to Lead with Emotional Intelligence.* Boston, MA: Harvard Business School Press.

Golembiewski, Robert T. 1997. "Perspectives on Public-Sector OD, VIII, Part 1: Aspects of Planned Change, Mostly Macro: A Symposium." *Public Administration Quarterly* 21 (3): 253–58.

Government Accounting Standards Board. 1994. *Concept Statement No. 2. Service Efforts and Accomplishments Reporting.* Norwalk, CT: Government Accounting Standards Board.

Government Performance Project. 2003. *Paths to Performance in State and Local Government.* Syracuse, NY: Maxwell School.

Gramlich, Edward M. 1997. *A Guide to Benefit-Cost Analysis.* Long Grove, IL: Waveland Press.

Guajardo, Salomon A., and Rosemary McDonnell. 2000. *An Elected Official's Guide to Performance Measurement.* Chicago: Government Finance Officers Association.

Gullick, Luther, and Lindall Urwick. 1937. *Papers on the Science of Administration.* New York: Institute of Public Administration.

Halachmi, Arie, ed. 1999. *Performance and Quality Measurement in Government.* Burke, VA: Chatelaine Press.

Hammer, Michael. 1995. *The Reengineering Revolution.* New York: HarperBusiness.

Hammer, Michael, and James A. Champy. 2001. *Reengineering the Corporation: A Manifesto for Business Revolution.* New York: HarperBusiness.

Handy, Femida, and Narasimhan Srinivasan. 2004. "Valuing Volunteers: An Economic Evaluation of the Net Benefits of Hospital Volunteers." *Nonprofit & Voluntary Sector Quarterly* 33 (1): 28–56.

Harrison, Michael I. 2004. *Diagnosing Organizations.* 3rd ed. Thousand Oaks, CA: Sage.

Haynes, Marion E. 1989. *Project Management.* Menlo Park, CA: Crisp.

Haynes, Patricia. 1980. "Industrial Engineering Techniques." In Washnis 1980, 204–36. New York: John Wiley & Sons.

Hendriks, Frank, and Pieter W. Tops. 2003. "Local Public Management Reforms in the Netherlands: Fads, Fashions and Winds of Change." *Public Administration* 81 (2): 301–24.

Henry, Nicholas. 1995. *Public Administration and Public Affairs.* Upper Saddle River, NJ: Prentice Hall.

Herman, Robert D., ed. 2004. *Handbook of Nonprofit Leadership and Management.* San Francisco: Jossey-Bass.

Herman, Robert D., and David O. Renz. 1998. "Nonprofit Organizational Effectiveness: Contrasts Between Especially Effective and Less Effective Organizations." *Nonprofit Management & Leadership* 9 (1): 23–39.

Herzberg, Frederick. 1959. *The Motivation to Work.* New York: Wiley.

Ho, Alfred T. 2002. Reinventing Local Government and the E-Government Initiative. *Public Administration Review* 62 (4): 434–43.

Holden, Stephen H., Donald F. Norris, and Patricia D. Fletcher. 2003. "Electronic Government at the Local Level." *Public Performance & Management Review* 26 (4): 325–44.

Holley, Lyn M., Donna Dufner, and B.J. Reed. 2004. "Strategic Information Systems Planning (SISP) in U. S. County Governments: Will the Real SISP Model Please Stand Up?" *Public Performance and Management Review* 27 (3): 102–26.

Holzer, Marc, and Hwang-Sun Kang. 2004. "Balanced Measurement in the Public Sector: Stakeholder-Driven Measurement." In Holzer and Lee 2004, 3285–96. New York: Marcel Dekker.

Holzer, Marc, and Seok-Hwan Lee. 2004. *Public Productivity Handbook.* New York: Marcel Dekker.

Hudson, Bob. 2004. "Analyzing Network Partnerships." *Public Management Review* 6 (1): 75–95.

Hyde, Al C. 1995. "A Primer on Process Re-engineering." *Public Manager* 24 (1): 55–69.

Independent Sector. 2001. *Given and Volunteering in the U.S.* Washington, DC: Independent Sector.

Internet Security Alliance. 2004. *Common Sense Guide to Cyber Security for Small Business.* www.us-cert.gov/reading _room/CSG-small-business.pdf (accessed July 5, 2005).

Jennings, Jason. 2002. *Less Is More: How Great Companies Use Productivity as a Competitive Tool in Business.* East Rutherford, NJ: Portfolio.

Johnston, Van R. 1996. "Optimizing Productivity Through Privatization and Entrepreneurial Management." *Policy Studies Journal* 24 (3): 444–63.

Julnes, Patria de Lancer. 2004. "The Utilization of Performance Measurement Information." In Holzer and Lee 2004, 353–76. New York: Marcel Dekker.

Kanter, Rosabeth Moss. 1985. *The Change Masters.* New York: Free Press.

Kaplan, Robert S., and David P. Norton. 1992. "The Balanced Scorecard-Measures That Drive Performance." *Harvard Business Review* 70 (1): 71–79.

———. 1996. *The Balanced Scorecard: Translating Strategy into Action.* Boston: Harvard Business School.

Keegan, P. Burke. 1994. *Fundraising for Nonprofits: How to Build a Community Partnership.* New York: HarperResource.

Kettl, Donald F. 2000. *The Global Public Management Revolution: A Report on the Transformation of Governance.* Washington, DC: Brookings Institution Press.

Kettl, Donald F., and John J. DiIulio. 1995. *Inside the Reinvention Machine.* Washington, DC: Brookings Institution Press.

King, Cheryl S., and Lisa A. Zanetti. 2005. *Transformational Public Service.* Armonk, NY: M.E. Sharpe.

Korosec, Ronnie L., and Evan M. Berman. 2005. *National Survey of Public Administration in U.S. Cities.* Unpublished data.

Krug, Kersti, and Charles B. Weinberg. 2004. "Mission, Money, and Merit: Strategic Decision Making by Nonprofit Managers." *Nonprofit Management & Leadership* 14 (3): 325–43.

Lawther, Wendell C. 2004. "Ethical Challenges in Privatizing Government Services." *Public Integrity* 6 (2): 141–54.

Lemberg, Paul. 2004. "If You're Not Growing, You're Dying: Steps to Breakthrough Growth for Your Organization." *Nonprofit World* 22 (5): 20–21.

Lian Kok Fei, Teddy, and Hal G. Rainey. 2003. "Total Quality Management in Malaysian Government Agencies: Conditions for Successful Implementation of Organizational Change." *International Public Management Journal* 6 (2): 145–73.

Light, Paul C. 2002a. *Pathways to Nonprofit Excellence.* Washington, DC: Brookings Institution Press.

———. 2002b. "The State of the Nonprofit Workforce." *The Nonprofit Quarterly* 9 (3): 6–16.

———. 2003. *Fact Sheet on the New True Size of Government.* Washington, DC: Brookings Institution. www.brook.edu/gs/cps/light20030905.htm (accessed July 11, 2005).

———. 2005. *The Four Pillars of High Performance.* New York: McGraw-Hill.

Linden, Russell M. 1998. *Workbook for Seamless Government: A Hands-on Guide to Implementing Organizational Change.* San Francisco: Jossey-Bass.

Little, Helen. 1999. *Volunteers: How to Get Them, How to Keep Them.* Naperville, IL: Panacea Press.

Locke, Edwin A., Gary P. Latham, Ken J. Smith, and Robert E. Wood. 1990. *A Theory of Goal Setting and Task Performance.* Englewood Cliffs, NJ: Prentice Hall.

Long, Donna J. 2004. "Providing Outstanding Service to Diverse Customers and Citizens." *Public Management* 86 (1): 33–36.

Long, Edward, and Aimee L. Franklin. 2004. "The Paradox of Implementing the Government Performance and Results Act: Top-Down Direction for Bottom-Up Implementation." *Public Administration Review* 64 (3): 309–20.

Lubit, Roy. 2004. "The Tyranny of Toxic Managers: Applying Emotional Intelligence to Deal With Difficult Personalities." *Ivey Business Journal* 68 (4): 1–7.

Luke, Jeffrey S. 1998. *Catalytic Leadership: Strategies for an Interconnected World.* San Francisco: Jossey-Bass.

Mara, Cynthia M. 2000. "A Strategic Planning Process for a Small Nonprofit Organization." *Nonprofit Management & Leadership* 11 (2): 211–24.

Maranville, Steven J. 1999. "Requisite Variety of Strategic Management Modes: A Cultural Study of Strategic Actions in a Deterministic Environment." *Nonprofit Management & Leadership* 9 (3): 277–92.

Maslow, Abraham H. 1954. *Motivation and Personality.* New York: Harper & Row.

McClelland, David C. 1985. *Human Motivation.* Glenview, IL: Scott, Foresman.

McClendon, Bruce. 1992. *Customer Service in Local Government.* Chicago: American Planning Association.

McGregor, Douglas. 1960. *The Human Side of Enterprise.* New York: McGraw-Hill.

McLain, David L., and Katarina Hackman. 1999. "Trust, Risk, and Decision-Making in Organizational Change." *Public Administration Quarterly* 23 (2): 152–77.

Melitski, James. 2003. "Capacity and E-Government Performance." *Public Performance & Management Review* 26 (4): 376–90.

———. 2004. "E-Government and Information Technology in the Public Sector." In Holzer and Lee 2004, 649–72. *Public Productivity Handbook,* New York: Marcel Dekker.

Melkers, Julia E., and Katherine G. Willoughby. 2005. "Models of Performance-Measurement Use in Local Governments: Understanding Budgeting, Communication, and Lasting Effects." *Public Administration Review* 65 (2): 180–91.

Mento, Anthony J., Raymond M. Jones, and Walter Dirndorfer. 2002. "A Change Management Process: Grounded in Both Theory and Practice." *Journal of Change Management* 3 (1): 45–69.

Meredith, Jack R., and Samuel J. Mantel. 2003. *Project Management: A Managerial Approach.* New York: Wiley.

Miller, Patrick W. 2002. *Grantwriting: Strategies for Developing Winning Proposals.* Munster, IL: Miller & Associates.

Miller, Thomas I., and Michelle M. Kobayashi. 2000. *Citizen Surveys: How to Do Them, How to Use Them, What They Mean.* Washington, DC: International City/County Management Association.

Mitchell, Jerry M. 2001. "Business Improvement Districts and the Management of Innovation." *American Review of Public Administration* 31 (2): 201–18.

Mittenthal, Richard A. 2004. "Don't Give Up On Strategic Planning: 10 Keys to Success." *Nonprofit World* 22 (3): 21–26.

Mulroy, Elizabeth A. 2003. "Community as a Factor in Implementing Inter-Organizational Partnerships: Issues, Constraints, and Adaptations." *Nonprofit Management & Leadership* 14 (1): 47–67.

Nadler, David A., and Edward E. Lawler. 1977. "Motivation: A Diagnostic Approach." In *Perspectives on Behavior in Organizations,* ed. J. Richard Hackman and Edward E. Lawler, 26–34. New York: McGraw-Hill.

Nanus, Burt. 1999. *Leaders Who Make a Difference: Essential Strategies for Meeting the Nonprofit Challenge.* San Francisco: Jossey-Bass.

National Telecommunications and Information Administration. 2002. *A Nation Online: How Americans Are Expanding Their Use of the Internet.* Washington, DC: National Telecommunications and Information Administration.

Newland, Chester A. 1972. "Symposium on Productivity in Government." *Public Administration Review* 32 (6): 739–850.

Nicholls, Walter J. 2003. "Forging a 'New' Organizational Infrastructure for Los Angeles' Progressive Community." *International Journal of Urban & Regional Research* 27 (4): 881–97.

Niven, Paul R. 2003. *Balanced Scorecard Step by Step for Government and Nonprofit Agencies.* New York: John Wiley & Sons.

Nonprofit Business Advisor. 2004. "The Top Five Ways Nonprofits Cut Compensation Costs." 7 (1): 4–7.

Nutt, Paul C. 2004. "Prompting the Transformation of Public Organizations." *Public Performance & Management Review* 27 (4): 9–33.

Nyhan, Ronald C., and Larry Martin. 1999. "Comparative Performance Measurement: A Primer on Data Envelopment Analysis." *Public Performance & Management Review* 22 (3): 348–64.

Olsen, Ron, Audrey Seymour, and Robin Weaver. 2004. "Downsizing Is Rough." *Public Management* 86 (11): 10–15.

Orange County. 2001. *Citizen Survey.* Orlando: University of Central Florida, Institute of Government.

Oregon Progress Board. 1995. *Oregon Benchmarks: Standards for Measuring Statewide Progress and Institutional Performance: Report to the 1995 Legislature.* Salem, OR: Oregon Progress Board.

Organization for Economic Cooperation and Development. 2002. *Measuring Up: Improving Health System Performance in OECD Countries.* Paris: Organization for Economic Cooperation and Development.

Osborne, David E., and Ted Gaebler. 1992. *Reinventing Government.* Reading, MA: Addison-Wesley.

Osborne, David E., and Peter Plastrik. 1997. *Banishing Bureaucracy.* Reading, MA: Addison-Wesley.

———. 2000. *The Reinventor's Fieldbook.* San Francisco: Jossey-Bass.

Osborne, Stephen P., ed. 2000. *Public-Private Partnerships: Theory and Practice in International Perspective.* Florence, KY: Routledge.

Osland, Joyce S., David A. Kolb, and Irwin M. Rubin. 2000. *Organizational Behavior: An Experiential Approach.* 7th ed. Englewood Cliffs, NJ: Prentice-Hall.

Ott, Steven J., ed. 2000. *The Nature of the Nonprofit Sector.* Boulder, CO: Westview Press.

PA Times. 2003. *Special Issue: How to Measure IT Return On Investment.* Washington, DC: American Society for Public Administration.

Palm, David W. 2005. "Designing and Building New Local Public Health Agencies in Nebraska." *Journal of Public Health Management Practice* 11 (2): 139–49.

Phillips, Joseph. 2004. *IT Project Management: On Track from Start to Finish.* New York: McGraw-Hill.

Pinto, Jeffrey K., and Ido Millet. 1999. *Successful Information System Implementation: The Human Side.* 2nd ed. Upper Darby, PA: Project Management Institute.

Plunkett, Lorne C., and Robert Fournier. 1991. *Participative Management: Implementing Empowerment.* New York: John Wiley.

Poister, Theodore H. 2003. *Measuring Performance in Public and Nonprofit Organizations.* New York: John Wiley & Sons.

Poister, Theodore H., and Greg Streib. 1994. "Municipal Management Tools from 1976 to 1993." *Public Productivity & Management Review* 18 (2): 115–25.

———. 2005. "Elements of Strategic Planning and Management in Municipal Government: Status After Two Decades." *Public Administration Review* 65 (1): 45–57.

Poister, Theodore H., and David Van Slyke. 2002. "Strategic Management Innovations in State Transportation Departments." *Public Performance & Management Review* 26 (1): 58–75.

Rainey, Hal G. 1999. "Assessing Innovative Attitudes." *Public Performance & Management Review* 23 (2): 150–69.

Rainey, Hal G., and Sergio Fernandez. 2004. "A Response to 'Prompting the Transformation of Public Organizations.'" *Public Performance & Management Review* 27 (4): 34–40.

Riggio, Ronald E., Sarah S. Orr, and Jack Shakely. 2003. *Improving Leadership in Nonprofit Organizations.* San Francisco: Jossey-Bass.

Rogers, Everett M. 1995. *Diffusion of Innovations.* New York: Free Press.

Rosander, Arlyn C. 1989. *The Quest for Quality in Services.* Milwaukee, WI: Quality Press.

Rossi, Peter H., Mark W. Lipsey, and Howard E. Freeman. 2004. *Evaluation: A Systematic Approach.* 7th ed. Thousand Oaks, CA: Sage.

Rousseau, Denise M. 1995. *Psychological Contracts in Organizations: Understanding Written and Unwritten Agreements.* Thousand Oaks, CA: Sage.

Salamon, Lester M. 2003. *The State of Nonprofit America.* Washington, DC: Brookings Institution Press.

Savas, Emanuel S. 1999. *Privatization and Public-Private Partnerships.* Chatham, NJ: Chatham House.

Schachter, Hindy L. 2004. "Public Productivity in the Classical Age of Public Administration." In Holzer and Lee 2004, 17–30. New York: Marcel Dekker.

Schwalbe, Kathy. 2003. *Information Technology Project Management.* Cambridge, MA: Thomson.

Segal, Lydia. 1997. "The Pitfalls of Political Decentralization and Proposals for Reform: The Case of New York City Public Schools." *Public Administration Review* 57 (2):141–49.

Service to America Medals. 2005. *Award Recipients.* Washington, DC: Partnership for Public Service. http://www2.govexec.com/SAM/ (accessed July 12, 2005).

Shafritz, Jay M., and Al C. Hyde. 1992. *Classics of Public Administration.* 3rd ed. Belmont, CA: Wadsworth.

Shapiro, Andrea. 2003. *Creating Contagious Commitment: Applying the Tipping Point to Organizational Change.* Hillsborough, NC: Strategy Perspective.

Shaw, Mary M. 2003. "Successful Collaboration Between the Nonprofit and Public Sectors." *Nonprofit Management & Leadership* 14 (1): 107–21.

Simmons, John. 2003. "Rules of Engagement." *Public Management Review* 5 (4): 585–96.

Skinner, Burrhus F. 1971. *Beyond Freedom and Dignity.* New York: Bantam Books.

Spicer, Michael W. 2004. "Public Administration, the History of Ideas, and the Reinventing Government Movement." *Public Administration Review* 64 (3): 353–63.

Stauber, Karl N. 2001. "Mission-Driven Philanthropy: What Do We Want to Accomplish and How Do We Do It?" *Nonprofit & Voluntary Sector Quarterly* 30 (2): 393–400.

Stephens, James E. 1999. "Turnaround at the Alabama Rehabilitation Agency." In *Public Sector Performance: Management, Motivation and Measurement* (ASPA Classics Series), ed. Richard Kearney and Evan Berman, 65–82. Boulder, CO: Westview Press.

Stokey, Edith, and Richard J. Zeckhauser. 1978. *A Primer for Policy Analysis.* New York: Norton & Co.

Swanson, Richard A. 1996. *Analysis for Improving Performance: Tools for Diagnosing Organizations & Documenting Workplace Expertise.* San Francisco: Berrett-Koehler.

Swiss, James E. 1992. "Adapting TQM to Government." *Public Administration Review* 52 (4): 356–62.

Taylor, Frederick W. 1911. *The Principles of Scientific Management.* New York: Harper Brothers.

Teisman, Geert R., and Erik-Hans Klijn. 2002. "Partnership Arrangements: Governmental Rhetoric or Governance Scheme?" *Public Administration Review* 62 (2): 197–206.

Teratanavat, Ratapol, and Brian Kleiner. 2005. "When It's Time to Say Good-Bye." *Nonprofit World* 23 (2): 12–15.

Tetrault, Jessica. 2004. "Surveys Provide Crucial Feedback." *Nonprofit World* 22 (5): 22–23.

Tigue, Patricia, and Dennis Strachota. 1994. *The Use of Performance Measures in City and County Budgets.* Chicago: Government Finance Officers Association.

Times Picayune (New Orleans, LA). 2005. "Hatchet Men," June 26.

Torres, Lourdes. 2004. "Trajectories in Public Administration Reforms in European Continental Countries." *Australian Journal of Public Administration* 63 (3): 99–113.

U.S. Census Bureau. 1997. *Finances of Special District Governments.* Vol. 4. Washington, DC: Government Printing Office.

———. 2002. *Preliminary Report: The 2002 Census of Governments Finances of Special District Governments.* Vol. 4. Washington, DC: U.S. Department of Commerce. www.census.gov/govs/www/cog2002.html (accessed July 11, 2005).

———. 1989. Computer Use in the United States: 1989. (Washington, D.C.). Special Studies Series P-23, No. 171.

———. 2001. Computer and Internet Use in the United States: 2001. (Washington, D.C.). Detailed Tables PPL-175.

U.S. Department of Homeland Security. 2003. *National Strategy to Secure Cyberspace.* Washington, DC: U.S. Department of Homeland Security. www.dhs.gov/interweb/ assetlibrary/ National_Cyberspace_Strategy.pdf (accessed July 5, 2005).

U.S. Department of Justice. 2005. *Freedom of Information Act Reference Guide.* Washington, DC: U.S. Department of Justice. www.usdoj.gov/04foia/04_3.html (accessed July 5, 2005).